Book of Joshua

Joshua
God

King James Bible
Douay Rheims
American Standard Bible
Bible in Basic English
Webster Bible

Matthew Henry

ISBN-10: 1497354633
ISBN-13: 978-1497354630

"When the trumpets sounded, the people shouted, and at the sound of the trumpet, when the people gave a loud shout, the wall collapsed; so every man charged straight in, and they took the city."

CONTENTS

JOSHUA

JOSHUA

KING JAMES BIBLE

1

1:1 Now after the death of Moses the servant of the LORD it came to pass,
that the LORD spake unto Joshua the son of Nun, Moses' minister, saying,
1:2 Moses my servant is dead; now therefore arise, go over this Jordan,
thou, and all this people, unto the land which I do give to them, even to the
children of Israel.
1:3 Every place that the sole of your foot shall tread upon, that have I given
unto you, as I said unto Moses.
1:4 From the wilderness and this Lebanon even unto the great river, the
river Euphrates, all the land of the Hittites, and unto the great sea toward
the going down of the sun, shall be your coast.
1:5 There shall not any man be able to stand before thee all the days of thy
life: as I was with Moses, so I will be with thee: I will not fail thee, nor
forsake thee.
1:6 Be strong and of a good courage: for unto this people shalt thou divide
for an inheritance the land, which I sware unto their fathers to give them.
1:7 Only be thou strong and very courageous, that thou mayest observe to
do according to all the law, which Moses my servant commanded thee: turn
not from it to the right hand or to the left, that thou mayest prosper
withersoever thou goest.
1:8 This book of the law shall not depart out of thy mouth; but thou shalt
meditate therein day and night, that thou mayest observe to do according to
all that is written therein: for then thou shalt make thy way prosperous, and
then thou shalt have good success.

1:9 Have not I commanded thee? Be strong and of a good courage; be not afraid, neither be thou dismayed: for the LORD thy God is with thee whithersoever thou goest.

1:10 Then Joshua commanded the officers of the people, saying, 1:11 Pass through the host, and command the people, saying, Prepare you victuals; for within three days ye shall pass over this Jordan, to go in to possess the land, which the LORD your God giveth you to possess it.

1:12 And to the Reubenites, and to the Gadites, and to half the tribe of Manasseh, spake Joshua, saying, 1:13 Remember the word which Moses the servant of the LORD commanded you, saying, The LORD your God hath given you rest, and hath given you this land.

1:14 Your wives, your little ones, and your cattle, shall remain in the land which Moses gave you on this side Jordan; but ye shall pass before your brethren armed, all the mighty men of valour, and help them; 1:15 Until the LORD have given your brethren rest, as he hath given you, and they also have possessed the land which the LORD your God giveth them: then ye shall return unto the land of your possession, and enjoy it, which Moses the LORD's servant gave you on this side Jordan toward the sunrising.

1:16 And they answered Joshua, saying, All that thou commandest us we will do, and whithersoever thou sendest us, we will go.

1:17 According as we hearkened unto Moses in all things, so will we hearken unto thee: only the LORD thy God be with thee, as he was with Moses.

1:18 Whosoever he be that doth rebel against thy commandment, and will not hearken unto thy words in all that thou commandest him, he shall be put to death: only be strong and of a good courage.

2

2:1 And Joshua the son of Nun sent out of Shittim two men to spy secretly, saying, Go view the land, even Jericho. And they went, and came into an harlot's house, named Rahab, and lodged there.

2:2 And it was told the king of Jericho, saying, Behold, there came men in hither to night of the children of Israel to search out the country.

2:3 And the king of Jericho sent unto Rahab, saying, Bring forth the men that are come to thee, which are entered into thine house: for they be come to search out all the country.

2:4 And the woman took the two men, and hid them, and said thus, There came men unto me, but I wist not whence they were: 2:5 And it came to pass about the time of shutting of the gate, when it was dark, that the men went out: whither the men went I wot not: pursue after them quickly; for ye shall overtake them.

2:6 But she had brought them up to the roof of the house, and hid them
with the stalks of flax, which she had laid in order upon the roof.
2:7 And the men pursued after them the way to Jordan unto the fords: and
as soon as they which pursued after them were gone out, they shut the gate.
2:8 And before they were laid down, she came up unto them upon the roof;
2:9 And she said unto the men, I know that the LORD hath given you the
land, and that your terror is fallen upon us, and that all the inhabitants of
the land faint because of you.
2:10 For we have heard how the LORD dried up the water of the Red sea
for you, when ye came out of Egypt; and what ye did unto the two kings of
the Amorites, that were on the other side Jordan, Sihon and Og, whom ye
utterly destroyed.
2:11 And as soon as we had heard these things, our hearts did melt, neither
did there remain any more courage in any man, because of you: for the
LORD your God, he is God in heaven above, and in earth beneath.
2:12 Now therefore, I pray you, swear unto me by the LORD, since I have
shewed you kindness, that ye will also shew kindness unto my father's
house, and give me a true token: 2:13 And that ye will save alive my father,
and my mother, and my brethren, and my sisters, and all that they have, and
deliver our lives from death.
2:14 And the men answered her, Our life for yours, if ye utter not this our
business. And it shall be, when the LORD hath given us the land, that we
will deal kindly and truly with thee.
2:15 Then she let them down by a cord through the window: for her house
was upon the town wall, and she dwelt upon the wall.
2:16 And she said unto them, Get you to the mountain, lest the pursuers
meet you; and hide yourselves there three days, until the pursuers be
returned: and afterward may ye go your way.
2:17 And the men said unto her, We will be blameless of this thine oath
which thou hast made us swear.
2:18 Behold, when we come into the land, thou shalt bind this line of
scarlet thread in the window which thou didst let us down by: and thou
shalt bring thy father, and thy mother, and thy brethren, and all thy father's
household, home unto thee.
2:19 And it shall be, that whosoever shall go out of the doors of thy house
into the street, his blood shall be upon his head, and we will be guiltless:
and whosoever shall be with thee in the house, his blood shall be on our
head, if any hand be upon him.
2:20 And if thou utter this our business, then we will be quit of thine oath
which thou hast made us to swear.
2:21 And she said, According unto your words, so be it. And she sent them
away, and they departed: and she bound the scarlet line in the window.
2:22 And they went, and came unto the mountain, and abode there three

days, until the pursuers were returned: and the pursuers sought them throughout all the way, but found them not.
2:23 So the two men returned, and descended from the mountain, and passed over, and came to Joshua the son of Nun, and told him all things
that befell them: 2:24 And they said unto Joshua, Truly the LORD hath
delivered into our hands all the land; for even all the inhabitants of the country do faint because of us.

3

3:1 And Joshua rose early in the morning; and they removed from Shittim, and came to Jordan, he and all the children of Israel, and lodged there before they passed over.
3:2 And it came to pass after three days, that the officers went through the
host; 3:3 And they commanded the people, saying, When ye see the ark of the covenant of the LORD your God, and the priests the Levites bearing it, then ye shall remove from your place, and go after it.
3:4 Yet there shall be a space between you and it, about two thousand cubits by measure: come not near unto it, that ye may know the way by which ye must go: for ye have not passed this way heretofore.
3:5 And Joshua said unto the people, Sanctify yourselves: for to morrow the LORD will do wonders among you.
3:6 And Joshua spake unto the priests, saying, Take up the ark of the covenant, and pass over before the people. And they took up the ark of the covenant, and went before the people.
3:7 And the LORD said unto Joshua, This day will I begin to magnify thee in the sight of all Israel, that they may know that, as I was with Moses, so I will be with thee.
3:8 And thou shalt command the priests that bear the ark of the covenant, saying, When ye are come to the brink of the water of Jordan, ye shall stand still in Jordan.
3:9 And Joshua said unto the children of Israel, Come hither, and hear the words of the LORD your God.
3:10 And Joshua said, Hereby ye shall know that the living God is among you, and that he will without fail drive out from before you the Canaanites, and the Hittites, and the Hivites, and the Perizzites, and the Girgashites, and the Amorites, and the Jebusites.
3:11 Behold, the ark of the covenant of the LORD of all the earth passeth over before you into Jordan.
3:12 Now therefore take you twelve men out of the tribes of Israel, out of every tribe a man.
3:13 And it shall come to pass, as soon as the soles of the feet of the priests

that bear the ark of the LORD, the LORD of all the earth, shall rest in the
waters of Jordan, that the waters of Jordan shall be cut off from the waters
that come down from above; and they shall stand upon an heap.
3:14 And it came to pass, when the people removed from their tents, to
pass over Jordan, and the priests bearing the ark of the covenant before the
people; 3:15 And as they that bare the ark were come unto Jordan, and the
feet of the priests that bare the ark were dipped in the brim of the water,
(for Jordan overfloweth all his banks all the time of harvest,) 3:16 That the
waters which came down from above stood and rose up upon an heap very
far from the city Adam, that is beside Zaretan: and those that came down
toward the sea of the plain, even the salt sea, failed, and were cut off: and
the people passed over right against Jericho.
3:17 And the priests that bare the ark of the covenant of the LORD stood
firm on dry ground in the midst of Jordan, and all the Israelites passed over
on dry ground, until all the people were passed clean over Jordan.

4

4:1 And it came to pass, when all the people were clean passed over Jordan,
that the LORD spake unto Joshua, saying, 4:2 Take you twelve men out of
the people, out of every tribe a man, 4:3 And command ye them, saying,
Take you hence out of the midst of Jordan, out of the place where the
priests' feet stood firm, twelve stones, and ye shall carry them over with
you, and leave them in the lodging place, where ye shall lodge this night.
4:4 Then Joshua called the twelve men, whom he had prepared of the
children of Israel, out of every tribe a man: 4:5 And Joshua said unto them,
Pass over before the ark of the LORD your God into the midst of Jordan,
and take you up every man of you a stone upon his shoulder, according
unto the number of the tribes of the children of Israel: 4:6 That this may be
a sign among you, that when your children ask their fathers in time to
come, saying, What mean ye by these stones? 4:7 Then ye shall answer
them, That the waters of Jordan were cut off before the ark of the covenant
of the LORD; when it passed over Jordan, the waters of Jordan were cut
off: and these stones shall be for a memorial unto the children of Israel for
ever.
4:8 And the children of Israel did so as Joshua commanded, and took up
twelve stones out of the midst of Jordan, as the LORD spake unto Joshua,
according to the number of the tribes of the children of Israel, and carried
them over with them unto the place where they lodged, and laid them down
there.
4:9 And Joshua set up twelve stones in the midst of Jordan, in the place
where the feet of the priests which bare the ark of the covenant stood: and

they are there unto this day.
4:10 For the priests which bare the ark stood in the midst of Jordan, until everything was finished that the LORD commanded Joshua to speak unto the people, according to all that Moses commanded Joshua: and the people hasted and passed over.
4:11 And it came to pass, when all the people were clean passed over, that the ark of the LORD passed over, and the priests, in the presence of the people.
4:12 And the children of Reuben, and the children of Gad, and half the tribe of Manasseh, passed over armed before the children of Israel, as Moses spake unto them: 4:13 About forty thousand prepared for war passed over before the LORD unto battle, to the plains of Jericho.
4:14 On that day the LORD magnified Joshua in the sight of all Israel; and they feared him, as they feared Moses, all the days of his life.
4:15 And the LORD spake unto Joshua, saying, 4:16 Command the priests that bear the ark of the testimony, that they come up out of Jordan.
4:17 Joshua therefore commanded the priests, saying, Come ye up out of Jordan.
4:18 And it came to pass, when the priests that bare the ark of the covenant of the LORD were come up out of the midst of Jordan, and the soles of the priests' feet were lifted up unto the dry land, that the waters of Jordan returned unto their place, and flowed over all his banks, as they did before.
4:19 And the people came up out of Jordan on the tenth day of the first month, and encamped in Gilgal, in the east border of Jericho.
4:20 And those twelve stones, which they took out of Jordan, did Joshua pitch in Gilgal.
4:21 And he spake unto the children of Israel, saying, When your children shall ask their fathers in time to come, saying, What mean these stones?
4:22 Then ye shall let your children know, saying, Israel came over this Jordan on dry land.
4:23 For the LORD your God dried up the waters of Jordan from before you, until ye were passed over, as the LORD your God did to the Red sea, which he dried up from before us, until we were gone over: 4:24 That all the people of the earth might know the hand of the LORD, that it is mighty: that ye might fear the LORD your God for ever.

5

5:1 And it came to pass, when all the kings of the Amorites, which were on the side of Jordan westward, and all the kings of the Canaanites, which were by the sea, heard that the LORD had dried up the waters of Jordan from before the children of Israel, until we were passed over, that their heart

melted, neither was there spirit in them any more, because of the children of Israel.
5:2 At that time the LORD said unto Joshua, Make thee sharp knives, and circumcise again the children of Israel the second time.
5:3 And Joshua made him sharp knives, and circumcised the children of Israel at the hill of the foreskins.
5:4 And this is the cause why Joshua did circumcise: All the people that came out of Egypt, that were males, even all the men of war, died in the wilderness by the way, after they came out of Egypt.
5:5 Now all the people that came out were circumcised: but all the people that were born in the wilderness by the way as they came forth out of Egypt, them they had not circumcised.
5:6 For the children of Israel walked forty years in the wilderness, till all the people that were men of war, which came out of Egypt, were consumed, because they obeyed not the voice of the LORD: unto whom the LORD sware that he would not shew them the land, which the LORD sware unto their fathers that he would give us, a land that floweth with milk and honey.
5:7 And their children, whom he raised up in their stead, them Joshua circumcised: for they were uncircumcised, because they had not circumcised them by the way.
5:8 And it came to pass, when they had done circumcising all the people, that they abode in their places in the camp, till they were whole.
5:9 And the LORD said unto Joshua, This day have I rolled away the reproach of Egypt from off you. Wherefore the name of the place is called Gilgal unto this day.
5:10 And the children of Israel encamped in Gilgal, and kept the passover on the fourteenth day of the month at even in the plains of Jericho.
5:11 And they did eat of the old corn of the land on the morrow after the passover, unleavened cakes, and parched corn in the selfsame day.
5:12 And the manna ceased on the morrow after they had eaten of the old corn of the land; neither had the children of Israel manna any more; but they did eat of the fruit of the land of Canaan that year.
5:13 And it came to pass, when Joshua was by Jericho, that he lifted up his eyes and looked, and, behold, there stood a man over against him with his sword drawn in his hand: and Joshua went unto him, and said unto him, Art thou for us, or for our adversaries? 5:14 And he said, Nay; but as captain of the host of the LORD am I now come. And Joshua fell on his face to the earth, and did worship, and said unto him, What saith my Lord unto his servant? 5:15 And the captain of the LORD's host said unto Joshua, Loose thy shoe from off thy foot; for the place whereon thou standest is holy. And Joshua did so.

6

6:1 Now Jericho was straitly shut up because of the children of Israel: none went out, and none came in.
6:2 And the LORD said unto Joshua, See, I have given into thine hand Jericho, and the king thereof, and the mighty men of valour.
6:3 And ye shall compass the city, all ye men of war, and go round about the city once. Thus shalt thou do six days.
6:4 And seven priests shall bear before the ark seven trumpets of rams' horns: and the seventh day ye shall compass the city seven times, and the priests shall blow with the trumpets.
6:5 And it shall come to pass, that when they make a long blast with the ram's horn, and when ye hear the sound of the trumpet, all the people shall shout with a great shout; and the wall of the city shall fall down flat, and the people shall ascend up every man straight before him.
6:6 And Joshua the son of Nun called the priests, and said unto them, Take up the ark of the covenant, and let seven priests bear seven trumpets of rams' horns before the ark of the LORD.
6:7 And he said unto the people, Pass on, and compass the city, and let him that is armed pass on before the ark of the LORD.
6:8 And it came to pass, when Joshua had spoken unto the people, that the seven priests bearing the seven trumpets of rams' horns passed on before the LORD, and blew with the trumpets: and the ark of the covenant of the LORD followed them.
6:9 And the armed men went before the priests that blew with the trumpets, and the rereward came after the ark, the priests going on, and blowing with the trumpets.
6:10 And Joshua had commanded the people, saying, Ye shall not shout, nor make any noise with your voice, neither shall any word proceed out of your mouth, until the day I bid you shout; then shall ye shout.
6:11 So the ark of the LORD compassed the city, going about it once: and they came into the camp, and lodged in the camp.
6:12 And Joshua rose early in the morning, and the priests took up the ark of the LORD.
6:13 And seven priests bearing seven trumpets of rams' horns before the ark of the LORD went on continually, and blew with the trumpets: and the armed men went before them; but the rereward came after the ark of the LORD, the priests going on, and blowing with the trumpets.
6:14 And the second day they compassed the city once, and returned into the camp: so they did six days.
6:15 And it came to pass on the seventh day, that they rose early about the dawning of the day, and compassed the city after the same manner seven times: only on that day they compassed the city seven times.

6:16 And it came to pass at the seventh time, when the priests blew with the trumpets, Joshua said unto the people, Shout; for the LORD hath given you the city.

6:17 And the city shall be accursed, even it, and all that are therein, to the LORD: only Rahab the harlot shall live, she and all that are with her in the house, because she hid the messengers that we sent.

6:18 And ye, in any wise keep yourselves from the accursed thing, lest ye make yourselves accursed, when ye take of the accursed thing, and make the camp of Israel a curse, and trouble it.

6:19 But all the silver, and gold, and vessels of brass and iron, are consecrated unto the LORD: they shall come into the treasury of the LORD.

6:20 So the people shouted when the priests blew with the trumpets: and it came to pass, when the people heard the sound of the trumpet, and the people shouted with a great shout, that the wall fell down flat, so that the people went up into the city, every man straight before him, and they took the city.

6:21 And they utterly destroyed all that was in the city, both man and woman, young and old, and ox, and sheep, and ass, with the edge of the sword.

6:22 But Joshua had said unto the two men that had spied out the country, Go into the harlot's house, and bring out thence the woman, and all that she hath, as ye sware unto her.

6:23 And the young men that were spies went in, and brought out Rahab, and her father, and her mother, and her brethren, and all that she had; and they brought out all her kindred, and left them without the camp of Israel.

6:24 And they burnt the city with fire, and all that was therein: only the silver, and the gold, and the vessels of brass and of iron, they put into the treasury of the house of the LORD.

6:25 And Joshua saved Rahab the harlot alive, and her father's household, and all that she had; and she dwelleth in Israel even unto this day; because she hid the messengers, which Joshua sent to spy out Jericho.

6:26 And Joshua adjured them at that time, saying, Cursed be the man before the LORD, that riseth up and buildeth this city Jericho: he shall lay the foundation thereof in his firstborn, and in his youngest son shall he set up the gates of it.

6:27 So the LORD was with Joshua; and his fame was noised throughout all the country.

7

7:1 But the children of Israel committed a trespass in the accursed thing: for Achan, the son of Carmi, the son of Zabdi, the son of Zerah, of the tribe of Judah, took of the accursed thing: and the anger of the LORD was kindled against the children of Israel.
7:2 And Joshua sent men from Jericho to Ai, which is beside Bethaven, on the east of Bethel, and spake unto them, saying, Go up and view the country.
And the men went up and viewed Ai.
7:3 And they returned to Joshua, and said unto him, Let not all the people go up; but let about two or three thousand men go up and smite Ai; and make not all the people to labour thither; for they are but few.
7:4 So there went up thither of the people about three thousand men: and they fled before the men of Ai.
7:5 And the men of Ai smote of them about thirty and six men: for they chased them from before the gate even unto Shebarim, and smote them in the going down: wherefore the hearts of the people melted, and became as water.
7:6 And Joshua rent his clothes, and fell to the earth upon his face before the ark of the LORD until the eventide, he and the elders of Israel, and put dust upon their heads.
7:7 And Joshua said, Alas, O LORD God, wherefore hast thou at all brought this people over Jordan, to deliver us into the hand of the Amorites, to destroy us? would to God we had been content, and dwelt on
the other side Jordan! 7:8 O LORD, what shall I say, when Israel turneth
their backs before their enemies! 7:9 For the Canaanites and all the
inhabitants of the land shall hear of it, and shall environ us round, and cut off our name from the earth: and what wilt thou do unto thy great name?
7:10 And the LORD said unto Joshua, Get thee up; wherefore liest thou
thus upon thy face? 7:11 Israel hath sinned, and they have also transgressed
my covenant which I commanded them: for they have even taken of the accursed thing, and have also stolen, and dissembled also, and they have put it even among their own stuff.
7:12 Therefore the children of Israel could not stand before their enemies, but turned their backs before their enemies, because they were accursed: neither will I be with you any more, except ye destroy the accursed from among you.
7:13 Up, sanctify the people, and say, Sanctify yourselves against to morrow: for thus saith the LORD God of Israel, There is an accursed thing in the midst of thee, O Israel: thou canst not stand before thine enemies, until ye take away the accursed thing from among you.
7:14 In the morning therefore ye shall be brought according to your tribes: and it shall be, that the tribe which the LORD taketh shall come according to the families thereof; and the family which the LORD shall take shall

come by households; and the household which the LORD shall take shall come man by man.

7:15 And it shall be, that he that is taken with the accursed thing shall be burnt with fire, he and all that he hath: because he hath transgressed the covenant of the LORD, and because he hath wrought folly in Israel.

7:16 So Joshua rose up early in the morning, and brought Israel by their
tribes; and the tribe of Judah was taken: 7:17 And he brought the family of
Judah; and he took the family of the Zarhites: and he brought the family of
the Zarhites man by man; and Zabdi was taken: 7:18 And he brought his
household man by man; and Achan, the son of Carmi, the son of Zabdi, the
son of Zerah, of the tribe of Judah, was taken.

7:19 And Joshua said unto Achan, My son, give, I pray thee, glory to the LORD God of Israel, and make confession unto him; and tell me now what thou hast done; hide it not from me.

7:20 And Achan answered Joshua, and said, Indeed I have sinned against
the LORD God of Israel, and thus and thus have I done: 7:21 When I saw
among the spoils a goodly Babylonish garment, and two hundred shekels of
silver, and a wedge of gold of fifty shekels weight, then I coveted them, and
took them; and, behold, they are hid in the earth in the midst of my tent,
and the silver under it.

7:22 So Joshua sent messengers, and they ran unto the tent; and, behold, it was hid in his tent, and the silver under it.

7:23 And they took them out of the midst of the tent, and brought them unto Joshua, and unto all the children of Israel, and laid them out before the LORD.

7:24 And Joshua, and all Israel with him, took Achan the son of Zerah, and the silver, and the garment, and the wedge of gold, and his sons, and his daughters, and his oxen, and his asses, and his sheep, and his tent, and all that he had: and they brought them unto the valley of Achor.

7:25 And Joshua said, Why hast thou troubled us? the LORD shall trouble thee this day. And all Israel stoned him with stones, and burned them with fire, after they had stoned them with stones.

7:26 And they raised over him a great heap of stones unto this day. So the LORD turned from the fierceness of his anger. Wherefore the name of that place was called, The valley of Achor, unto this day.

8

8:1 And the LORD said unto Joshua, Fear not, neither be thou dismayed:
take all the people of war with thee, and arise, go up to Ai: see, I have given
into thy hand the king of Ai, and his people, and his city, and his land: 8:2

And thou shalt do to Ai and her king as thou didst unto Jericho and her king: only the spoil thereof, and the cattle thereof, shall ye take for a prey unto yourselves: lay thee an ambush for the city behind it.
8:3 So Joshua arose, and all the people of war, to go up against Ai: and Joshua chose out thirty thousand mighty men of valour, and sent them away by night.
8:4 And he commanded them, saying, Behold, ye shall lie in wait against the city, even behind the city: go not very far from the city, but be ye all ready:
8:5 And I, and all the people that are with me, will approach unto the city: and it shall come to pass, when they come out against us, as at the first, that we will flee before them, 8:6 (For they will come out after us) till we have drawn them from the city; for they will say, They flee before us, as at the first: therefore we will flee before them.
8:7 Then ye shall rise up from the ambush, and seize upon the city: for the LORD your God will deliver it into your hand.
8:8 And it shall be, when ye have taken the city, that ye shall set the city on fire: according to the commandment of the LORD shall ye do. See, I have commanded you.
8:9 Joshua therefore sent them forth: and they went to lie in ambush, and abode between Bethel and Ai, on the west side of Ai: but Joshua lodged that night among the people.
8:10 And Joshua rose up early in the morning, and numbered the people, and went up, he and the elders of Israel, before the people to Ai.
8:11 And all the people, even the people of war that were with him, went up, and drew nigh, and came before the city, and pitched on the north side of Ai: now there was a valley between them and Ai.
8:12 And he took about five thousand men, and set them to lie in ambush between Bethel and Ai, on the west side of the city.
8:13 And when they had set the people, even all the host that was on the north of the city, and their liers in wait on the west of the city, Joshua went that night into the midst of the valley.
8:14 And it came to pass, when the king of Ai saw it, that they hasted and rose up early, and the men of the city went out against Israel to battle, he and all his people, at a time appointed, before the plain; but he wist not that there were liers in ambush against him behind the city.
8:15 And Joshua and all Israel made as if they were beaten before them, and fled by the way of the wilderness.
8:16 And all the people that were in Ai were called together to pursue after them: and they pursued after Joshua, and were drawn away from the city.
8:17 And there was not a man left in Ai or Bethel, that went not out after Israel: and they left the city open, and pursued after Israel.
8:18 And the LORD said unto Joshua, Stretch out the spear that is in thy hand toward Ai; for I will give it into thine hand. And Joshua stretched out

the spear that he had in his hand toward the city.
8:19 And the ambush arose quickly out of their place, and they ran as soon as he had stretched out his hand: and they entered into the city, and took it, and hasted and set the city on fire.
8:20 And when the men of Ai looked behind them, they saw, and, behold, the smoke of the city ascended up to heaven, and they had no power to flee this way or that way: and the people that fled to the wilderness turned back upon the pursuers.
8:21 And when Joshua and all Israel saw that the ambush had taken the city, and that the smoke of the city ascended, then they turned again, and slew the men of Ai.
8:22 And the other issued out of the city against them; so they were in the midst of Israel, some on this side, and some on that side: and they smote them, so that they let none of them remain or escape.
8:23 And the king of Ai they took alive, and brought him to Joshua.
8:24 And it came to pass, when Israel had made an end of slaying all the inhabitants of Ai in the field, in the wilderness wherein they chased them, and when they were all fallen on the edge of the sword, until they were consumed, that all the Israelites returned unto Ai, and smote it with the edge of the sword.
8:25 And so it was, that all that fell that day, both of men and women, were twelve thousand, even all the men of Ai.
8:26 For Joshua drew not his hand back, wherewith he stretched out the spear, until he had utterly destroyed all the inhabitants of Ai.
8:27 Only the cattle and the spoil of that city Israel took for a prey unto themselves, according unto the word of the LORD which he commanded Joshua.
8:28 And Joshua burnt Ai, and made it an heap for ever, even a desolation unto this day.
8:29 And the king of Ai he hanged on a tree until eventide: and as soon as the sun was down, Joshua commanded that they should take his carcase down from the tree, and cast it at the entering of the gate of the city, and raise thereon a great heap of stones, that remaineth unto this day.
8:30 Then Joshua built an altar unto the LORD God of Israel in mount
Ebal, 8:31 As Moses the servant of the LORD commanded the children of
Israel, as it is written in the book of the law of Moses, an altar of whole stones, over which no man hath lift up any iron: and they offered thereon burnt offerings unto the LORD, and sacrificed peace offerings.
8:32 And he wrote there upon the stones a copy of the law of Moses, which he wrote in the presence of the children of Israel.
8:33 And all Israel, and their elders, and officers, and their judges, stood on this side the ark and on that side before the priests the Levites, which bare the ark of the covenant of the LORD, as well the stranger, as he that was

born among them; half of them over against mount Gerizim, and half of them over against mount Ebal; as Moses the servant of the LORD had commanded before, that they should bless the people of Israel.
8:34 And afterward he read all the words of the law, the blessings and cursings, according to all that is written in the book of the law.
8:35 There was not a word of all that Moses commanded, which Joshua read not before all the congregation of Israel, with the women, and the little ones, and the strangers that were conversant among them.

9

9:1 And it came to pass, when all the kings which were on this side Jordan, in the hills, and in the valleys, and in all the coasts of the great sea over against Lebanon, the Hittite, and the Amorite, the Canaanite, the Perizzite,
the Hivite, and the Jebusite, heard thereof; 9:2 That they gathered
themselves together, to fight with Joshua and with Israel, with one accord.
9:3 And when the inhabitants of Gibeon heard what Joshua had done unto
Jericho and to Ai, 9:4 They did work wilily, and went and made as if they
had been ambassadors, and took old sacks upon their asses, and wine
bottles, old, and rent, and bound up; 9:5 And old shoes and clouted upon
their feet, and old garments upon them; and all the bread of their provision was dry and mouldy.
9:6 And they went to Joshua unto the camp at Gilgal, and said unto him, and to the men of Israel, We be come from a far country: now therefore make ye a league with us.
9:7 And the men of Israel said unto the Hivites, Peradventure ye dwell
among us; and how shall we make a league with you? 9:8 And they said
unto Joshua, We are thy servants. And Joshua said unto them, Who are ye?
and from whence come ye? 9:9 And they said unto him, From a very far
country thy servants are come because of the name of the LORD thy God:
for we have heard the fame of him, and all that he did in Egypt, 9:10 And
all that he did to the two kings of the Amorites, that were beyond Jordan, to Sihon king of Heshbon, and to Og king of Bashan, which was at Ashtaroth.
9:11 Wherefore our elders and all the inhabitants of our country spake to us, saying, Take victuals with you for the journey, and go to meet them, and say unto them, We are your servants: therefore now make ye a league with us.
9:12 This our bread we took hot for our provision out of our houses on the
day we came forth to go unto you; but now, behold, it is dry, and it is
mouldy: 9:13 And these bottles of wine, which we filled, were new; and,
behold, they be rent: and these our garments and our shoes are become old

by reason of the very long journey.
9:14 And the men took of their victuals, and asked not counsel at the
mouth of the LORD.
9:15 And Joshua made peace with them, and made a league with them, to
let them live: and the princes of the congregation sware unto them.
9:16 And it came to pass at the end of three days after they had made a
league with them, that they heard that they were their neighbours, and that
they dwelt among them.
9:17 And the children of Israel journeyed, and came unto their cities on the
third day. Now their cities were Gibeon, and Chephirah, and Beeroth, and
Kirjathjearim.
9:18 And the children of Israel smote them not, because the princes of the
congregation had sworn unto them by the LORD God of Israel. And all
the congregation murmured against the princes.
9:19 But all the princes said unto all the congregation, We have sworn unto
them by the LORD God of Israel: now therefore we may not touch them.
9:20 This we will do to them; we will even let them live, lest wrath be upon
us, because of the oath which we sware unto them.
9:21 And the princes said unto them, Let them live; but let them be hewers
of wood and drawers of water unto all the congregation; as the princes had
promised them.
9:22 And Joshua called for them, and he spake unto them, saying,
Wherefore have ye beguiled us, saying, We are very far from you; when ye
dwell among us? 9:23 Now therefore ye are cursed, and there shall none of
you be freed from being bondmen, and hewers of wood and drawers of
water for the house of my God.
9:24 And they answered Joshua, and said, Because it was certainly told thy
servants, how that the LORD thy God commanded his servant Moses to
give you all the land, and to destroy all the inhabitants of the land from
before you, therefore we were sore afraid of our lives because of you, and
have done this thing.
9:25 And now, behold, we are in thine hand: as it seemeth good and right
unto thee to do unto us, do.
9:26 And so did he unto them, and delivered them out of the hand of the
children of Israel, that they slew them not.
9:27 And Joshua made them that day hewers of wood and drawers of water
for the congregation, and for the altar of the LORD, even unto this day, in
the place which he should choose.

10

10:1 Now it came to pass, when Adonizedec king of Jerusalem had heard how Joshua had taken Ai, and had utterly destroyed it; as he had done to Jericho and her king, so he had done to Ai and her king; and how the inhabitants of Gibeon had made peace with Israel, and were among them;
10:2 That they feared greatly, because Gibeon was a great city, as one of the royal cities, and because it was greater than Ai, and all the men thereof were mighty.
10:3 Wherefore Adonizedec king of Jerusalem, sent unto Hoham king of Hebron, and unto Piram king of Jarmuth, and unto Japhia king of Lachish,
and unto Debir king of Eglon, saying, 10:4 Come up unto me, and help me, that we may smite Gibeon: for it hath made peace with Joshua and with the children of Israel.
10:5 Therefore the five kings of the Amorites, the king of Jerusalem, the king of Hebron, the king of Jarmuth, the king of Lachish, the king of Eglon, gathered themselves together, and went up, they and all their hosts, and encamped before Gibeon, and made war against it.
10:6 And the men of Gibeon sent unto Joshua to the camp to Gilgal, saying, Slack not thy hand from thy servants; come up to us quickly, and save us, and help us: for all the kings of the Amorites that dwell in the mountains are gathered together against us.
10:7 So Joshua ascended from Gilgal, he, and all the people of war with him, and all the mighty men of valour.
10:8 And the LORD said unto Joshua, Fear them not: for I have delivered them into thine hand; there shall not a man of them stand before thee.
10:9 Joshua therefore came unto them suddenly, and went up from Gilgal all night.
10:10 And the LORD discomfited them before Israel, and slew them with a great slaughter at Gibeon, and chased them along the way that goeth up to Bethhoron, and smote them to Azekah, and unto Makkedah.
10:11 And it came to pass, as they fled from before Israel, and were in the going down to Bethhoron, that the LORD cast down great stones from heaven upon them unto Azekah, and they died: they were more which died with hailstones than they whom the children of Israel slew with the sword.
10:12 Then spake Joshua to the LORD in the day when the LORD delivered up the Amorites before the children of Israel, and he said in the sight of Israel, Sun, stand thou still upon Gibeon; and thou, Moon, in the valley of Ajalon.
10:13 And the sun stood still, and the moon stayed, until the people had avenged themselves upon their enemies. Is not this written in the book of Jasher? So the sun stood still in the midst of heaven, and hasted not to go down about a whole day.
10:14 And there was no day like that before it or after it, that the LORD hearkened unto the voice of a man: for the LORD fought for Israel.

10:15 And Joshua returned, and all Israel with him, unto the camp to Gilgal.
10:16 But these five kings fled, and hid themselves in a cave at Makkedah.
10:17 And it was told Joshua, saying, The five kings are found hid in a cave at Makkedah.
10:18 And Joshua said, Roll great stones upon the mouth of the cave, and
set men by it for to keep them: 10:19 And stay ye not, but pursue after your
enemies, and smite the hindmost of them; suffer them not to enter into their cities: for the LORD your God hath delivered them into your hand.
10:20 And it came to pass, when Joshua and the children of Israel had made an end of slaying them with a very great slaughter, till they were consumed, that the rest which remained of them entered into fenced cities.
10:21 And all the people returned to the camp to Joshua at Makkedah in peace: none moved his tongue against any of the children of Israel.
10:22 Then said Joshua, Open the mouth of the cave, and bring out those five kings unto me out of the cave.
10:23 And they did so, and brought forth those five kings unto him out of the cave, the king of Jerusalem, the king of Hebron, the king of Jarmuth, the king of Lachish, and the king of Eglon.
10:24 And it came to pass, when they brought out those kings unto Joshua, that Joshua called for all the men of Israel, and said unto the captains of the men of war which went with him, Come near, put your feet upon the necks of these kings. And they came near, and put their feet upon the necks of them.
10:25 And Joshua said unto them, Fear not, nor be dismayed, be strong and of good courage: for thus shall the LORD do to all your enemies against whom ye fight.
10:26 And afterward Joshua smote them, and slew them, and hanged them on five trees: and they were hanging upon the trees until the evening.
10:27 And it came to pass at the time of the going down of the sun, that Joshua commanded, and they took them down off the trees, and cast them into the cave wherein they had been hid, and laid great stones in the cave's mouth, which remain until this very day.
10:28 And that day Joshua took Makkedah, and smote it with the edge of the sword, and the king thereof he utterly destroyed, them, and all the souls that were therein; he let none remain: and he did to the king of Makkedah as he did unto the king of Jericho.
10:29 Then Joshua passed from Makkedah, and all Israel with him, unto
Libnah, and fought against Libnah: 10:30 And the LORD delivered it also,
and the king thereof, into the hand of Israel; and he smote it with the edge of the sword, and all the souls that were therein; he let none remain in it; but did unto the king thereof as he did unto the king of Jericho.
10:31 And Joshua passed from Libnah, and all Israel with him, unto
Lachish, and encamped against it, and fought against it: 10:32 And the

LORD delivered Lachish into the hand of Israel, which took it on the
second day, and smote it with the edge of the sword, and all the souls that
were therein, according to all that he had done to Libnah.
10:33 Then Horam king of Gezer came up to help Lachish; and Joshua
smote him and his people, until he had left him none remaining.
10:34 And from Lachish Joshua passed unto Eglon, and all Israel with him;
and they encamped against it, and fought against it: 10:35 And they took it
on that day, and smote it with the edge of the sword, and all the souls that
were therein he utterly destroyed that day, according to all that he had done
to Lachish.
10:36 And Joshua went up from Eglon, and all Israel with him, unto
Hebron; and they fought against it: 10:37 And they took it, and smote it
with the edge of the sword, and the king thereof, and all the cities thereof,
and all the souls that were therein; he left none remaining, according to all
that he had done to Eglon; but destroyed it utterly, and all the souls that
were therein.
10:38 And Joshua returned, and all Israel with him, to Debir; and fought
against it: 10:39 And he took it, and the king thereof, and all the cities
thereof; and they smote them with the edge of the sword, and utterly
destroyed all the souls that were therein; he left none remaining: as he had
done to Hebron, so he did to Debir, and to the king thereof; as he had
done also to Libnah, and to her king.
10:40 So Joshua smote all the country of the hills, and of the south, and of
the vale, and of the springs, and all their kings: he left none remaining, but
utterly destroyed all that breathed, as the LORD God of Israel commanded.
10:41 And Joshua smote them from Kadeshbarnea even unto Gaza, and all
the country of Goshen, even unto Gibeon.
10:42 And all these kings and their land did Joshua take at one time,
because the LORD God of Israel fought for Israel.
10:43 And Joshua returned, and all Israel with him, unto the camp to Gilgal.

11

11:1 And it came to pass, when Jabin king of Hazor had heard those things,
that he sent to Jobab king of Madon, and to the king of Shimron, and to
the king of Achshaph, 11:2 And to the kings that were on the north of the
mountains, and of the plains south of Chinneroth, and in the valley, and in
the borders of Dor on the west, 11:3 And to the Canaanite on the east and
on the west, and to the Amorite, and the Hittite, and the Perizzite, and the
Jebusite in the mountains, and to the Hivite under Hermon in the land of
Mizpeh.

11:4 And they went out, they and all their hosts with them, much people,
even as the sand that is upon the sea shore in multitude, with horses and
chariots very many.
11:5 And when all these kings were met together, they came and pitched
together at the waters of Merom, to fight against Israel.
11:6 And the LORD said unto Joshua, Be not afraid because of them: for
to morrow about this time will I deliver them up all slain before Israel: thou
shalt hough their horses, and burn their chariots with fire.
11:7 So Joshua came, and all the people of war with him, against them by
the waters of Merom suddenly; and they fell upon them.
11:8 And the LORD delivered them into the hand of Israel, who smote
them, and chased them unto great Zidon, and unto Misrephothmaim, and
unto the valley of Mizpeh eastward; and they smote them, until they left
them none remaining.
11:9 And Joshua did unto them as the LORD bade him: he houghed their
horses, and burnt their chariots with fire.
11:10 And Joshua at that time turned back, and took Hazor, and smote the
king thereof with the sword: for Hazor beforetime was the head of all those
kingdoms.
11:11 And they smote all the souls that were therein with the edge of the
sword, utterly destroying them: there was not any left to breathe: and he
burnt Hazor with fire.
11:12 And all the cities of those kings, and all the kings of them, did Joshua
take, and smote them with the edge of the sword, and he utterly destroyed
them, as Moses the servant of the LORD commanded.
11:13 But as for the cities that stood still in their strength, Israel burned
none of them, save Hazor only; that did Joshua burn.
11:14 And all the spoil of these cities, and the cattle, the children of Israel
took for a prey unto themselves; but every man they smote with the edge of
the sword, until they had destroyed them, neither left they any to breathe.
11:15 As the LORD commanded Moses his servant, so did Moses
command Joshua, and so did Joshua; he left nothing undone of all that the
LORD commanded Moses.
11:16 So Joshua took all that land, the hills, and all the south country, and
all the land of Goshen, and the valley, and the plain, and the mountain of
Israel, and the valley of the same; 11:17 Even from the mount Halak, that
goeth up to Seir, even unto Baalgad in the valley of Lebanon under mount
Hermon: and all their kings he took, and smote them, and slew them.
11:18 Joshua made war a long time with all those kings.
11:19 There was not a city that made peace with the children of Israel, save
the Hivites the inhabitants of Gibeon: all other they took in battle.
11:20 For it was of the LORD to harden their hearts, that they should come
against Israel in battle, that he might destroy them utterly, and that they

might have no favour, but that he might destroy them, as the LORD commanded Moses.
11:21 And at that time came Joshua, and cut off the Anakims from the mountains, from Hebron, from Debir, from Anab, and from all the mountains of Judah, and from all the mountains of Israel: Joshua destroyed them utterly with their cities.
11:22 There was none of the Anakims left in the land of the children of Israel: only in Gaza, in Gath, and in Ashdod, there remained.
11:23 So Joshua took the whole land, according to all that the LORD said unto Moses; and Joshua gave it for an inheritance unto Israel according to their divisions by their tribes. And the land rested from war.

12

12:1 Now these are the kings of the land, which the children of Israel
smote, and possessed their land on the other side Jordan toward the rising
of the sun, from the river Arnon unto mount Hermon, and all the plain on
the east: 12:2 Sihon king of the Amorites, who dwelt in Heshbon, and ruled
from Aroer, which is upon the bank of the river Arnon, and from the
middle of the river, and from half Gilead, even unto the river Jabbok, which
is the border of the children of Ammon; 12:3 And from the plain to the sea
of Chinneroth on the east, and unto the sea of the plain, even the salt sea
on the east, the way to Bethjeshimoth; and from the south, under
Ashdothpisgah: 12:4 And the coast of Og king of Bashan, which was of the
remnant of the giants, that dwelt at Ashtaroth and at Edrei, 12:5 And
reigned in mount Hermon, and in Salcah, and in all Bashan, unto the border
of the Geshurites and the Maachathites, and half Gilead, the border of
Sihon king of Heshbon.
12:6 Them did Moses the servant of the LORD and the children of Israel smite: and Moses the servant of the LORD gave it for a possession unto the Reubenites, and the Gadites, and the half tribe of Manasseh.
12:7 And these are the kings of the country which Joshua and the children
of Israel smote on this side Jordan on the west, from Baalgad in the valley
of Lebanon even unto the mount Halak, that goeth up to Seir; which
Joshua gave unto the tribes of Israel for a possession according to their
divisions; 12:8 In the mountains, and in the valleys, and in the plains, and in
the springs, and in the wilderness, and in the south country; the Hittites, the
Amorites, and the Canaanites, the Perizzites, the Hivites, and the Jebusites:
12:9 The king of Jericho, one; the king of Ai, which is beside Bethel, one;
12:10 The king of Jerusalem, one; the king of Hebron, one; 12:11 The king
of Jarmuth, one; the king of Lachish, one; 12:12 The king of Eglon, one;

the king of Gezer, one; 12:13 The king of Debir, one; the king of Geder, one; 12:14 The king of Hormah, one; the king of Arad, one; 12:15 The king of Libnah, one; the king of Adullam, one; 12:16 The king of Makkedah, one; the king of Bethel, one; 12:17 The king of Tappuah, one; the king of Hepher, one; 12:18 The king of Aphek, one; the king of Lasharon, one; 12:19 The king of Madon, one; the king of Hazor, one; 12:20 The king of Shimronmeron, one; the king of Achshaph, one; 12:21 The king of Taanach, one; the king of Megiddo, one; 12:22 The king of Kedesh, one; the king of Jokneam of Carmel, one; 12:23 The king of Dor in the coast of Dor, one; the king of the nations of Gilgal, one; 12:24 The king of Tirzah, one: all the kings thirty and one.

13

13:1 Now Joshua was old and stricken in years; and the LORD said unto him, Thou art old and stricken in years, and there remaineth yet very much land to be possessed.
13:2 This is the land that yet remaineth: all the borders of the Philistines, and all Geshuri, 13:3 From Sihor, which is before Egypt, even unto the borders of Ekron northward, which is counted to the Canaanite: five lords of the Philistines; the Gazathites, and the Ashdothites, the Eshkalonites, the Gittites, and the Ekronites; also the Avites: 13:4 From the south, all the land of the Canaanites, and Mearah that is beside the Sidonians unto Aphek, to the borders of the Amorites: 13:5 And the land of the Giblites, and all Lebanon, toward the sunrising, from Baalgad under mount Hermon unto the entering into Hamath.
13:6 All the inhabitants of the hill country from Lebanon unto Misrephothmaim, and all the Sidonians, them will I drive out from before the children of Israel: only divide thou it by lot unto the Israelites for an inheritance, as I have commanded thee.
13:7 Now therefore divide this land for an inheritance unto the nine tribes, and the half tribe of Manasseh, 13:8 With whom the Reubenites and the Gadites have received their inheritance, which Moses gave them, beyond Jordan eastward, even as Moses the servant of the LORD gave them; 13:9 From Aroer, that is upon the bank of the river Arnon, and the city that is in the midst of the river, and all the plain of Medeba unto Dibon; 13:10 And all the cities of Sihon king of the Amorites, which reigned in Heshbon, unto the border of the children of Ammon; 13:11 And Gilead, and the border of the Geshurites and Maachathites, and all mount Hermon, and all Bashan unto Salcah; 13:12 All the kingdom of Og in Bashan, which reigned in Ashtaroth and in Edrei, who remained of the remnant of the giants: for

these did Moses smite, and cast them out.
13:13 Nevertheless the children of Israel expelled not the Geshurites, nor the Maachathites: but the Geshurites and the Maachathites dwell among the Israelites until this day.
13:14 Only unto the tribes of Levi he gave none inheritance; the sacrifices of the LORD God of Israel made by fire are their inheritance, as he said unto them.
13:15 And Moses gave unto the tribe of the children of Reuben inheritance according to their families.
13:16 And their coast was from Aroer, that is on the bank of the river Arnon, and the city that is in the midst of the river, and all the plain by
Medeba; 13:17 Heshbon, and all her cities that are in the plain; Dibon, and
Bamothbaal, and Bethbaalmeon, 13:18 And Jahaza, and Kedemoth, and
Mephaath, 13:19 And Kirjathaim, and Sibmah, and Zarethshahar in the
mount of the valley, 13:20 And Bethpeor, and Ashdothpisgah, and
Bethjeshimoth, 13:21 And all the cities of the plain, and all the kingdom of Sihon king of the Amorites, which reigned in Heshbon, whom Moses smote with the princes of Midian, Evi, and Rekem, and Zur, and Hur, and Reba, which were dukes of Sihon, dwelling in the country.
13:22 Balaam also the son of Beor, the soothsayer, did the children of Israel slay with the sword among them that were slain by them.
13:23 And the border of the children of Reuben was Jordan, and the border thereof. This was the inheritance of the children of Reuben after their families, the cities and the villages thereof.
13:24 And Moses gave inheritance unto the tribe of Gad, even unto the children of Gad according to their families.
13:25 And their coast was Jazer, and all the cities of Gilead, and half the land of the children of Ammon, unto Aroer that is before Rabbah; 13:26
And from Heshbon unto Ramathmizpeh, and Betonim; and from
Mahanaim unto the border of Debir; 13:27 And in the valley, Betharam, and Bethnimrah, and Succoth, and Zaphon, the rest of the kingdom of Sihon king of Heshbon, Jordan and his border, even unto the edge of the sea of Chinnereth on the other side Jordan eastward.
13:28 This is the inheritance of the children of Gad after their families, the cities, and their villages.
13:29 And Moses gave inheritance unto the half tribe of Manasseh: and this was the possession of the half tribe of the children of Manasseh by their families.
13:30 And their coast was from Mahanaim, all Bashan, all the kingdom of Og king of Bashan, and all the towns of Jair, which are in Bashan,
threescore cities: 13:31 And half Gilead, and Ashtaroth, and Edrei, cities of
the kingdom of Og in Bashan, were pertaining unto the children of Machir the son of Manasseh, even to the one half of the children of Machir by their

families.
13:32 These are the countries which Moses did distribute for inheritance in the plains of Moab, on the other side Jordan, by Jericho, eastward.
13:33 But unto the tribe of Levi Moses gave not any inheritance: the LORD God of Israel was their inheritance, as he said unto them.

14

14:1 And these are the countries which the children of Israel inherited in the land of Canaan, which Eleazar the priest, and Joshua the son of Nun, and the heads of the fathers of the tribes of the children of Israel, distributed for inheritance to them.
14:2 By lot was their inheritance, as the LORD commanded by the hand of Moses, for the nine tribes, and for the half tribe.
14:3 For Moses had given the inheritance of two tribes and an half tribe on the other side Jordan: but unto the Levites he gave none inheritance among them.
14:4 For the children of Joseph were two tribes, Manasseh and Ephraim: therefore they gave no part unto the Levites in the land, save cities to dwell in, with their suburbs for their cattle and for their substance.
14:5 As the LORD commanded Moses, so the children of Israel did, and they divided the land.
14:6 Then the children of Judah came unto Joshua in Gilgal: and Caleb the son of Jephunneh the Kenezite said unto him, Thou knowest the thing that the LORD said unto Moses the man of God concerning me and thee in Kadeshbarnea.
14:7 Forty years old was I when Moses the servant of the LORD sent me from Kadeshbarnea to espy out the land; and I brought him word again as it was in mine heart.
14:8 Nevertheless my brethren that went up with me made the heart of the people melt: but I wholly followed the LORD my God.
14:9 And Moses sware on that day, saying, Surely the land whereon thy feet have trodden shall be thine inheritance, and thy children's for ever, because thou hast wholly followed the LORD my God.
14:10 And now, behold, the LORD hath kept me alive, as he said, these forty and five years, even since the LORD spake this word unto Moses, while the children of Israel wandered in the wilderness: and now, lo, I am this day fourscore and five years old.
14:11 As yet I am as strong this day as I was in the day that Moses sent me: as my strength was then, even so is my strength now, for war, both to go out, and to come in.

14:12 Now therefore give me this mountain, whereof the LORD spake in that day; for thou heardest in that day how the Anakims were there, and that the cities were great and fenced: if so be the LORD will be with me, then I shall be able to drive them out, as the LORD said.
14:13 And Joshua blessed him, and gave unto Caleb the son of Jephunneh Hebron for an inheritance.
14:14 Hebron therefore became the inheritance of Caleb the son of Jephunneh the Kenezite unto this day, because that he wholly followed the LORD God of Israel.
14:15 And the name of Hebron before was Kirjatharba; which Arba was a great man among the Anakims. And the land had rest from war.

15

15:1 This then was the lot of the tribe of the children of Judah by their families; even to the border of Edom the wilderness of Zin southward was the uttermost part of the south coast.
15:2 And their south border was from the shore of the salt sea, from the
bay that looketh southward: 15:3 And it went out to the south side to
Maalehacrabbim, and passed along to Zin, and ascended up on the south side unto Kadeshbarnea, and passed along to Hezron, and went up to Adar,
and fetched a compass to Karkaa: 15:4 From thence it passed toward
Azmon, and went out unto the river of Egypt; and the goings out of that coast were at the sea: this shall be your south coast.
15:5 And the east border was the salt sea, even unto the end of Jordan.
And their border in the north quarter was from the bay of the sea at the
uttermost part of Jordan: 15:6 And the border went up to Bethhogla, and
passed along by the north of Betharabah; and the border went up to the
stone of Bohan the son of Reuben: 15:7 And the border went up toward
Debir from the valley of Achor, and so northward, looking toward Gilgal, that is before the going up to Adummim, which is on the south side of the river: and the border passed toward the waters of Enshemesh, and the
goings out thereof were at Enrogel: 15:8 And the border went up by the
valley of the son of Hinnom unto the south side of the Jebusite; the same is Jerusalem: and the border went up to the top of the mountain that lieth before the valley of Hinnom westward, which is at the end of the valley of
the giants northward: 15:9 And the border was drawn from the top of the
hill unto the fountain of the water of Nephtoah, and went out to the cities of mount Ephron; and the border was drawn to Baalah, which is
Kirjathjearim: 15:10 And the border compassed from Baalah westward unto
mount Seir, and passed along unto the side of mount Jearim, which is

Chesalon, on the north side, and went down to Bethshemesh, and passed
on to Timnah: 15:11 And the border went out unto the side of Ekron
northward: and the border was drawn to Shicron, and passed along to
mount Baalah, and went out unto Jabneel; and the goings out of the border
were at the sea.
15:12 And the west border was to the great sea, and the coast thereof.
This is the coast of the children of Judah round about according to their
families.
15:13 And unto Caleb the son of Jephunneh he gave a part among the
children of Judah, according to the commandment of the LORD to Joshua,
even the city of Arba the father of Anak, which city is Hebron.
15:14 And Caleb drove thence the three sons of Anak, Sheshai, and
Ahiman, and Talmai, the children of Anak.
15:15 And he went up thence to the inhabitants of Debir: and the name of
Debir before was Kirjathsepher.
15:16 And Caleb said, He that smiteth Kirjathsepher, and taketh it, to him
will I give Achsah my daughter to wife.
15:17 And Othniel the son of Kenaz, the brother of Caleb, took it: and he
gave him Achsah his daughter to wife.
15:18 And it came to pass, as she came unto him, that she moved him to
ask of her father a field: and she lighted off her ass; and Caleb said unto her,
What wouldest thou? 15:19 Who answered, Give me a blessing; for thou
hast given me a south land; give me also springs of water. And he gave her
the upper springs, and the nether springs.
15:20 This is the inheritance of the tribe of the children of Judah according
to their families.
15:21 And the uttermost cities of the tribe of the children of Judah toward
the coast of Edom southward were Kabzeel, and Eder, and Jagur, 15:22
And Kinah, and Dimonah, and Adadah, 15:23 And Kedesh, and Hazor,
and Ithnan, 15:24 Ziph, and Telem, and Bealoth, 15:25 And Hazor,
Hadattah, and Kerioth, and Hezron, which is Hazor, 15:26 Amam, and
Shema, and Moladah, 15:27 And Hazargaddah, and Heshmon, and
Bethpalet, 15:28 And Hazarshual, and Beersheba, and Bizjothjah, 15:29
Baalah, and Iim, and Azem, 15:30 And Eltolad, and Chesil, and Hormah,
15:31 And Ziklag, and Madmannah, and Sansannah, 15:32 And Lebaoth,
and Shilhim, and Ain, and Rimmon: all the cities are twenty and nine, with
their villages: 15:33 And in the valley, Eshtaol, and Zoreah, and Ashnah,
15:34 And Zanoah, and Engannim, Tappuah, and Enam, 15:35 Jarmuth,
and Adullam, Socoh, and Azekah, 15:36 And Sharaim, and Adithaim, and
Gederah, and Gederothaim; fourteen cities with their villages: 15:37 Zenan,
and Hadashah, and Migdalgad, 15:38 And Dilean, and Mizpeh, and
Joktheel, 15:39 Lachish, and Bozkath, and Eglon, 15:40 And Cabbon, and
Lahmam, and Kithlish, 15:41 And Gederoth, Bethdagon, and Naamah, and

Makkedah; sixteen cities with their villages: 15:42 Libnah, and Ether, and Ashan, 15:43 And Jiphtah, and Ashnah, and Nezib, 15:44 And Keilah, and Achzib, and Mareshah; nine cities with their villages: 15:45 Ekron, with her towns and her villages: 15:46 From Ekron even unto the sea, all that lay near Ashdod, with their villages: 15:47 Ashdod with her towns and her villages, Gaza with her towns and her villages, unto the river of Egypt, and the great sea, and the border thereof: 15:48 And in the mountains, Shamir, and Jattir, and Socoh, 15:49 And Dannah, and Kirjathsannah, which is Debir, 15:50 And Anab, and Eshtemoh, and Anim, 15:51 And Goshen, and Holon, and Giloh; eleven cities with their villages: 15:52 Arab, and Dumah, and Eshean, 15:53 And Janum, and Bethtappuah, and Aphekah, 15:54 And Humtah, and Kirjatharba, which is Hebron, and Zior; nine cities with their villages: 15:55 Maon, Carmel, and Ziph, and Juttah, 15:56 And Jezreel, and Jokdeam, and Zanoah, 15:57 Cain, Gibeah, and Timnah; ten cities with their villages: 15:58 Halhul, Bethzur, and Gedor, 15:59 And Maarath, and Bethanoth, and Eltekon; six cities with their villages: 15:60 Kirjathbaal, which is Kirjathjearim, and Rabbah; two cities with their villages: 15:61 In the wilderness, Betharabah, Middin, and Secacah, 15:62 And Nibshan, and the city of Salt, and Engedi; six cities with their villages.

15:63 As for the Jebusites the inhabitants of Jerusalem, the children of Judah could not drive them out; but the Jebusites dwell with the children of Judah at Jerusalem unto this day.

16

16:1 And the lot of the children of Joseph fell from Jordan by Jericho, unto the water of Jericho on the east, to the wilderness that goeth up from Jericho throughout mount Bethel, 16:2 And goeth out from Bethel to Luz, and passeth along unto the borders of Archi to Ataroth, 16:3 And goeth down westward to the coast of Japhleti, unto the coast of Bethhoron the nether, and to Gezer; and the goings out thereof are at the sea.

16:4 So the children of Joseph, Manasseh and Ephraim, took their inheritance.

16:5 And the border of the children of Ephraim according to their families was thus: even the border of their inheritance on the east side was Atarothaddar, unto Bethhoron the upper; 16:6 And the border went out toward the sea to Michmethah on the north side; and the border went about eastward unto Taanathshiloh, and passed by it on the east to Janohah; 16:7 And it went down from Janohah to Ataroth, and to Naarath, and came to Jericho, and went out at Jordan.

16:8 The border went out from Tappuah westward unto the river Kanah;

and the goings out thereof were at the sea. This is the inheritance of the tribe of the children of Ephraim by their families.
16:9 And the separate cities for the children of Ephraim were among the inheritance of the children of Manasseh, all the cities with their villages.
16:10 And they drave not out the Canaanites that dwelt in Gezer: but the Canaanites dwell among the Ephraimites unto this day, and serve under tribute.

17

17:1 There was also a lot for the tribe of Manasseh; for he was the firstborn of Joseph; to wit, for Machir the firstborn of Manasseh, the father of Gilead: because he was a man of war, therefore he had Gilead and Bashan.
17:2 There was also a lot for the rest of the children of Manasseh by their families; for the children of Abiezer, and for the children of Helek, and for the children of Asriel, and for the children of Shechem, and for the children of Hepher, and for the children of Shemida: these were the male children of Manasseh the son of Joseph by their families.
17:3 But Zelophehad, the son of Hepher, the son of Gilead, the son of Machir, the son of Manasseh, had no sons, but daughters: and these are the names of his daughters, Mahlah, and Noah, Hoglah, Milcah, and Tirzah.
17:4 And they came near before Eleazar the priest, and before Joshua the son of Nun, and before the princes, saying, The LORD commanded Moses to give us an inheritance among our brethren. Therefore according to the commandment of the LORD he gave them an inheritance among the brethren of their father.
17:5 And there fell ten portions to Manasseh, beside the land of Gilead and
Bashan, which were on the other side Jordan; 17:6 Because the daughters of
Manasseh had an inheritance among his sons: and the rest of Manasseh's sons had the land of Gilead.
17:7 And the coast of Manasseh was from Asher to Michmethah, that lieth before Shechem; and the border went along on the right hand unto the inhabitants of Entappuah.
17:8 Now Manasseh had the land of Tappuah: but Tappuah on the border
of Manasseh belonged to the children of Ephraim; 17:9 And the coast
descended unto the river Kanah, southward of the river: these cities of
Ephraim are among the cities of Manasseh: the coast of Manasseh also was
on the north side of the river, and the outgoings of it were at the sea: 17:10
Southward it was Ephraim's, and northward it was Manasseh's, and the sea
is his border; and they met together in Asher on the north, and in Issachar
on the east.

17:11 And Manasseh had in Issachar and in Asher Bethshean and her towns, and Ibleam and her towns, and the inhabitants of Dor and her towns, and the inhabitants of Endor and her towns, and the inhabitants of Taanach and her towns, and the inhabitants of Megiddo and her towns, even three countries.
17:12 Yet the children of Manasseh could not drive out the inhabitants of those cities; but the Canaanites would dwell in that land.
17:13 Yet it came to pass, when the children of Israel were waxen strong, that they put the Canaanites to tribute, but did not utterly drive them out.
17:14 And the children of Joseph spake unto Joshua, saying, Why hast thou
given me but one lot and one portion to inherit, seeing I am a great people,
forasmuch as the LORD hath blessed me hitherto? 17:15 And Joshua
answered them, If thou be a great people, then get thee up to the wood
country, and cut down for thyself there in the land of the Perizzites and of
the giants, if mount Ephraim be too narrow for thee.
17:16 And the children of Joseph said, The hill is not enough for us: and all the Canaanites that dwell in the land of the valley have chariots of iron, both they who are of Bethshean and her towns, and they who are of the valley of Jezreel.
17:17 And Joshua spake unto the house of Joseph, even to Ephraim and to
Manasseh, saying, Thou art a great people, and hast great power: thou shalt
not have one lot only: 17:18 But the mountain shall be thine; for it is a
wood, and thou shalt cut it down: and the outgoings of it shall be thine: for
thou shalt drive out the Canaanites, though they have iron chariots, and
though they be strong.

18

18:1 And the whole congregation of the children of Israel assembled together at Shiloh, and set up the tabernacle of the congregation there. And the land was subdued before them.
18:2 And there remained among the children of Israel seven tribes, which had not yet received their inheritance.
18:3 And Joshua said unto the children of Israel, How long are ye slack to
go to possess the land, which the LORD God of your fathers hath given
you? 18:4 Give out from among you three men for each tribe: and I will
send them, and they shall rise, and go through the land, and describe it
according to the inheritance of them; and they shall come again to me.
18:5 And they shall divide it into seven parts: Judah shall abide in their coast on the south, and the house of Joseph shall abide in their coasts on the north.

18:6 Ye shall therefore describe the land into seven parts, and bring the description hither to me, that I may cast lots for you here before the LORD our God.
18:7 But the Levites have no part among you; for the priesthood of the LORD is their inheritance: and Gad, and Reuben, and half the tribe of Manasseh, have received their inheritance beyond Jordan on the east, which Moses the servant of the LORD gave them.
18:8 And the men arose, and went away: and Joshua charged them that went to describe the land, saying, Go and walk through the land, and describe it, and come again to me, that I may here cast lots for you before the LORD in Shiloh.
18:9 And the men went and passed through the land, and described it by cities into seven parts in a book, and came again to Joshua to the host at Shiloh.
18:10 And Joshua cast lots for them in Shiloh before the LORD: and there Joshua divided the land unto the children of Israel according to their divisions.
18:11 And the lot of the tribe of the children of Benjamin came up according to their families: and the coast of their lot came forth between the children of Judah and the children of Joseph.
18:12 And their border on the north side was from Jordan; and the border went up to the side of Jericho on the north side, and went up through the mountains westward; and the goings out thereof were at the wilderness of Bethaven.
18:13 And the border went over from thence toward Luz, to the side of Luz, which is Bethel, southward; and the border descended to Atarothadar, near the hill that lieth on the south side of the nether Bethhoron.
18:14 And the border was drawn thence, and compassed the corner of the sea southward, from the hill that lieth before Bethhoron southward; and the goings out thereof were at Kirjathbaal, which is Kirjathjearim, a city of the children of Judah: this was the west quarter.
18:15 And the south quarter was from the end of Kirjathjearim, and the border went out on the west, and went out to the well of waters of
Nephtoah: 18:16 And the border came down to the end of the mountain
that lieth before the valley of the son of Hinnom, and which is in the valley
of the giants on the north, and descended to the valley of Hinnom, to the
side of Jebusi on the south, and descended to Enrogel, 18:17 And was
drawn from the north, and went forth to Enshemesh, and went forth
toward Geliloth, which is over against the going up of Adummim, and
descended to the stone of Bohan the son of Reuben, 18:18 And passed
along toward the side over against Arabah northward, and went down unto
Arabah: 18:19 And the border passed along to the side of Bethhoglah
northward: and the outgoings of the border were at the north bay of the salt

sea at the south end of Jordan: this was the south coast.
18:20 And Jordan was the border of it on the east side. This was the
inheritance of the children of Benjamin, by the coasts thereof round about,
according to their families.
18:21 Now the cities of the tribe of the children of Benjamin according to
their families were Jericho, and Bethhoglah, and the valley of Keziz, 18:22
And Betharabah, and Zemaraim, and Bethel, 18:23 And Avim, and Pharah,
and Ophrah, 18:24 And Chepharhaammonai, and Ophni, and Gaba; twelve
cities with their villages: 18:25 Gibeon, and Ramah, and Beeroth, 18:26 And
Mizpeh, and Chephirah, and Mozah, 18:27 And Rekem, and Irpeel, and
Taralah, 18:28 And Zelah, Eleph, and Jebusi, which is Jerusalem, Gibeath,
and Kirjath; fourteen cities with their villages. This is the inheritance of the
children of Benjamin according to their families.

19

19:1 And the second lot came forth to Simeon, even for the tribe of the
children of Simeon according to their families: and their inheritance was
within the inheritance of the children of Judah.
19:2 And they had in their inheritance Beersheba, and Sheba, and Moladah,
19:3 And Hazarshual, and Balah, and Azem, 19:4 And Eltolad, and Bethul,
and Hormah, 19:5 And Ziklag, and Bethmarcaboth, and Hazarsusah, 19:6
And Bethlebaoth, and Sharuhen; thirteen cities and their villages: 19:7 Ain,
Remmon, and Ether, and Ashan; four cities and their villages: 19:8 And all
the villages that were round about these cities to Baalathbeer, Ramath of
the south. This is the inheritance of the tribe of the children of Simeon
according to their families.
19:9 Out of the portion of the children of Judah was the inheritance of the
children of Simeon: for the part of the children of Judah was too much for
them: therefore the children of Simeon had their inheritance within the
inheritance of them.
19:10 And the third lot came up for the children of Zebulun according to
their families: and the border of their inheritance was unto Sarid: 19:11 And
their border went up toward the sea, and Maralah, and reached to
Dabbasheth, and reached to the river that is before Jokneam; 19:12 And
turned from Sarid eastward toward the sunrising unto the border of
Chislothtabor, and then goeth out to Daberath, and goeth up to Japhia,
19:13 And from thence passeth on along on the east to Gittahhepher, to
Ittahkazin, and goeth out to Remmonmethoar to Neah; 19:14 And the
border compasseth it on the north side to Hannathon: and the outgoings
thereof are in the valley of Jiphthahel: 19:15 And Kattath, and Nahallal, and

Shimron, and Idalah, and Bethlehem: twelve cities with their villages.
19:16 This is the inheritance of the children of Zebulun according to their
families, these cities with their villages.
19:17 And the fourth lot came out to Issachar, for the children of Issachar
according to their families.
19:18 And their border was toward Jezreel, and Chesulloth, and Shunem,
19:19 And Haphraim, and Shihon, and Anaharath, 19:20 And Rabbith, and
Kishion, and Abez, 19:21 And Remeth, and Engannim, and Enhaddah, and
Bethpazzez; 19:22 And the coast reacheth to Tabor, and Shahazimah, and
Bethshemesh; and the outgoings of their border were at Jordan: sixteen
cities with their villages.
19:23 This is the inheritance of the tribe of the children of Issachar
according to their families, the cities and their villages.
19:24 And the fifth lot came out for the tribe of the children of Asher
according to their families.
19:25 And their border was Helkath, and Hali, and Beten, and Achshaph,
19:26 And Alammelech, and Amad, and Misheal; and reacheth to Carmel
westward, and to Shihorlibnath; 19:27 And turneth toward the sunrising to
Bethdagon, and reacheth to Zebulun, and to the valley of Jiphthahel toward
the north side of Bethemek, and Neiel, and goeth out to Cabul on the left
hand, 19:28 And Hebron, and Rehob, and Hammon, and Kanah, even unto
great Zidon; 19:29 And then the coast turneth to Ramah, and to the strong
city Tyre; and the coast turneth to Hosah; and the outgoings thereof are at
the sea from the coast to Achzib: 19:30 Ummah also, and Aphek, and
Rehob: twenty and two cities with their villages.
19:31 This is the inheritance of the tribe of the children of Asher according
to their families, these cities with their villages.
19:32 The sixth lot came out to the children of Naphtali, even for the
children of Naphtali according to their families.
19:33 And their coast was from Heleph, from Allon to Zaanannim, and
Adami, Nekeb, and Jabneel, unto Lakum; and the outgoings thereof were at
Jordan: 19:34 And then the coast turneth westward to Aznothtabor, and
goeth out from thence to Hukkok, and reacheth to Zebulun on the south
side, and reacheth to Asher on the west side, and to Judah upon Jordan
toward the sunrising.
19:35 And the fenced cities are Ziddim, Zer, and Hammath, Rakkath, and
Chinnereth, 19:36 And Adamah, and Ramah, and Hazor, 19:37 And
Kedesh, and Edrei, and Enhazor, 19:38 And Iron, and Migdalel, Horem,
and Bethanath, and Bethshemesh; nineteen cities with their villages.
19:39 This is the inheritance of the tribe of the children of Naphtali
according to their families, the cities and their villages.
19:40 And the seventh lot came out for the tribe of the children of Dan
according to their families.

19:41 And the coast of their inheritance was Zorah, and Eshtaol, and
Irshemesh, 19:42 And Shaalabbin, and Ajalon, and Jethlah, 19:43 And Elon,
and Thimnathah, and Ekron, 19:44 And Eltekeh, and Gibbethon, and
Baalath, 19:45 And Jehud, and Beneberak, and Gathrimmon, 19:46 And
Mejarkon, and Rakkon, with the border before Japho.
19:47 And the coast of the children of Dan went out too little for them:
therefore the children of Dan went up to fight against Leshem, and took it,
and smote it with the edge of the sword, and possessed it, and dwelt
therein, and called Leshem, Dan, after the name of Dan their father.
19:48 This is the inheritance of the tribe of the children of Dan according
to their families, these cities with their villages.
19:49 When they had made an end of dividing the land for inheritance by
their coasts, the children of Israel gave an inheritance to Joshua the son of
Nun among them: 19:50 According to the word of the LORD they gave
him the city which he asked, even Timnathserah in mount Ephraim: and he
built the city, and dwelt therein.
19:51 These are the inheritances, which Eleazar the priest, and Joshua the
son of Nun, and the heads of the fathers of the tribes of the children of
Israel, divided for an inheritance by lot in Shiloh before the LORD, at the
door of the tabernacle of the congregation. So they made an end of dividing
the country.

20

20:1 The LORD also spake unto Joshua, saying, 20:2 Speak to the children
of Israel, saying, Appoint out for you cities of refuge, whereof I spake unto
you by the hand of Moses: 20:3 That the slayer that killeth any person
unawares and unwittingly may flee thither: and they shall be your refuge
from the avenger of blood.
20:4 And when he that doth flee unto one of those cities shall stand at the
entering of the gate of the city, and shall declare his cause in the ears of the
elders of that city, they shall take him into the city unto them, and give him
a place, that he may dwell among them.
20:5 And if the avenger of blood pursue after him, then they shall not
deliver the slayer up into his hand; because he smote his neighbour
unwittingly, and hated him not beforetime.
20:6 And he shall dwell in that city, until he stand before the congregation
for judgment, and until the death of the high priest that shall be in those
days: then shall the slayer return, and come unto his own city, and unto his
own house, unto the city from whence he fled.
20:7 And they appointed Kedesh in Galilee in mount Naphtali, and

Shechem in mount Ephraim, and Kirjatharba, which is Hebron, in the mountain of Judah.

20:8 And on the other side Jordan by Jericho eastward, they assigned Bezer in the wilderness upon the plain out of the tribe of Reuben, and Ramoth in Gilead out of the tribe of Gad, and Golan in Bashan out of the tribe of Manasseh.

20:9 These were the cities appointed for all the children of Israel, and for the stranger that sojourneth among them, that whosoever killeth any person at unawares might flee thither, and not die by the hand of the avenger of blood, until he stood before the congregation.

21

21:1 Then came near the heads of the fathers of the Levites unto Eleazar
the priest, and unto Joshua the son of Nun, and unto the heads of the
fathers of the tribes of the children of Israel; 21:2 And they spake unto
them at Shiloh in the land of Canaan, saying, The LORD commanded by
the hand of Moses to give us cities to dwell in, with the suburbs thereof for
our cattle.

21:3 And the children of Israel gave unto the Levites out of their inheritance, at the commandment of the LORD, these cities and their suburbs.

21:4 And the lot came out for the families of the Kohathites: and the children of Aaron the priest, which were of the Levites, had by lot out of the tribe of Judah, and out of the tribe of Simeon, and out of the tribe of Benjamin, thirteen cities.

21:5 And the rest of the children of Kohath had by lot out of the families of the tribe of Ephraim, and out of the tribe of Dan, and out of the half tribe of Manasseh, ten cities.

21:6 And the children of Gershon had by lot out of the families of the tribe of Issachar, and out of the tribe of Asher, and out of the tribe of Naphtali, and out of the half tribe of Manasseh in Bashan, thirteen cities.

21:7 The children of Merari by their families had out of the tribe of Reuben, and out of the tribe of Gad, and out of the tribe of Zebulun, twelve cities.

21:8 And the children of Israel gave by lot unto the Levites these cities with their suburbs, as the LORD commanded by the hand of Moses.

21:9 And they gave out of the tribe of the children of Judah, and out of the tribe of the children of Simeon, these cities which are here mentioned by name.

21:10 Which the children of Aaron, being of the families of the Kohathites, who were of the children of Levi, had: for theirs was the first lot.

21:11 And they gave them the city of Arba the father of Anak, which city is Hebron, in the hill country of Judah, with the suburbs thereof round about it.
21:12 But the fields of the city, and the villages thereof, gave they to Caleb the son of Jephunneh for his possession.
21:13 Thus they gave to the children of Aaron the priest Hebron with her suburbs, to be a city of refuge for the slayer; and Libnah with her suburbs,
21:14 And Jattir with her suburbs, and Eshtemoa with her suburbs, 21:15
And Holon with her suburbs, and Debir with her suburbs, 21:16 And Ain
with her suburbs, and Juttah with her suburbs, and Bethshemesh with her suburbs; nine cities out of those two tribes.
21:17 And out of the tribe of Benjamin, Gibeon with her suburbs, Geba
with her suburbs, 21:18 Anathoth with her suburbs, and Almon with her suburbs; four cities.
21:19 All the cities of the children of Aaron, the priests, were thirteen cities with their suburbs.
21:20 And the families of the children of Kohath, the Levites which remained of the children of Kohath, even they had the cities of their lot out of the tribe of Ephraim.
21:21 For they gave them Shechem with her suburbs in mount Ephraim, to
be a city of refuge for the slayer; and Gezer with her suburbs, 21:22 And
Kibzaim with her suburbs, and Bethhoron with her suburbs; four cities.
21:23 And out of the tribe of Dan, Eltekeh with her suburbs, Gibbethon
with her suburbs, 21:24 Aijalon with her suburbs, Gathrimmon with her suburbs; four cities.
21:25 And out of the half tribe of Manasseh, Tanach with her suburbs, and Gathrimmon with her suburbs; two cities.
21:26 All the cities were ten with their suburbs for the families of the children of Kohath that remained.
21:27 And unto the children of Gershon, of the families of the Levites, out of the other half tribe of Manasseh they gave Golan in Bashan with her suburbs, to be a city of refuge for the slayer; and Beeshterah with her suburbs; two cities.
21:28 And out of the tribe of Issachar, Kishon with her suburbs, Dabareh
with her suburbs, 21:29 Jarmuth with her suburbs, Engannim with her suburbs; four cities.
21:30 And out of the tribe of Asher, Mishal with her suburbs, Abdon with
her suburbs, 21:31 Helkath with her suburbs, and Rehob with her suburbs; four cities.
21:32 And out of the tribe of Naphtali, Kedesh in Galilee with her suburbs, to be a city of refuge for the slayer; and Hammothdor with her suburbs, and Kartan with her suburbs; three cities.
21:33 All the cities of the Gershonites according to their families were

thirteen cities with their suburbs.
21:34 And unto the families of the children of Merari, the rest of the
Levites, out of the tribe of Zebulun, Jokneam with her suburbs, and Kartah
with her suburbs, 21:35 Dimnah with her suburbs, Nahalal with her
suburbs; four cities.
21:36 And out of the tribe of Reuben, Bezer with her suburbs, and Jahazah
with her suburbs, 21:37 Kedemoth with her suburbs, and Mephaath with
her suburbs; four cities.
21:38 And out of the tribe of Gad, Ramoth in Gilead with her suburbs, to
be a city of refuge for the slayer; and Mahanaim with her suburbs, 21:39
Heshbon with her suburbs, Jazer with her suburbs; four cities in all.
21:40 So all the cities for the children of Merari by their families, which
were remaining of the families of the Levites, were by their lot twelve cities.
21:41 All the cities of the Levites within the possession of the children of
Israel were forty and eight cities with their suburbs.
21:42 These cities were every one with their suburbs round about them:
thus were all these cities.
21:43 And the LORD gave unto Israel all the land which he sware to give
unto their fathers; and they possessed it, and dwelt therein.
21:44 And the LORD gave them rest round about, according to all that he
sware unto their fathers: and there stood not a man of all their enemies
before them; the LORD delivered all their enemies into their hand.
21:45 There failed not ought of any good thing which the LORD had
spoken unto the house of Israel; all came to pass.

22

22:1 Then Joshua called the Reubenites, and the Gadites, and the half tribe
of Manasseh, 22:2 And said unto them, Ye have kept all that Moses the
servant of the LORD commanded you, and have obeyed my voice in all
that I commanded you: 22:3 Ye have not left your brethren these many
days unto this day, but have kept the charge of the commandment of the
LORD your God.
22:4 And now the LORD your God hath given rest unto your brethren, as
he promised them: therefore now return ye, and get you unto your tents,
and unto the land of your possession, which Moses the servant of the
LORD gave you on the other side Jordan.
22:5 But take diligent heed to do the commandment and the law, which
Moses the servant of the LORD charged you, to love the LORD your God,
and to walk in all his ways, and to keep his commandments, and to cleave
unto him, and to serve him with all your heart and with all your soul.

22:6 So Joshua blessed them, and sent them away: and they went unto their
tents.
22:7 Now to the one half of the tribe of Manasseh Moses had given
possession in Bashan: but unto the other half thereof gave Joshua among
their brethren on this side Jordan westward. And when Joshua sent them
away also unto their tents, then he blessed them, 22:8 And he spake unto
them, saying, Return with much riches unto your tents, and with very much
cattle, with silver, and with gold, and with brass, and with iron, and with
very much raiment: divide the spoil of your enemies with your brethren.
22:9 And the children of Reuben and the children of Gad and the half tribe
of Manasseh returned, and departed from the children of Israel out of
Shiloh, which is in the land of Canaan, to go unto the country of Gilead, to
the land of their possession, whereof they were possessed, according to the
word of the LORD by the hand of Moses.
22:10 And when they came unto the borders of Jordan, that are in the land
of Canaan, the children of Reuben and the children of Gad and the half
tribe of Manasseh built there an altar by Jordan, a great altar to see to.
22:11 And the children of Israel heard say, Behold, the children of Reuben
and the children of Gad and the half tribe of Manasseh have built an altar
over against the land of Canaan, in the borders of Jordan, at the passage of
the children of Israel.
22:12 And when the children of Israel heard of it, the whole congregation
of the children of Israel gathered themselves together at Shiloh, to go up to
war against them.
22:13 And the children of Israel sent unto the children of Reuben, and to
the children of Gad, and to the half tribe of Manasseh, into the land of
Gilead, Phinehas the son of Eleazar the priest, 22:14 And with him ten
princes, of each chief house a prince throughout all the tribes of Israel; and
each one was an head of the house of their fathers among the thousands of
Israel.
22:15 And they came unto the children of Reuben, and to the children of
Gad, and to the half tribe of Manasseh, unto the land of Gilead, and they
spake with them, saying, 22:16 Thus saith the whole congregation of the
LORD, What trespass is this that ye have committed against the God of
Israel, to turn away this day from following the LORD, in that ye have
builded you an altar, that ye might rebel this day against the LORD? 22:17
Is the iniquity of Peor too little for us, from which we are not cleansed until
this day, although there was a plague in the congregation of the LORD,
22:18 But that ye must turn away this day from following the LORD? and it
will be, seeing ye rebel to day against the LORD, that to morrow he will be
wroth with the whole congregation of Israel.
22:19 Notwithstanding, if the land of your possession be unclean, then pass
ye over unto the land of the possession of the LORD, wherein the LORD's

tabernacle dwelleth, and take possession among us: but rebel not against the LORD, nor rebel against us, in building you an altar beside the altar of the LORD our God.

22:20 Did not Achan the son of Zerah commit a trespass in the accursed thing, and wrath fell on all the congregation of Israel? and that man perished not alone in his iniquity.

22:21 Then the children of Reuben and the children of Gad and the half
tribe of Manasseh answered, and said unto the heads of the thousands of
Israel, 22:22 The LORD God of gods, the LORD God of gods, he
knoweth, and Israel he shall know; if it be in rebellion, or if in transgression
against the LORD, (save us not this day,) 22:23 That we have built us an
altar to turn from following the LORD, or if to offer thereon burnt offering
or meat offering, or if to offer peace offerings thereon, let the LORD
himself require it; 22:24 And if we have not rather done it for fear of this
thing, saying, In time to come your children might speak unto our children,
saying, What have ye to do with the LORD God of Israel? 22:25 For the
LORD hath made Jordan a border between us and you, ye children of
Reuben and children of Gad; ye have no part in the LORD: so shall your
children make our children cease from fearing the LORD.

22:26 Therefore we said, Let us now prepare to build us an altar, not for
burnt offering, nor for sacrifice: 22:27 But that it may be a witness between
us, and you, and our generations after us, that we might do the service of
the LORD before him with our burnt offerings, and with our sacrifices, and
with our peace offerings; that your children may not say to our children in
time to come, Ye have no part in the LORD.

22:28 Therefore said we, that it shall be, when they should so say to us or to our generations in time to come, that we may say again, Behold the pattern of the altar of the LORD, which our fathers made, not for burnt offerings, nor for sacrifices; but it is a witness between us and you.

22:29 God forbid that we should rebel against the LORD, and turn this day from following the LORD, to build an altar for burnt offerings, for meat offerings, or for sacrifices, beside the altar of the LORD our God that is before his tabernacle.

22:30 And when Phinehas the priest, and the princes of the congregation and heads of the thousands of Israel which were with him, heard the words that the children of Reuben and the children of Gad and the children of Manasseh spake, it pleased them.

22:31 And Phinehas the son of Eleazar the priest said unto the children of Reuben, and to the children of Gad, and to the children of Manasseh, This day we perceive that the LORD is among us, because ye have not committed this trespass against the LORD: now ye have delivered the children of Israel out of the hand of the LORD.

22:32 And Phinehas the son of Eleazar the priest, and the princes, returned

from the children of Reuben, and from the children of Gad, out of the land of Gilead, unto the land of Canaan, to the children of Israel, and brought them word again.
22:33 And the thing pleased the children of Israel; and the children of Israel blessed God, and did not intend to go up against them in battle, to destroy the land wherein the children of Reuben and Gad dwelt.
22:34 And the children of Reuben and the children of Gad called the altar Ed: for it shall be a witness between us that the LORD is God.

23

23:1 And it came to pass a long time after that the LORD had given rest unto Israel from all their enemies round about, that Joshua waxed old and stricken in age.
23:2 And Joshua called for all Israel, and for their elders, and for their heads, and for their judges, and for their officers, and said unto them, I am
old and stricken in age: 23:3 And ye have seen all that the LORD your God
hath done unto all these nations because of you; for the LORD your God is he that hath fought for you.
23:4 Behold, I have divided unto you by lot these nations that remain, to be an inheritance for your tribes, from Jordan, with all the nations that I have cut off, even unto the great sea westward.
23:5 And the LORD your God, he shall expel them from before you, and drive them from out of your sight; and ye shall possess their land, as the LORD your God hath promised unto you.
23:6 Be ye therefore very courageous to keep and to do all that is written in the book of the law of Moses, that ye turn not aside therefrom to the right
hand or to the left; 23:7 That ye come not among these nations, these that
remain among you; neither make mention of the name of their gods, nor cause to swear by them, neither serve them, nor bow yourselves unto them:
23:8 But cleave unto the LORD your God, as ye have done unto this day.
23:9 For the LORD hath driven out from before you great nations and strong: but as for you, no man hath been able to stand before you unto this day.
23:10 One man of you shall chase a thousand: for the LORD your God, he it is that fighteth for you, as he hath promised you.
23:11 Take good heed therefore unto yourselves, that ye love the LORD your God.
23:12 Else if ye do in any wise go back, and cleave unto the remnant of these nations, even these that remain among you, and shall make marriages
with them, and go in unto them, and they to you: 23:13 Know for a

certainty that the LORD your God will no more drive out any of these nations from before you; but they shall be snares and traps unto you, and scourges in your sides, and thorns in your eyes, until ye perish from off this good land which the LORD your God hath given you.
23:14 And, behold, this day I am going the way of all the earth: and ye know in all your hearts and in all your souls, that not one thing hath failed of all the good things which the LORD your God spake concerning you; all are come to pass unto you, and not one thing hath failed thereof.
23:15 Therefore it shall come to pass, that as all good things are come upon you, which the LORD your God promised you; so shall the LORD bring upon you all evil things, until he have destroyed you from off this good land which the LORD your God hath given you.
23:16 When ye have transgressed the covenant of the LORD your God, which he commanded you, and have gone and served other gods, and bowed yourselves to them; then shall the anger of the LORD be kindled against you, and ye shall perish quickly from off the good land which he hath given unto you.

24

24:1 And Joshua gathered all the tribes of Israel to Shechem, and called for the elders of Israel, and for their heads, and for their judges, and for their officers; and they presented themselves before God.
24:2 And Joshua said unto all the people, Thus saith the LORD God of Israel, Your fathers dwelt on the other side of the flood in old time, even Terah, the father of Abraham, and the father of Nachor: and they served other gods.
24:3 And I took your father Abraham from the other side of the flood, and led him throughout all the land of Canaan, and multiplied his seed, and gave him Isaac.
24:4 And I gave unto Isaac Jacob and Esau: and I gave unto Esau mount Seir, to possess it; but Jacob and his children went down into Egypt.
24:5 I sent Moses also and Aaron, and I plagued Egypt, according to that which I did among them: and afterward I brought you out.
24:6 And I brought your fathers out of Egypt: and ye came unto the sea; and the Egyptians pursued after your fathers with chariots and horsemen unto the Red sea.
24:7 And when they cried unto the LORD, he put darkness between you and the Egyptians, and brought the sea upon them, and covered them; and your eyes have seen what I have done in Egypt: and ye dwelt in the wilderness a long season.

24:8 And I brought you into the land of the Amorites, which dwelt on the other side Jordan; and they fought with you: and I gave them into your hand, that ye might possess their land; and I destroyed them from before you.

24:9 Then Balak the son of Zippor, king of Moab, arose and warred against
Israel, and sent and called Balaam the son of Beor to curse you: 24:10 But I
would not hearken unto Balaam; therefore he blessed you still: so I
delivered you out of his hand.

24:11 And you went over Jordan, and came unto Jericho: and the men of Jericho fought against you, the Amorites, and the Perizzites, and the Canaanites, and the Hittites, and the Girgashites, the Hivites, and the Jebusites; and I delivered them into your hand.

24:12 And I sent the hornet before you, which drave them out from before you, even the two kings of the Amorites; but not with thy sword, nor with thy bow.

24:13 And I have given you a land for which ye did not labour, and cities which ye built not, and ye dwell in them; of the vineyards and oliveyards which ye planted not do ye eat.

24:14 Now therefore fear the LORD, and serve him in sincerity and in truth: and put away the gods which your fathers served on the other side of the flood, and in Egypt; and serve ye the LORD.

24:15 And if it seem evil unto you to serve the LORD, choose you this day whom ye will serve; whether the gods which your fathers served that were on the other side of the flood, or the gods of the Amorites, in whose land ye dwell: but as for me and my house, we will serve the LORD.

24:16 And the people answered and said, God forbid that we should
forsake the LORD, to serve other gods; 24:17 For the LORD our God, he
it is that brought us up and our fathers out of the land of Egypt, from the
house of bondage, and which did those great signs in our sight, and
preserved us in all the way wherein we went, and among all the people
through whom we passed: 24:18 And the LORD drave out from before us
all the people, even the Amorites which dwelt in the land: therefore will we
also serve the LORD; for he is our God.

24:19 And Joshua said unto the people, Ye cannot serve the LORD: for he is an holy God; he is a jealous God; he will not forgive your transgressions nor your sins.

24:20 If ye forsake the LORD, and serve strange gods, then he will turn and do you hurt, and consume you, after that he hath done you good.

24:21 And the people said unto Joshua, Nay; but we will serve the LORD.

24:22 And Joshua said unto the people, Ye are witnesses against yourselves that ye have chosen you the LORD, to serve him. And they said, We are witnesses.

24:23 Now therefore put away, said he, the strange gods which are among

you, and incline your heart unto the LORD God of Israel.
24:24 And the people said unto Joshua, The LORD our God will we serve, and his voice will we obey.
24:25 So Joshua made a covenant with the people that day, and set them a statute and an ordinance in Shechem.
24:26 And Joshua wrote these words in the book of the law of God, and took a great stone, and set it up there under an oak, that was by the sanctuary of the LORD.
24:27 And Joshua said unto all the people, Behold, this stone shall be a witness unto us; for it hath heard all the words of the LORD which he spake unto us: it shall be therefore a witness unto you, lest ye deny your God.
24:28 So Joshua let the people depart, every man unto his inheritance.
24:29 And it came to pass after these things, that Joshua the son of Nun, the servant of the LORD, died, being an hundred and ten years old.
24:30 And they buried him in the border of his inheritance in Timnathserah, which is in mount Ephraim, on the north side of the hill of Gaash.
24:31 And Israel served the LORD all the days of Joshua, and all the days of the elders that overlived Joshua, and which had known all the works of the LORD, that he had done for Israel.
24:32 And the bones of Joseph, which the children of Israel brought up out of Egypt, buried they in Shechem, in a parcel of ground which Jacob bought of the sons of Hamor the father of Shechem for an hundred pieces of silver: and it became the inheritance of the children of Joseph.
24:33 And Eleazar the son of Aaron died; and they buried him in a hill that pertained to Phinehas his son, which was given him in mount Ephraim.

THE BOOK OF JOSUE

DOUAY RHEIMS BIBLE

This Book is called JOSUE, because it contains the history of what passed under him, and according to the common opinion was written by him. The Greeks call him Jesus: for Josue and Jesus in the Hebrew, are the same name, and have the same signification, viz., A SAVIOUR. And it was not without a mystery that he who was to bring the people into the land of promise should have his name changed from OSEE (for so he was called before, Num. 13.17,) to JOSUE or JESUS, to give us to understand, that Moses by his law could only bring the people within sight of the promised inheritance, but that our Saviour JESUS was to bring us into it.

Josue Chapter 1

Josue, encouraged by the Lord, admonisheth the people to prepare themselves to pass over the Jordan.
1:1. Now it came to pass after the death of Moses, the servant of the Lord, that the Lord spoke to Josue, the son of Nun, the minister of Moses, and said to him:
1:2. Moses my servant is dead: arise, and pass over this Jordan, thou and thy people with thee, into the land which I will give to the children of Israel.
1:3. I will deliver to you every place that the sole of your foot shall tread upon, as I have said to Moses.
1:4. From the desert, and from Libanus unto the great river Euphrates, all the land of the Hethites, unto the great sea toward the going down of the sun, shall be your border.

1:5. No man shall be able to resist you all the days of thy life: as I have been with Moses, so will I be with thee: I will not leave thee, nor forsake thee.
1:6. Take courage, and be strong: for thou shalt divide by lot to this people the land for which I swore to their fathers, that I would deliver it to them.
1:7. Take courage therefore, and be very valiant: that thou mayst observe and do all the law, which Moses my servant hath commanded thee: turn not from it to the right hand or to the left, that thou mayst understand all things which thou dost.
1:8. Let not the book of this law depart from thy mouth: but thou shalt meditate on it day and night, that thou mayst observe and do all things that are written in it: then shalt thou direct thy way, and understand it.
1:9. Behold I command thee, take courage, and be strong. Fear not, and be not dismayed: because the Lord thy God is with thee in all things whatsoever thou shalt go to.
1:10. And Josue commanded the princes of the people, saying: Pass through the midst of the camp, and command the people, and say:
1:11. Prepare your victuals: for after the third day you shall pass over the Jordan, and shall go in to possess the land, which the Lord your God will give you.
1:12. And he said to the Rubenites, and the Gadites, and the half tribe of Manasses:
1:13. Remember the word, which Moses the servant of the Lord commanded you, saying: The Lord your God hath given you rest, and all this land.
1:14. Your wives, and children; and cattle, shall remain in the land which Moses gave you on this side of the Jordan: but pass you over armed before your brethren all of you that are strong of hand, and fight for them,
1:15. Until the Lord give rest to your brethren, as he hath given you, and they also possess the land which the Lord your God will give them: and so you shall return into the land of your possession, and you shall dwell in it, which Moses the servant of the Lord gave you beyond the Jordan, toward the rising of the sun.
1:16. And they made answer to Josue, and said: All that thou hast commanded us, we will do: and whither soever thou shalt send us, we will go.
1:17. As we obeyed Moses in all things, so will we obey thee also: only be the Lord thy God with thee, as he was with Moses.
1:18. He that shall gainsay thy mouth, and not obey all thy words, that thou shalt command him, let him die: only take thou courage, and do manfully.

Josue Chapter 2

Two spies are sent to Jericho, who are received and concealed by Rahab.

2:1. And Josue, the son of Nun, sent from Setim two men, to spy secretly: and said to them: Go, and view the land, and the city of Jericho. They went, and entered into the house of a woman that was a harlot, named Rahab, and lodged with her.
2:2. And it was told the king of Jericho, and was said: Behold there are men come in hither, by night, of the children of Israel, to spy the land.
2:3. And the king of Jericho sent to Rahab, saying: Bring forth the men that came to thee, and are entered into thy house: for they are spies, and are come to view all the land.
2:4. And the woman taking the men, hid them, and said: I confess they came to me, but I knew not whence they were:
2:5. And at the time of shutting the gate in the dark, they also went out together. I know not whither they are gone: pursue after them quickly, and you will overtake them.
2:6. But she made the men go up to the top of her house, and covered them with the stalks of flax, which was there.
2:7. Now they that were sent, pursued after them, by the way that leadeth to the fords of the Jordan: and as soon as they were gone out, the gate was presently shut.
2:8. The men that were hid were not yet asleep, when behold the woman went up to them, and said:
2:9. I know that the Lord hath given this land to you: for the dread of you is fallen upon us, and all the inhabitants of the land have lost all strength.
2:10. We have heard that the Lord dried up the water of the Red Sea, at your going in, when you came out of Egypt: and what things you did to the two kings of the Amorrhites, that were beyond the Jordan, Sehon and Og whom you slew.
2:11. And at the hearing these things, we were affrighted, and our heart fainted away, neither did there remain any spirit in us, at your coming in: for the Lord your God he is God in heaven above, and in the earth beneath.
2:12. Now, therefore, swear ye to me by the Lord, that as I have shewed mercy to you, so you also will shew mercy to my father's house: and give me a true token.
2:13. That you will save my father and mother, my brethren and sisters, and all things that are theirs, and deliver our souls from death.
2:14. They answered her: Be our lives for you unto death, only if thou betray us not. And when the Lord shall have delivered us the land, we will shew thee mercy and truth.
2:15. Then she let them down with a cord out of a window: for her house joined close to the wall.
2:16. And she said to them: Get ye up to the mountains, lest perhaps they

meet you as they return: and there lie ye hid three days, till they come back, and so you shall go on yonr way.
2:17. And they said to her: We shall be blameless of this oath, which thou hast made us swear,
2:18. If, when we come into the land, this scarlet cord be a sign, and thou tie it in the window, by which thou hast let us down: and gather together thy father and mother, and brethren, and all thy kindred into thy house.
2:19. Whosoever shall go out of the door of thy house, his blood shall be upon his own head, and we shall be quit. But the blood of all that shall be with thee in the house, shall light upon our head, if any man touch them.
2:20. But if thou wilt betray us, and utter this word abroad, we shall be quit of this oath, which thou hast made us swear.
2:21. And she answered: As you have spoken, so be it done: and sending them on their way, she hung the scarlet cord in the window.
2:22. But they went and came to the mountains, and stayed there three days, till they that pursued them were returned. For having sought them through all the way, they found them not.
2:23. And when they were gone back into the city, the spies returned, and came down from the mountain: and passing over the Jordan, they came to Josue, the son of Nun, and told him all that befel them,
2:24. And said: the Lord hath delivered all this land into our hands, and all the inhabitants thereof are overthrown with fear.

Josue Chapter 3

The river Jordan is miraculously dried up for the passage of the children of Israel.

3:1. And Josue rose before daylight, and removed the camp: and they departed from Setim, and came to the Jordan: he, and all the children of Israel, and they abode there for three days.
3:2. After which, the heralds went through the midst of the camp,
3:3. And began to proclaim: When you shall see the ark of the covenant of the Lord your God, and the priests of the race of Levi carrying it, rise you up also, and follow them as they go before:
3:4. And let there be between you and the ark the space of two thousand cubits: that you may see it afar off, and know which way you must go: for you have not gone this way before: and take care you come not near the ark.
3:5. And Josue said to the people: Be ye sanctified: for tomorrow the Lord will do wonders among you.
3:6. And he said to the priests: Take up the ark of the covenant, and go

before the people. And they obeyed his commands, and took it up, and walked before them.
3:7. And the Lord said to Josue: This day will I begin to exalt thee before Israel: that they may know that as I was with Moses, so I am with thee also.
3:8. And do thou command the priests, that carry the ark of the covenant, and say to them: When you shall have entered into part of the water of the Jordan, stand in it.
3:9. And Josue said to the children of Israel: Come hither, and hear the word of the Lord your God.
3:10. And again he said: By this you shall know, that the Lord, the living God, is in the midst of you, and that he shall destroy, before your sight, the Chanaanite and the Hethite, the Hevite and the Pherezite, the Gergesite also, and the Jebusite, and the Amorrhite.
3:11. Behold, the ark of the covenant of the Lord of all the earth shall go before you into the Jordan.
3:12. Prepare ye twelve men of the tribes of Israel, one of every tribe.
3:13. And when the priests, that carry the ark of the Lord the God of the whole earth, shall set the soles of their feet in the waters of the Jordan, the waters that are beneath shall run down and go off: and those that come from above, shall stand together upon a heap.
3:14. So the people went out of their tents, to pass over the Jordan: and the priests that carried the ark of the covenant, went on before them.
3:15. And as soon as they came into the Jordan, and their feet were dipped in part of the water, (now the Jordan, it being harvest time, had filled the banks of its channel,)
3:16. The waters that came down from above stood in one place, and swelling up like a mountain, were seen afar off, from the city that is called Adom, to the place of Sarthan: but those that were beneath, ran down into the sea of the wilderness, (which now is called the Dead Sea) until they wholly failed.
3:17. And the people marched over against Jericho: and the priests that carried the ark of the covenant of the Lord, stood girded upon the dry ground in the midst of the Jordan, and all the people passed over, through the channel that was dried up.

Josue Chapter 4

Twelve stones are taken out of the river to be set up for a monument of the miracle; and other twelve are placed in the midst of the river.

4:1. And when they were passed over, the Lord said to Josue:
4:2. Choose twelve men, one of every tribe:

4:3. And command them to take out of the midst of the Jordan, where the feet of the priests stood, twelve very hard stones, which you shall set in the place of the camp, where you shall pitch your tents this night.
4:4. And Josue called twelve men, whom he had chosen out of the children of Israel, one out of every tribe,
4:5. And he said to them: Go before the ark of the Lord your God to the midst of the Jordan, and carry from thence every man a stone on your shoulders, according to the number of the children of Israel,
4:6. That it may be a sign among you: and when your children shall ask you tomorrow, saying: What means these stones?
4:7. You shall answer them: The waters of the Jordan ran off before the ark of the covenant of the Lord when it passed over the same: therefore were these stones set for a monument of the children of Israel forever.
4:8. The children of Israel therefore did as Josue commanded them, carrying out of the channel of the Jordan twelve stones, as the Lord had commanded him according to the number of the children of Israel unto the place wherein they camped, and there they set them.
4:9. And Josue put other twelve stones in the midst of the channel of the Jordan, where the priests stood that carried the ark of the covenant: and they are there until this present day.
4:10. Now the priests that carried the ark, stood in the midst of the Jordan, till all things were accomplished, which the Lord had commanded Josue to speak to the people, and Moses had said to him. And the people made haste, and passed over.
4:11. And when they had all passed over, the ark also of the Lord passed over, and the priests went before the people.
4:12. The children of Ruben also, and Gad, and half the tribe of Manasses, went armed before the children of Israel, as Moses had commanded them.
4:13. And forty thousand fighting men by their troops and bands, marched through the plains and fields of the city of Jericho.
4:14. In that day the Lord magnified Josue in the sight of all Israel, that they should fear him, as they had feared Moses, while he lived.
4:15. And he said to him:
4:16. Command the priests, that carry the ark of the covenant, to come up out of the Jordan.
4:17. And he commanded them, saying: Come ye up out of the Jordan.
4:18. And when they that carried the ark of the covenant of the Lord, were come up, and began to tread on the dry ground, the waters returned into their channel, and ran as they were wont before.
4:19. And the people came up out of the Jordan, the tenth day of the first month, and camped in Galgal, over against the east side of the city of Jericho.
4:20. And the twelve stones, which they had taken out of the channel of the

Jordan, Josue pitched in Galgal,
4:21. And said to the children of Israel: When your children shall ask their fathers tomorrow, and shall say to them: What mean these stones?
4:22. You shall teach them, and say: Israel passed over this Jordan through the dry channel,
4:23. The Lord your God drying up the waters thereof in your sight, until you passed over:
4:24. As he had done before in the Red Sea, which he dried up till we passed through:
4:25. That all the people of the earth may learn the most mighty hand of the Lord, that you also may fear the Lord your God for ever.

Josue Chapter 5

The people are circumcised: they keep the pasch. The manna ceaseth. An angel appeareth to Josue.

5:1. Now when all the kings of the Amorrhites, who dwelt beyond the Jordan, westward, and all the kings of Chanaan, who possessed the places near the great sea, had heard that the Lord had dried up the waters of the Jordan before the children of Israel, till they passed over, their heart failed them, and there remained no spirit in them, fearing the coming in of the children of Israel.
5:2. At that time the Lord said to Josue: Make thee knives of stone, and circumcise the second time the children of Israel.
The second time... Not that such as had been circumcised before were to be circumcised again; but that they were now to renew, and take up again the practice of circumcision; which had been omitted during their forty years' sojourning in the wilderness; by reason of their being always uncertain when they should be obliged to march.
5:3. He did what the Lord had commanded, and he circumcised the children of Israel in the hill of the foreskins.
5:4. Now this is the cause of the second circumcision: All the people that came out of Egypt that were males, all the men fit for war, died in the desert, during the time of the long going about in the way:
5:6. Now these were all circumcised. But the people that were born in the desert,
5:6. During the forty years of the journey in the wide wilderness, were uncircumcised: till all they were consumed that had not heard the voice of the Lord, and to whom he had sworn before, that he would not shew them the land flowing with milk and honey.
5:7. The children of these succeeded in the place of their fathers, and were

circumcised by Josue: for they were uncircumcised even as they were born, and no one had circumcised them in the way.
5:8. Now after they were all circumcised, they remained in the same place of the camp, until they were healed.
5:9. And the Lord said to Josue: This day have I taken away from you the reproach of Egypt. And the name of that place was called Galgal, until this present day.
5:10. And the children of Israel abode in Galgal, and they kept the phase, on the fourteenth day of the month at evening, in the plains of Jericho:
5:11. And they ate on the next day unleavened bread of the corn of the land, and frumenty of the same year.
5:12. And the manna ceased after they ate of the corn of the land, neither did the children of Israel use that food any more, but they ate of the corn of the present year of the land of Chanaan.
5:13. And when Josue was in the field of the city of Jericho, he lifted up his eyes, and saw a man standing over against him, holding a drawn sword, and he went to him, and said: Art thou one of ours, or of our adversaries?
5:14. And he answered: No: but I am prince of the host of the Lord, and now I am come.
Prince of the host of the Lord, etc... St. Michael, who is called prince of the people of Israel, Dan. 10.21.
5:15. Josue fell on his face to the ground. And worshipping, said: What saith my lord to his servant?
Worshipping... Not with divine honour, but with a religious veneration of an inferior kind, suitable to the dignity of his person.
5:16. Loose, saith he, thy shoes from off thy feet: for the place whereon thou standest is holy. And Josue did as was commanded him.

Josue Chapter 6

After seven days' processions, the priests sounding the trumpets, the walls of Jericho fall down: and the city is taken and destroyed.

6:1. Now Jericho was close shut up and fenced, for fear of the children of Israel, and no man durst go out or come in.
6:2. And the Lord said to Josue: Behold I have given into thy hands Jericho, and the king thereof, and all the valiant men.
6:3. Go round about the city all ye fighting men once a day: so shall ye do for six days.
6:4. And on the seventh day the priests shall take the seven trumpets, which are used in the jubilee, and shall go before the ark of the covenant: and you shall go about the city seven times, and the priests shall sound the trumpets.

6:5. And when the voice of the trumpet shall give a longer and broken tune, and shall sound in your ears, all the people shall shout together with a very great shout, and the walls of the city shall fall to the ground, and they shall enter in every one at the place against which they shall stand.
6:6. Then Josue, the son of Nun, called the priests, and said to them: Take the ark of the covenant: and let seven other priests take the seven trumpets of the jubilee, and march before the ark of the Lord.
6:7. And he said to the people: Go, and compass the city, armed, marching before the ark of the Lord.
6:8. And when Josue had ended his words, and the seven priests blew the seven trumpets before the ark of the covenant of the Lord,
6:9. And all the armed men went before, the rest of the common people followed the ark, and the sound of the trumpets was heard on all sides.
6:10. But Josue had commanded the people, saying: You shall not shout, nor shall your voice be heard, nor any word go out of your mouth: until the day come wherein I shall say to you: Cry, and shout.
6:11. So the ark of the Lord went about the city once a day, and returning into the camp, abode there.
6:12. And Josue rising before day, the priests took the ark of the Lord,
6:13. And seven of them seven trumpets, which are used in the jubilee: and they went before the ark of the Lord, walking and sounding the trumpets: and the armed men went before them, and the rest of the common people followed the ark, and they blew the trumpets.
6:14. And they went round about the city the second day once, and returned into the camp. So they did six days.
6:15. But the seventh day, rising up early, they went about the city, as it was ordered, seven times.
6:16. And when in the seventh going about the priests sounded with the trumpets, Josue said to all Israel: Shout: for the Lord hath delivered the city to you:
6:17. And let this city be an anathema, and all things that are in it, to the Lord. Let only Rahab, the harlot, live, with all that are with her in the house: for she hid the messengers whom we sent.
6:18. But beware ye lest you touch ought of those things that are forbidden, and you be guilty of transgression, and all the camp of Israel be under sin, and be troubled.
6:19. But whatsoever gold or silver there shall be, or vessels of brass and iron, let it be consecrated to the Lord, laid up in his treasures.
6:20. So all the people making a shout, and the trumpets sounding, when the voice and the sound thundered in the ears of the multitude, the walls forthwith fell down: and every man went up by the place that was over against him: and they took the city,
6:21. And killed all that were in it, man and woman, young and old. The

oxen also, and the sheep, and the asses, they slew with the edge of the sword.
6:22. But Josue said to the two men that had been sent for spies: Go into the harlot's house, and bring her out, and all things that are hers, as you assured her by oath.
6:23. And the young men went in, and brought out Rahab, and her parents, her brethren also, and all her goods, and her kindred, and made them to stay without the camp.
6:24. But they burned the city, and all things that were therein; except the gold and silver, and vessels of brass and iron, which they consecrated unto the treasury of the Lord.
6:25. But Josue saved Rahab the harlot, and her father's house, and all she had, and they dwelt in the midst of Israel until this present day: because she hid the messengers whom he had sent to spy out Jericho. At that time, Josue made an imprecation, saying:
6:26. Cursed be the man before the Lord, that shall raise up and build the city of Jericho. In his firstborn may he lay the foundation thereof, and in the last of his children set up its gates.
Cursed, etc... Jericho, in the mystical sense, signifies iniquity: the sounding of the trumpets by the priests, the preaching of the word of God; by which the walls of Jericho are thrown down, when sinners are converted; and a dreadful curse will light on them who build them up again.
6:27. And the Lord was with Josue, and his name was noised throughout all the land.

Josue Chapter 7

For the sins of Achan, the Israelites are defeated at Hai. The offender is found out; and stoned to death, and God's wrath is turned from them.

7:1. But the children of Israel transgressed the commandment, and took to their own use of that which was accursed. For Achan, the son of Charmi, the son of Zabdi, the son of Zare, of the tribe of Juda, took something of the anathema: and the Lord was angry against the children of Israel.
7:2. And when Josue sent men from Jericho against Hai, which is beside Bethaven, on the east side of the town of Bethel, he said to them: Go up, and view the country: and they fulfilled his command, and viewed Hai.
7:3. And returning, they said to him: Let not all the people go up, but let two or three thousand men go, and destroy the city: why should all the people be troubled in vain, against enemies that are very few?
7:4. There went up therefore three thousand fighting men: who immediately turned their backs,

7:5. And were defeated by the men of the city of Hai, and there fell of them six and thirty men: and the enemies pursued them from the gate as far as Sabarim, and they slew them as they fled by the descent: and the heart of the people was struck with fear, and melted like water.
7:6. But Josue rent his garments, and fell flat on the ground, before the ark of the Lord, until the evening, both he and all the ancients of Israel: and they put dust upon their heads.
7:7. And Josue said: Alas, O Lord God, why wouldst thou bring this people over the river Jordan, to deliver us into the hand of the Amorrhite, and to destroy us? would God we had stayed beyond the Jordan, as we began.
7:8. My Lord God, what shall I say, seeing Israel turning their backs to their enemies?
7:9. The Chanaanites, and all the inhabitants of the land, will hear of it, and being gathered together will surround us, and cut off our name from the earth: and what wilt thou do to thy great name?
7:10. And the Lord said to Josue: Arise, why liest thou flat on the ground?
7:11. Israel hath sinned, and transgressed my covenant: and they have taken of the anathema, and have stolen and lied, and have hid it among their goods.
7:12. Neither can Israel stand before his enemies, but he shall flee from them: because he is defiled with the anathema. I will be no more with you, till you destroy him that is guilty of this wickedness.
7:13. Arise, sanctify the people, and say to them: Be ye sanctified against tomorrow: for thus saith the Lord God of Israel: The curse is in the midst of thee, O Israel: thou canst not stand before thy enemies, till he be destroyed out of thee, that is defiled with this wickedness.
7:14. And you shall come in the morning, every one by your tribes: and what tribe soever the lot shall find, it shall come by its kindreds, and the kindred by its houses and tho house by the men.
7:15. And whosoever he be that shall be found guilty of this fact, he shall be burnt with fire, with all his substance, because he hath transgressed the covenant of the Lord, and hath done wickedness in Israel.
7:16. Josue, therefore, when he rose in the morning, made Israel to come by their tribes, and the tribe of Juda was found.
7:17. Which being brought by in families, it was found to be the family of Zare. Bringing that also by the houses, he found it to be Zabdi:
7:18. And bringing his house man by man, he found Achan, the son of Charmi, the son of Zabdi, the son of Zare, of the tribe of Juda.
7:19. And Josue said to Achan: My son, give glory to the Lord God of Israel, and confess, and tell me what thou hast done, hide it not.
7:20. And Achan answered Josue, and said to him: Indeed I have sinned against the Lord, the God of Israel, and thus and thus have I done.
7:21. For I saw among the spoils a scarlet garment, exceeding good, and

two hundred sicles of silver, and a golden rule of fifty sicles: and I coveted them, and I took them away, and hid them in the ground in the midst of my tent, and the silver I covered with the earth that I dug up.
7:22. Josue therefore sent ministers: who running to his tent, found all hid in the same place, together with the silver.
7:23. And taking them away out of the tent, they brought them to Josue, and to all the children of Israel, and threw them down before the Lord.
7:24. Then Josue, and all Israel with him, took Achan, the son of Zare, and the silver, and the garment, and the golden rule, his sons also, and his daughters, his oxen, and asses, and sheep, the tent also, and all the goods: and brought them to the valley of Achor:
His sons, etc... Probably conscious to, or accomplices of, the crime of their father.
7:25. Where Josue said: Because thou hast troubled us, the Lord trouble thee this day. And all Israel stoned him: and all things that were his, were consumed with fire.
7:26. And they gathered together upon him a great heap of stones, which remaineth until this present day And the wrath of the Lord was turned away from them. And the name of that place was called the Valley of Achor, until this day.
Achor... That is, trouble.

Josue Chapter 8

Hai is taken and burnt, and all the inhabitants slain. An altar is built, and sacrifices offered. The law is written on stones, and the blessings and cursings are read before all the people.

8:1. And the Lord said to Josue: Fear not, nor be thou dismayed: take with thee all the multitude of fighting men, arise, and go up to the town of Hai: Behold I have delivered into thy hand the king thereof, and the people, and the city, and the land.
8:2. And thou shalt do to the city of Hai, and to the king thereof, as thou hast done to Jericho, and to the king thereof: but the spoils, and all the cattle, you shall take for a prey to yourselves: lay an ambush for the city behind it.
8:3. And Josue arose, and all the army of the fighting men with him, to go up against Hai: and he sent thirty thousand chosen valiant men in the night,
8:4. And commanded them, saying: Lay an ambush behind the city: and go not very far from it: and be ye all ready.
8:5. But I, and the rest of the multitude which is with me, will approach on the contrary side against the city. And when they shall come out against us,

we will flee, and turn our backs, as we did before:
8:6. Till they pursuing us be drawn farther from the city: for they will think that we flee as before.
8:7. And whilst we are fleeing, and they pursuing, you shall rise out of the ambush, and shall destroy the city: and the Lord your God will deliver it into your hands.
8:8. And when you shall have taken it, set it on fire, and you shall do all things so as I have commanded.
8:9. And he sent them away, and they went on to the place of the ambush, and abode between Bethel and Hai, on the west side of the city of Hai.
But Josue staid that night in the midst of the people,
8:10. And rising early in the morning, he mustered his soldiers, and went up with the ancients in the front of the army, environed with the aid of the fighting men.
8:11. And when they were come, and were gone up over against the city, they stood on the north side of the city, between which and them there was a valley in the midst.
8:12. And he had chosen five thousand men, and set them to lie in ambush between Bethel and Hai, on the west side of the same city:
Five thousand... These were part of the thirty thousand mentioned above, ver. 3.
8:13. But all the rest of the army went in battle array on the north side, so that the last of that multitude reached to the west side of the city. So Josue went that night, and stood in the midst of the valley.
8:14. And when the king of Hai saw this, he made haste in the morning, and went out with all the army of the city, and set it in battle array, toward the desert, not knowing that there lay an ambush behind his back.
8:15. But Josue, and all Israel gave back, making as if they were afraid, and fleeing by the way of the wilderness.
8:16. But they shouting together, and encouraging one another, pursued them. And when they were come from the city,
8:17. And not one remained in the city of Hai and of Bethel, that did not pursue after Israel, leaving the towns open as they had rushed out,
8:18. The Lord said to Josue: Lift up the shield that is in thy hand, towards the city of Hai, for I will deliver it to thee.
8:19. And when he had lifted up his shield towards the city, the ambush, that lay hid, rose up immediately: and going to the city, took it, and set it on fire.
8:20. And the men of the city, that pursued after Josue, looking back, and seeing the smoke of the city rise up to heaven, had no more power to flee this way or that way: especially as they that had counterfeited flight, and were going toward the wilderness, turned back most valiantly against them that pursued.

8:21. So Josue, and all Israel, seeing that the city was taken, and that the smoke of the city rose up, returned, and slew the men of Hai.
8:22. And they also that had taken and set the city on fire, issuing out of the city to meet their own men, began to cut off the enemies who were surrounded by them. So that the enemies being cut off on both sides, not one of so great a multitude was saved.
8:23. And they took the king of the city of Hai alive and brought him to Josue.
8:24. So all being slain that had pursued after Israel, in his flight to the wilderness, and falling by the sword in the same place, the children of Israel returned and laid waste the city.
8:25. And the number of them that fell that day, both of men and women, was twelve thousand persons, all of the city of Hai.
8:26. But Josue drew not back his hand, which he had stretched out on high, holding the shield, till all the inhabitants of Hai were slain.
8:27. And the children of Israel divided among them, the cattle and the prey of the city, as the Lord had commanded Josue.
8:28. And he burnt the city, and made it a heap forever:
8:29. And he hung the king thereof on a gibbet, until the evening and the going down of the sun. Then Josue commanded, and they took down his carcass from the gibbet: and threw it in the very entrance of the city, heaping upon it a great heap of stones, which remaineth until this present day.
8:30. Then Josue built an altar to the Lord, the God of Israel, in Mount Hebal,
8:31. As Moses, the servant of the Lord, had commanded the children of Israel, and it is written in the book of the law of Moses: an altar of unhewn stones, which iron had not touched: and he offered upon it holocausts to the Lord, and immolated victims of peace offerings.
8:32. And he wrote upon stones, the Deuteronomy of the law of Moses, which he had ordered before the children of Israel.
8:33. And all the people, and the ancients, and the princes, and judges, stood on both sides of the ark, before the priests that carried the ark of the covenant of the Lord, both the stranger and he that was born among them, half of them by Mount Garizim, and half by Mount Hebal, as Moses the servant of the Lord, had commanded. And first he blessed the people of Israel.
8:34. After this, he read all the words of the blessing and the cursing, and all things that were written in the book of the law.
8:35. He left out nothing of those things which Moses had commanded, but he repeated all before all the people of Israel, with the women and children, and strangers, that dwelt among them.

Josue Chapter 9

Josue is deceived by the Gabaonites: who being detected are condemned to be perpetual servants.

9:1. Now when these things were heard of, all the kings beyond the Jordan, that dwelt in the mountains, and in the plains, in the places near the sea, and on the coasts of the great sea, they also that dwell by Libanus, the Hethite, and the Amorrhite, the Chanaanite, the Pherezite, and the Hevite, and the Jebusite,
9:2. Gathered themselves together, to fight against Josue and Israel with one mind, and one resolution.
9:3. But they that dwelt in Gabaon, hearing all that Josue had done to Jericho and Hai:
9:4. Cunningly devising took for themselves provisions, laying old sacks upon their asses, and wine bottles rent and sewed up again,
9:5. And very old shoes, which for a show of age were clouted with patches, and old garments upon them: the loaves also, which they carried for provisions by the way, were hard, and broken into pieces:
9:6. And they went to Josue, who then abode in the camp at Galgal, and said to him, and to all Israel with him: We are come from a far country, desiring to make peace with you. And the children of Israel answered them, and said:
9:7. Perhaps you dwell in the land which falls to our lot; if so, we can make no league with you.
9:8. But they said to Josue: We are thy servants. Josue said to them: Who are you? and whence came you?
9:9. They answered: From a very far country thy servants are come in the name of the Lord thy God. For we have heard the fame of his power, all the things that he did in Egypt.
9:10. And to the two kings of the Amorrhites, that were beyond the Jordan, Sehon, king of Hesebon, and Og, king of Basan, that was in Astaroth:
9:11. And our ancients, and all the inhabitants of our country, said to us: Take with you victuals for a long way, and go meet them, and say: We are your servants, make ye a league with us.
9:12. Behold, these loaves we took hot, when we set out from our houses to come to you, now they are become dry, and broken in pieces by being exceeding old.
9:13. These bottles of wine when we filled them were new, now they are rent and burst. These garments we have on, and the shoes we have on our feet, by reason of the very long journey, are worn out, and almost consumed.

9:14. They took therefore of their victuals, and consulted not the mouth of the Lord.
9:15. And Josue made peace with them, and entering into a league, promised that they should not be slain: the princes also of the multitude swore to them.
9:16. Now three days after the league was made, they heard that they dwelt nigh, and they should be among them.
9:17. And the children of Israel removed the camp, and came into their cities on the third day, the names of which are, Gabaon, and Caphira, and Beroth, and Cariathiarim.
9:18. And they slew them not, because the princes of the multitude had sworn in the name of the Lord, the God of Israel. Then all the common people murmured against the princes.
9:19. And they answered them: We have sworn to them in the name of the Lord, the God of Israel, and therefore we may not touch them.
9:20. But this we will do to them: Let their lives be saved, lest the wrath of the Lord be stirred up against us, if we should be forsworn:
9:21. But so let them live, as to serve the whole multitude in hewing wood, and bringing in water. As they were speaking these things,
9;22. Josue called the Gabaonites, and said to them: Why would you impose upon us, saying: We dwell very far off from you, whereas you are in the midst of us?
9:23. Therefore you shall be under a curse, and your race shall always be hewers of wood, and carriers of water, into the house of my God.
9:24. They answered: It was told us, thy servants, that the Lord thy God had promised his servant Moses, to give you all the land, and to destroy all the inhabitants thereof. Therefore we feared exceedingly and provided for our lives, compelled by the dread we had of you, and we took this counsel.
9:25. And now we are in thy hand: deal with us as it seemeth good and right unto thee.
9:26. So Josue did as he had said, and delivered them from the hand of the children of Israel, that they should not be slain.
9:27. And he gave orders in that day, that they should be in the service of all the people, and of the altar of the Lord, hewing wood, and carrying water, until this present time, in the place which the Lord hath chosen.

Josue Chapter 10

Five kings war against Gabaon. Josue defeateth them: many are slain with hailstones. At the prayer of Josue the sun and moon stand still the space of one day. The five kings are hanged. Divers cities are taken.

10:1. When Adonisedec, king of Jerusalem, had heard these things, to wit, that Josue had taken Hai, and had destroyed it, (for as he had done to Jericho and the king thereof, so did he to Hai and its king) and that the Gabaonites were gone over to Israel, and were their confederates,
10:2. He was exceedingly afraid. For Gabaon was a great city, and one of the royal cities, and greater than the town of Hai, and all its fighting men were most valiant.
10:3. Therefore Adonisedec, king of Jerusalem, sent to Oham, king of Hebron, and to Pharam, king of Jerimoth, and to Japhia, king of Lachis, and to Dabir, king of Eglon, saying:
10:4. Come up to me, and bring help, that we may take Gabaon, because it hath gone over to Josue, and to the children of Israel.
10:5. So the five kings of the Amorrhites being assembled together, went up: the king of Jerusalem, the king of Hebron, the king of Jerimoth, the king of Lachis, the king of Eglon, they and their armies, and camped about Gabaon, laying siege to it.
10:6. But the inhabitants of the city of Gabaon, which was besieged, sent to Josue, who then abode in the camp at Galgal, and said to him: Withdraw not thy hands from helping thy servants: come up quickly, and save us, and bring us succour: for all the kings of the Amorrhites, who dwell in the mountains, are gathered together against us.
10:7. And Josue went up from Galgal, and all the army of the warriors with him, most valiant men.
10:8. But the Lord said to Josue: Fear them not: for I have delivered them into thy hands: none of them shall be able to stand against thee.
10:9. So Josue going up from Galgal all the night, came upon them suddenly.
10:10. And the Lord troubled them, at the sight of Israel: and he slew them with a great slaughter, in Gabaon, and pursued them by the way of the ascent to Bethoron, and cut them off all the way to Azeca and Maceda.
10:11. And when they were fleeing from the children of Israel, and were in the descent of Bethoron, the Lord cast down upon them great stones from heaven, as far as Azeca: and many more were killed with the hailstones, than were slain by the swords of the children of Israel,
10:12. Then Josue spoke to the Lord, in the day that he delivered the Amorrhite in the sight of the children of Israel, and he said before them: Move not, O sun, toward Gabaon, nor thou, O moon, toward the valley of Ajalon.
10:13. And the sun and the moon stood still, till the people revenged themselves of their enemies. Is not this written in the book of the just? So the sun stood still in the midst of heaven, and hasted not to go down the space of one day.
The book of the just... In Hebrew Jasher: an ancient book long since lost.

10:14. There was not before, nor after, so long a day, the Lord obeying the voice of a man, and fighting for Israel.
10:15. And Josue returned, with all Israel, into the camp of Galgal.
10:16. For the five kings were fled, and had hid themselves in a cave of the city of Maceda.
10:17. And it was told Josue, that the five kings were found hid in a cave of the city of Maceda.
10:18. And he commanded them that were with him, saying: Roll great stones to the mouth of the cave, and set careful men to keep them shut up:
10:19. And stay you not, but pursue after the enemies, and kill all the hindermost of them as they flee, and do not suffer them whom the Lord God hath delivered into your hands, to shelter themselves in their cities.
10:20. So the enemies being slain with a great slaughter, and almost utterly consumed, they that were able to escape from Israel, entered into fenced cities.
10:21. And all the army returned to Josue, in Maceda, where the camp then was, in good health, and without the loss of any one: and no man durst move his tongue against the children of Israel.
10:22. And Josue gave orders, saying: Open the mouth of the cave, and bring forth to me the five kings that lie hid therein.
10:23. And the ministers did as they were commanded: and they brought out to him the five kings out of the cave: the king of Jerusalem, the king of Hebron, the king of Jerimoth, the king of Lachis, the king of Eglon.
10:24. And when they were brought out to him, he called all the men of Israel, and said to the chiefs of the army that were with him: Go, and set your feet on the necks of these kings. And when they had gone, and put their feet upon the necks of them lying under them,
10:25. He said again to them: Fear not, neither be ye dismayed, take courage, and be strong: for so will the Lord do to all your enemies, against whom you fight.
10:26. And Josue struck, and slew them, and hanged them upon five gibbets; and they hung until the evening.
10:27. And when the sun was down, he commanded the soldiers to take them down from the gibbets. And after they were taken down, they cast them into the cave, where they had lain hid, and put great stones at the mouth thereof, which remain until this day.
10:28. The same day Josue took Maceda, and destroyed it with the edge of the sword, and killed the king and all the inhabitants thereof: he left not in it the least remains. And he did to the king of Maceda, as he had done to the king of Jericho.
10:29. And he passed from Maceda with all Israel to Lebna, and fought against it:
10:30. And the Lord delivered it with the king thereof into the hands of

Israel: and they destroyed the city with the edge of the sword, and all the inhabitants thereof. They left not in it any remains. And they did to the king of Lebna, as they had done to the king of Jericho.
10:31. From Lebna he passed unto Lachis, with all Israel: and investing it with his army, besieged it.
10:32. And the Lord delivered Lachis into the hands of Israel, and he took it the following day, and put it to the sword, and every soul that was in it, as he had done to Lebna.
10:33. At that time Horam, king of Gazer, came up to succour Lachis: and Josue slew him with all his people so as to leave none alive.
10:34. And he passed from Lachis to Eglon, and surrounded it,
10:35. And took it the same day: and put to the sword all the souls that were in it, according to all that he had done to Lachis.
10:36. He went up also with all Israel from Eglon to Hebron, and fought against it:
10:37. Took it, and destroyed it with the edge of the sword: the king also thereof, and all the towns of that country, and all the souls that dwelt in it: he left not therein any remains: as he had done to Eglon, so did he also to Hebron, putting to the sword all that he found in it.
The king... Viz., the new king, who succeeded him that was slain, ver. 26.
10:38. Returning from thence to Dabir,
10:39. He took it, and destroyed it: the king also thereof, and all the towns round about, he destroyed with the edge of the sword: he left not in it any remains: as he had done to Hebron and Lebna, and to their kings, so did he to Dabir, and to the king thereof.
10:40. So Josue conquered all the country of the hills, and of the south, and of the plain, and of Asedoth, with their kings: he left not any remains therein, but slew all that breathed, as the Lord, the God of Israel, had commanded him.
Any remains therein, but slew, etc... God ordered these people to be utterly destroyed, in punishment of their manifold abomination; and that they might not draw the Israelites into the like sins.
10:41. From Cadesbarne even to Gaza. All the land of Gosen even to Gabaon,
10:42. And all their kings, and their lands he took and wasted at one onset: for the Lord the God of Israel fought for him.
10:43. And he returned with all Israel to the place of the camp in Galgal.

Josue Chapter 11

The kings of the north are overthrown: the whole country is taken.

11:1. And when Jabin king of Asor had heard these things, he sent to Jobab king of Madon, and to the king of Semeron, and to the king of Achsaph:
11:2. And to the kings of the north, that dwelt in the mountains and in the plains over against the south side of Ceneroth, and in the levels and the countries of Dor by the sea side:
11:3. To the Chanaanites also on the east and on the west, and the Amorrhite, and the Hethite, and the Pherezite, and the Jebusite in the mountains: to the Hevite also who dwelt at the foot of Hermon in the land of Maspha.
11:4. And they all came out with their troops, a people exceeding numerous as the sand that is on the sea shore, their horses also and chariots a very great multitude,
11:5. And all these kings assembled together at the waters of Merom, to fight against Israel.
11:6. And the Lord said to Josue: Fear them not: for to morrow at this same hour I will deliver all these to be slain in the sight of Israel: thou shalt hamstring their horses, and thou shalt burn their chariots with fire.
Hamstring their horses, and burn their chariots with fire, etc... God so ordained, that his people might not trust in chariots and horses, but in him.
11:7. And Josue came, and all the army with him, against them to the waters of Merom on a sudden, and fell upon them.
11:8. And the Lord delivered them into the hands of Israel. And they defeated them, and chased them as far as the great Sidon and the waters of Maserophot, and the field of Masphe, which is on the east thereof. He slew them all, so as to leave no remains of them:
11:9. And he did as the Lord had commanded him, he hamstringed their horses and burned their chariots.
11:10. And presently turning back he took Asor: and slew the king thereof with the sword. Now Asor of old was the head of all these kingdoms.
11:11. And he cut off all the souls that abode there: he left not in it any remains, but utterly destroyed all, and burned the city itself with fire.
11:12. And he took and put to the sword and destroyed all the cities round about, and their kings, as Moses the servant of God had commanded him.
11:13. Except the cities that were on hills and high places, the rest Israel burned: only Asor that was very strong he consumed with fire.
11:14. And the children of Israel divided among themselves all the spoil of these cities and the cattle, killing all the men.
11:15. As the Lord had commanded Moses his servant, so did Moses command Josue, and he accomplished all: he left not one thing undone of all the commandments which the Lord had commanded Moses.
11:16. So Josue took all the country of the hills, and of the south, and the land of Gosen, and the plains and the west country, and the mountain of Israel, and the plains thereof:

11:17. And part of the mountain that goeth up to Seir as far as Baalgad, by the plain of Libanus under mount Hermon: all their kings he took, smote and slew.
11:18. Josue made war a long time against these kings.
A long time... Seven years, as appears from chap. 14.10.
11:19. There was not a city that delivered itself to the children of Israel, except the Hevite, who dwelt in Gabaon: for he took all by fight.
11:20. For it was the sentence of the Lord, that their hearts should be hardened, and they should fight against Israel, and fall, and should not deserve any clemency, and should be destroyed as the Lord had commanded Moses.
Hardened... This hardening of their hearts, was their having no thought of yielding or submitting: which was a sentence or judgment of God upon them in punishment of their enormous crimes.
11:21. At that time Josue came and cut off the Enancims from the mountains, from Hebron, and Dabir, and Anab, and from all the mountain of Juda and Israel, and destroyed their cities.
11:22. He left not any of the stock of the Enacims, in the land of the children of Israel: except the cities of Gaza, and Geth, and Azotus, in which alone they were left.
11:23. So Josue took all the land, as the Lord spoke to Moses, and delivered it in possession to the children of Israel, according to their divisions and tribes. And the land rested from wars.

Josue Chapter 12

A list of the kings slain by Moses and Josue.

12:1. These are the kings, whom the children of Israel slew and possessed their land beyond the Jordan towards the rising of the sun, from the torrent Arnon unto mount Hermon, and all the east country that looketh towards the wilderness.
12:2. Sehon king of the Amorrhites, who dwelt in Hesebon, and had dominion from Aroer, which is seated upon the bank of the torrent Arnon, and of the middle part in the valley, and of half Galaad, as far as the torrent Jaboc, which is the border of the children of Ammon.
12:3. And from the wilderness, to the sea of Ceneroth towards the east, and to the sea of the wilderness, which is the most salt sea, on the east side by the way that leadeth to Bethsimoth: and on the south side that lieth under Asedoth, Phasga.
12:4. The border of Og the king of Basan, of the remnant of the Raphaims who dwelt in Astaroth, and in Edrai, and had dominion in mount Hermon,

and in Salecha, and in all Basan, unto the borders
12:5. Of Gessuri and Machati, and of half Galaad: the borders of Sehon the king of Hesebon.
12:6. Moses the servant of the Lord, and the children of Israel slew them, and Moses delivered their land in possession to the Rubenites, and Gadites, and the half tribe of Manasses.
12:7. These are the kings of the land, whom Josue and the children of Israel slew beyond the Jordan on the west side from Baalgad in the field of Libanus, unto the mount, part of which goeth up into Seir: and Josue delivered it in possession to the tribes of Israel, to every one their divisions,
12:8. As well in the mountains as in the plains and the champaign countries. In Asedoth, and in the wilderness, and in the south was the Hethite and the Amorrhite, the Chanaanite and the Pherezite, the Hevite and the Jebusite.
12:9. The king of Jericho one: the king of Hai, which is on the side of Bethel, one:
12:10. The king of Jerusalem one, the king of Hebron one,
12:11. The king of Jerimoth one, thee king of Lachis one,
12:12. The king of Eglon one, the king of Gazer one,
12:13. The king of Dabir one, the king of Gader one,
12:14. The king of Herma one, the king of Hered one,
12:15. The king of Lebna one, the king of Odullam one,
12:16. The king of Maceda one, the king of Bethel one,
12:17. The king of Taphua one, the king of Opher one,
12:18. The king of Aphec one, the king of Saron one,
12:19. The king of Madon one, the king of Asor one,
12:20. The king of Semeron one, the king of Achsaph one,
12:21. The king of Thenac one, the king of Mageddo one,
12:22. Thee king of Cades one, the king of Jachanan of Carmel one,
12:23. The king of Dor, and of the province of Dor one, the king of the nations of Galgal one,
12:24. The king of Thersa one: all the kings thirty and one.
Josue Chapter 13
God commandeth Josue to divide the land: the possessions of Ruben, Gad, and half the tribe of Manasses, beyond the Jordan.

Josue Chapter 13

13:1. Josue was old, and far advanced in years, and the Lord said to him: Thou art grown old, and advanced in age, and there is a very large country left, which is not yet divided by lot:
Josue was old, and far advanced in years... He was then about one hundred and one years old.-And their is a very large country left, which is not yet

divided by lot... Not yet possessed by the children of Israel.
13:2. To wit, all Galilee, Philistia, and all Gessuri.
13:3. From the troubled river, that watereth Egypt, unto the border of Accaron northward: the land of Chanaan, which is divided among the lords of the Philistines, the Gazites, the Azotians, the Ascalonites, the Gethites, and the Accronites.
13:4. And on the south side are the Hevites, all the land of Chanaan, and Maara of the Sidonians as far as Apheca, and the borders of the Amorrhite,
13:5. And his confines. The country also of Libanus towards the east from Baalgad under mount Hermon to the entering into Emath.
13:6. Of all that dwell in the mountains from Libanus, to the waters of Maserephoth, and all the Sidonians. I am he that will cut them off from before the face of the children of Israel. So let their land come in as a part of the inheritance of Israel, as I have commanded thee.
13:7. And now divide the land in possession to the nine tribes, and to the half tribe of Manasses,
13:8. With whom Ruben and Gad have possessed the land, which Moses the servant of the Lord delivered to them beyond the river Jordan, on the east side.
With whom... That is, with the other half of that same tribe.
13:9. From Aroer, which is upon the bank of the torrent Arnon, and in the midst of the valley and all the plains of Medaba, as far as Dibon:
13:10. And all the cities of Sehon, king of the Amorrhites, who reigned in Hesebon, unto the borders of the children of Ammon.
13:11. And Galaad, and the borders of Gessuri and Machati, and all mount Hermon, and all Basan as far as Salecha,
13:12. All the kingdom of Og in Basan, who reigned in Astaroth and Edrai, he was of the remains of the Raphaims: and Moses overthrew and destroyed them.
13:13. And the children of Israel would not destroy Gessuri and Machati and they have dwelt in the midst of Israel, until this present day.
13:14. But to the tribe of Levi he gave no possession: but the sacrifices and victims of thee Lord God of Israel, are his inheritance, as he spoke to him.
13:15. And Moses gave a possession to the children of Ruben according to their kindreds.
13:16. And their border was from Aroer, which is on the bank of the torrent Arnon, and in the midst of the valley of the same torrent: all the plain, that leadeth to Medaba,
13:17. And Hesebon, and all their villages, which are in the plains.
Dibon also, and Bamothbaal, and the town of Baalmaon,
13:18. And Jassa, and Cidimoth, and Mephaath,
13:19. And Cariathaim, and Sabama, and Sarathasar in the mountain of the valley.

13:20. Bethphogor and Asedoth, Phasga and Bethiesimoth,
13:21. And all the cities of the plain, and all the kingdoms of Sehon king of the Amorrhites, that reigned in Hesebon, whom Moses slew with the princes of Madian: Hevi, and Recem, and Sur and Hur, and Rebe, dukes of Sehon inhabitants of the land.
The princes of Madian... It appears from hence that these were subjects of king Sehon: they are said to have been slain with him, that is, about the same time, but not in the same battle.
13:22. Balaam also the son of Beor the soothsayer, the children of Israel slew with the sword among the rest that were slain.
13:23. And the river Jordan was the border of the children of Ruben.
This is the possession of the Rubenites, by their kindreds, of cities and villages.
13:24. And Moses gave to the tribe of Gad and to his children by their kindreds a possession, of which this is the division.
13:25. The border of Jaser, and all the cities of Galaad, and half the land of the children of Ammon: as far as Aroer which is over against Rabba:
13:26. And from Hesebon unto Ramoth, Masphe and Betonim: and from Manaim unto the borders of Dabir.
13:27. And in the valley Betharan and Bethnemra, and Socoth, and Saphon the other part of the kingdom of Sehon king of Hesebon: the limit of this also is the Jordan, as far as the uttermost part of the sea of Cenereth beyond the Jordan on the east side,
13:28. This is the possession of the children of Gad by their families, their cities, and villages.
13:29. He gave also to the half tribe of Manasses and his children possession according to their kindreds,
13:30. The beginning whereof is this: from Manaim all Basan, and all the kingdoms of Og king of Basan, and all the villages of Jair, which are in Basan, threescore towns.
13:31. And half Galaad, and Astaroth, and Edrai, cities of the kingdom of Og in Basan: to the children of Machir, the son of Manasses, to one half of the children of Machir according to their kindreds.
13:32. This possession Moses divided in the plains of Moab, beyond the Jordan, over against Jericho on the east side,
13:33. But to the tribe of Levi he gave no possession: because the Lord the God of Israel himself is their possession, as he spoke to them.

Josue Chapter 14

Caleb's petition; Hebron is given to him and to his seed.

14:1. This is what the children of Israel possessed in the land of Chanaan, which Eleazar the priest, and Josue the son of Nun, and the princes of the families by the tribes of Israel gave to them.
14:2. Dividing all by lot, as the Lord had commanded the hand of Moses, to the nine tribes, and the half tribe.
14:3. For to two tribes and a half Moses had given possession beyond the Jordan: besides the Levites, who received no land among their brethren:
14:4. But in their place succeeded the children of Joseph divided into two tribes, of Manasses and Ephraim: neither did the Levites receive other portion of land, but cities to dwell in, and their suburbs to feed their beasts and flocks.
Hebron belonged, etc... All the country thereabouts, depending on Hebron, was given to Caleb; but the city itself with the suburbs, was one of those that were given to the priests to dwell in.
14:5. As the Lord had commanded Moses so did the children of Israel, and they divided the land.
14:6. Then the children of Juda came to Josue in Galgal, and Caleb the son of Jephone the Cenezite spoke to him: Thou knowest what the Lord spoke to Moses the man of God concerning me and thee in Cadesbarne.
14:7. I was forty years old when Moses the servant of the Lord sent me from Cadesbarne, to view the land, and I brought him word again as to me seemed true,
14:8. But my brethren, that had gone up with me, discouraged the heart of the people: and I nevertheless followed the Lord my God.
14:9. And Moses swore in that day, saying: The land which thy foot hath trodden upon shall be thy possession, and thy children for ever, because thou hast followed the Lord my God.
14:10. The Lord therefore hath granted me life, as he promised until this present day, It is forty and five years since the Lord spoke this word to Moses, when Israel journeyed through the wilderness: this day I am eighty-five years old,
14:11. As strong as I was at that time when I was sent to view the land: the strength of that time continueth in me until this day, as well to fight as to march.
14:12. Give me therefore this mountain, which the Lord promised, in thy hearing also, wherein are the Enacims, and cities great and strong: if so be the Lord will be with me, and I shall be able to destroy them, as he promised me.
14:13. And Josue blessed him, and gave him Hebron in possession.
14:14. And from that time Hebron belonged to Caleb the son of Jephone the Cenezite, until this present day: because he followed the Lord the God of Israel.
14:15. The name of Hebron before was called Cariath-Arbe: Adam the

greatest among the Enacims was laid there and the land rested from wars.

Josue Chapter 15

The borders of the lot of Juda. Caleb's portion and conquest. The cities of Juda.

15:1. Now the lot of the children of Juda by their kindreds was this: From the frontier of Edom, to the desert of Sin southward, and to the uttermost part of the south coast.
15:2. Its beginning was from the top of the most salt sea, and from the bay thereof, that looketh to the south.
15:3. And it goeth out towards the ascent of the Scorpion, and passeth on to Sina: and ascendeth into Cadesbarne, and reacheth into Esron, going up to Addar, and compassing Carcaa.
15:4. And from thence passing along into Asemona, and reaching the torrent of Egypt: and the bounds thereof shall be the great sea, this shall be the limit of the south coast.
15:5. But on the east side the beginning shall be the most salt sea even to the end of the Jordan: and towards the north from the bay of the sea unto the same river Jordan.
15:6. And the border goeth up into Beth-Hagla, and passeth by the north into Beth-Araba: going up to the stone of Boen the son of Ruben.
15:7. And reaching as far as the borders of Debara from the valley of Achor, and so northward looking towards Galgal, which is opposite to the ascent of Adommin, on the south side of the torrent, and the border passeth the waters that are called the fountain of the sun: and the goings out thereof shall be at the fountain Rogel.
15:8. And it goeth up by the valley of the son of Ennom on the side of the Jebusite towards the south, the same is Jerusalem: and thence ascending to the top of the mountain, which is over against Geennom to the west in the end of the valley of Raphaim, northward.
15:9. And it passeth on from the top of the mountain to the fountain of the water of Nephtoa: and reacheth to the towns of mount Ephron: and it bendeth towards Baala, which is Cariathiarim, that is to say, the city of the woods.
15:10. And it compasseth from Baala westward unto mount Seir: and passeth by the side of mount Jarim to the north into Cheslon: and goeth down into Bethsames, and passeth into Thamna.
15:11. And reacheth northward to a part of Accaron at the side: and bendeth to Sechrona, and passeth mount Baala: and cometh into Jebneel, and is bounded westward with the great sea.

15:12. These are the borders round about of the children of Juda in their kindreds.
15:13. But to Caleb the son of Jephone he gave a portion in the midst of the children of Juda, as the Lord had commanded him: Cariath-Arbe the father of Enac, which is Hebron.
15:14. And Caleb destroyed out of it the three sons of Enac, Sesai and Ahiman, and Tholmai of the race of Enac.
15:15. And going up from thence he came to the inhabitants of Dabir, which before was called Cariath-Sepher, that is to say, the city of letters.
15:16. And Caleb said: He that shall smite Cariath-Sepher, and take it, I will give him Axa my daughter to wife.
15:17. And Othoniel the son of Cenez, the younger brother of Caleb, took it: and he gave him Axa his daughter to wife.
15:18. And as they were going together, she was moved by her husband to ask a field of her father, and she sighed as she sat on her ass. And Caleb said to her: What aileth thee?
15:19. But she answered: Give me a blessing: thou hast given me a southern and dry land, give me also a land that Is watered. And Caleb gave her the upper and the nether watery ground.
15:20. This is the possession of the tribe of the children of Juda by their kindreds.
15:21. And the cities from the uttermost parts of the children of Juda by the borders of Edom to the south, were Cabseel and Eder and Jagur,
15:22. And Cina and Dimona and Adada,
15:23. And Cades and Asor and Jethnam,
15:24. Ziph and Telem and Baloth,
15:25. New Asor and Carioth, Hesron, which is Asor.
15:26. Amam, Sama and Molada,
15:27. And Asergadda and Hassemon and Bethphelet,
15:28. And Hasersual and Bersabee and Baziothia,
15:29. And Baala and Jim and Esem,
15:30. And Eltholad and Cesil and Harma,
15:31. And Siceleg and Medemena and Sensenna,
15:32. Lebaoth and Selim and Aen and Remmon: all the cities twenty-nine, and their villages.
15:33. But in the plains: Estaol and Sarea and Asena,
15:34. And Zanoe and Engannim and Taphua and Enaim,
15:35. And Jerimoth and Adullam, Socho and Azeca,
15:36. And Saraim and Adithaim and Gedera and Gederothaim: fourteen cities, and their villages.
15:37. Sanan and Hadassa and Magdalgad,
15:38. Delean and Masepha and Jecthel,
15:39. Lachis and Bascath and Eglon,

15:40. Chebbon and Leheman and Cethlis,
15:41. And Gideroth and Bethdagon and Naama and Maceda: sixteen cities, and their villages.
15:42. Labana and Ether and Asan,
15:43. Jephtha and Esna and Nesib,
15:44. And Ceila and Achzib and Maresa: nine cities, and their villages.
15:45. Accaron with the towns and villages thereof.
15:46. From Accaron even to the sea: all places that lie towards Azotus and the villages thereof.
15:47. Azotus with its towns and villages. Gaza with its towns and villages, even to the torrent of Egypt, and the great sea that is the border thereof.
15:48. And in the mountain Samir and Jether and Socoth,
15:49. And Danna and Cariath-senna, this is Dabir:
15:50. Anab and Istemo and Anim,
15:51. Gosen and Olon and Gilo: eleven cities and their villages.
15:52. Arab and Ruma and Esaan,
15:53. And Janum and Beththaphua and Apheca,
15:54. Athmatha and Cariath-Arbe, this is Hebron and Sior: nine cities and their villages.
15:55. Maon and Carmel and Ziph and Jota,
15:56. Jezrael and Jucadam and Zanoe,
15:57. Accain, Gabaa and Thamna: ten cities and their villages.
15:58. Halhul, and Bessur, and Gedor,
15:59. Mareth, and Bethanoth, and Eltecon: six cities and their villages.
15:60. Cariathbaal, the same is Cariathiarim the city of woods, and Arebba: two cities and their villages.
15:61. In the desert Betharaba, Meddin and Sachacha,
15:62. And Nebsan, and the city of salt, and Engaddi: six cities and their villages.
15:63. But the children of Juda could not destroy the Jebusite that dwelt in Jerusalem: and the Jebusite dwelt with the children of Juda in Jerusalem until this present day.

Josue Chapter 16

The lot of the sons of Joseph. The borders of the tribe of Ephraim.

16:1. And the lot of the sons of Joseph fell from the Jordan over against Jericho and the waters thereof, on the east: the wilderness which goeth up from Jericho to the mountain of Bethel:
16:2. And goeth out from Bethel to Luza: and passeth the border of Archi, to Ataroth,

16:3. And goeth down westward, by the border of Jephleti, unto the borders of Beth-horon the nether, and to Gazer: and the countries of it are ended by the great sea:
16:4. And Manasses and Ephraim the children of Joseph possessed it.
16:5. And the border of the children of Ephraim was according to their kindreds: and their possession towards the east was Ataroth-addar unto Beth-horon the upper.
16:6. And the confines go out unto the sea: but Machmethath looketh to the north, and it goeth round the borders eastward into Thanath-selo: and passeth along on the east side to Janoe.
Looketh to the north, etc... The meaning is, that the border went towards the north, by Machmethath; and then turned eastward to Thanath- selo.
16:7. And it goeth down from Janoe into Ataroth and Naaratha: and it cometh to Jericho, and goeth out to the Jordan.
16:8. From Taphua it passeth on towards the sea into the valley of reeds, and the goings out thereof are at the most salt sea. This is the possession of the tribe of the children of Ephraim by their families.
16:9. And there were cities with their villages separated for the children of Ephraim in the midst of the possession of the children of Manasses.
16:10. And the children of Ephraim slew not the Chanaanite, who dwelt in Gazer: and the Chanaanite dwelt in the midst of Ephraim until this day, paying tribute.

Josue Chapter 17

The lot of the half tribe of Manasses.

17:1. And this lot fell to the tribe of Manasses for he is the firstborn of Joseph to Machir the firstborn of Manasses the father of Galaad, who was a warlike man, and had for possession Galaad and Basan.
17:2. And to the rest of the children of Manasses according to their families: to the children of Abiezer, and to the children of Helec, and to the children of Esriel, and to the children of Sechem, and to the children of Hepher, and to the children of Semida: these are the male children of Manasses the son of Joseph, by their kindreds.
17:3. But Salphaad the son of Hepher the son of Galaad the son of Machir the son of Manasses had no sons, but only daughters: whose names are these, Maala and Noa and Hegla and Melcha and Thersa.
17:4. And they came in the presence of Eleazar the priest and of Josue the son of Nun, and of the princes, saying: The Lord commanded by the hand of Moses, that a possession should be given us in the midst of our brethren. And he gave them according to the commandment of the Lord a

possession amongst the brethren of their father.
17:5. And there fell ten portions to Manasses, beside the land of Galaad and Basan beyond the Jordan.
17:6. For the daughters of Manasses possessed inheritance in the midst of his sons. And the land of Galaad fell to the lot of the rest of the children of Manasses.
17:7. And the border of Manasses was from Aser, Machmethath which looketh towards Sichem: and it goeth out on the right hand by the inhabitants of the fountain of Taphua.
17:8. For the lot of Manasses took in the land of Taphua, which is on the borders of Manasses, and belongs to the children of Ephraim.
17:9. And the border goeth down to the valley of the reeds, to the south of the torrent of the cities of Ephraim, which are in the midst of the cities of Manasses: the border of Manasses is on the north side of the torrent, and the outgoings of it are at the sea:
17:10. So that the possession of Ephraim is on the south, and on the north that of Manasses, and the sea is the border of both, and they are joined together in the tribe of Aser on the north, and in the tribe of Issachar on the east.
17:11. And the inheritance of Manasses in Issachar and in Aser, was Bethsan and its villages, and Jeblaam with its villages, and the inhabitants of Dor, with the towns thereof: the inhabitants also of Endor with the villages thereof: and in like manner the inhabitants of Thenac with the villages thereof: and the inhabitants of Mageddo with their villages, and the third part of the city of Nopheth.
17:12. Neither could the children of Manasses overthrow these cities, but the Chanaanite began to dwell in his land.
17:13. But after that the children of Israel were grown strong, they subdued the Chanaanites, and made them their tributaries, and they did not kill them.
17:14. And the children of Joseph spoke to Josue, and said: Why hast thou given me but one lot and one portion to possess, whereas I am of so great a multitude, and the Lord hath blessed me?
17:15. And Josue said to them: If thou be a great people, go up into the woodland, and cut down room for thyself in the land of the Pherezite and the Raphaims: because the possession of mount Ephraim is too narrow for thee.
17:16. And the children of Joseph answered him: We cannot go up to the mountains, for the Chanaanites that dwell in the low lands, wherein are situate Bethsan with its towns, and Jezrael in the midst of the valley, have chariots of iron.
17:17. And Josue said to the house of Joseph, to Ephraim and Manasses: Thou art a great people, and of great strength, thou shalt not have one lot

only:
17:18. But thou shalt pass to the mountain, and shalt cut down the wood, and make thyself room to dwell in: and mayst proceed farther, when thou hast destroyed the Chanaanites, who as thou sayest have iron chariots, and are very strong.

Josue Chapter 18

Surveyors are sent to divide the rest of the land into seven tribes. The lot of Benjamin.

18:1. And all the children of Israel assembled together in Silo, and there they set up the tabernacle of the testimony, and the land was subdued before them.
18:2. But there remained seven tribes of the children of Israel, which as yet had not received their possessions.
18:3. And Josue said to them: How long are you indolent and slack, and go not in to possess the land which the Lord the God of your fathers hath given you?
18:4. Choose of every tribe three men, that I may send them, and they may go and compass the land, and mark it out according to the number of each multitude: and bring back to me what they have marked out.
18:5. Divide to yourselves the land into seven parts: let Juda be in his bounds on the south side, and the house of Joseph on the north.
18:6. The land in the midst between these mark ye out into seven parts; and you shall come hither to me, that I may cast lots for you before the Lord your God.
The land in the midst between these mark ye out into seven parts... That is to say, the rest of the land, which is not already assigned to Juda or Joseph.
18:7. For the Levites have no part among you, but the priesthood of the Lord is their inheritance. And Gad and Ruben, and the half tribe of Manasses have already received their possessions beyond the Jordan eastward: which Moses the servant of the Lord gave them.
18:8. And when the men were risen up, to go to mark out the land, Josue commanded them saying: Go round the land and mark it out, and return to me: that I may cast lots for you before the Lord in Silo.
18:9. So they went and surveying it divided it into seven parts, writing them down in a book. And they returned to Josue, to the camp in Silo.
18:10. And he cast lots before the Lord in Silo, and divided the land to the children of Israel into seven parts.
18:11. And first came up the lot of the children of Benjamin by their families, to possess the land between the children of Juda, and the children

of Joseph.
18:12. And their border northward was from the Jordan: going along by the side of Jericho on the north side, and thence going up westward to the mountains, and reaching to the wilderness of Bethaven,
18:13. And passing along southward by Luza, the same is Bethel, and it goeth down into Ataroth-addar to the mountain, that is on the south of the nether Beth-horon.
18:14. And it bendeth thence going round towards the sea, south of the mountain that looketh towards Beth-horon to the southwest: and the outgoings thereof are into Cariathbaal, which is called also Cariathiarim, a city of the children of Juda This is their coast towards the sea, westward.
18:15. But on the south side the border goeth out from part of Cariathiarim towards the sea, and cometh to the fountain of the waters of Nephtoa.
18:16. And it goeth down to that part of the mountain that looketh on the valley of the children of Ennom: and is over against the north quarter in the furthermost part of the valley of Raphaim, and it goeth down into Geennom (that is the valley of Ennom) by the side of the Jebusite to the south: and cometh to the fountain of Rogel,
18:17. Passing thence to the north, and going out to Ensemes, that is to say, the fountain of the sun:
18:18. And It passeth along to the hills that are over against the ascent of Adommim: and it goeth down to Abenboen, that is, the stone of Boen the son of Ruben: and it passeth on the north side to the champaign countries; and goeth down Into the plain,
18:19. And it passeth by Bethhagla northward: and the outgoings thereof are towards the north of the most salt sea at the south end of the Jordan.
18:20. Which is the border of it on the east side. This is the possession of the children of Benjamin by their borders round about, and their families.
18:21. And their cities were, Jericho and Bethhagla and Vale-Casis,
18:22. Betharaba and Samaraim and Bethel,
18:23. And Avim and Aphara and Ophera,
18:24. The town Emona and Ophni and Gabee: twelve cities, and their villages.
18:25. Gabam and Rama and Beroth,
18:26. And Mesphe, and Caphara, and Amosa,
18:27. And Recem, Jarephel, and Tharela,
18:28. And Sela, Eleph and Jebus, which is Jerusalem, Gabaath and Cariath: fourteen cities, and their villages. This is the possession of the children of Benjamin by their families.

Josue Chapter 19

The lots of the tribes of Simeon, Zabulon, Issachar, Aser, Nephtali and Dan. A city is given to Josue.

19:1. And the second lot came forth for the children of Simeon by their kindreds: and their inheritance was
19:2. In the midst of the possession of the children of Juda: Bersabee and Sabee and Molada,
19:3. And Hasersual, Bala and Asem,
19:4. And Eltholad, Bethul and Harma,
19:5. And Siceleg and Bethmarchaboth and Hasersusa,
19:6. And Bethlebaoth and Sarohen: thirteen cities, and their villages.
19:7. And Remmon and Athor and Asan: four cities, and their villages.
19:8. And all the villages round about these cities to Baalath Beer Ramath to the south quarter. This is the inheritance of the children of Simeon according to their kindreds,
19:9. In the possession and lot of the children of Juda: because it was too great, and therefore the children of Simeon had their possession in the midst of their inheritance.
19:10. And the third lot fell to the children of Zabulon by their kindreds: and the border of their possession was unto Sarid.
19:11. And It went up from the sea and from Merala, and came to Debbaseth: as far as the torrent, which is over against Jeconam.
19:12. And it returneth from Sarid eastward to the borders of Ceseleththabor: and it goeth out to Dabereth and ascendeth towards Japhie.
19:13. And it passeth along from thence to the east side of Gethhepher and Thacasin: and goeth out to Remmon, Amthar and Noa.
19:14. And it turneth about to the north of Hanathon: and the outgoings thereof are the valley of Jephtahel,
19:15. And Cateth and Naalol and Semeron and Jedala and Bethlehem: twelve cities and their villages.
19:16. This is the inheritance of the tribe of the children of Zabulon by their kindreds, the cities and their villages.
19:17. The fourth lot came out to Issachar by their kindreds.
19:18. And his inheritance was Jezrael and Casaloth and Sunem,
19:19. And Hapharaim and Seon and Anaharath,
19:20. And Rabboth and Cesion, Abes,
19:21. And Rameth and Engannim and Enhadda and Bethpheses.
19:22. And the border thereof cometh to Thabor and Sehesima and Bethsames: and the outgoings thereof shall be at the Jordan: sixteen cities, and their villages.
19:23. This is the possession of the sons of Issachar by their kindreds, the cities and their villages.
19:24. And the fifth lot fell to the tribe of the children of Aser by their

kindreds:
19:25. And their border was Halcath and Chali and Beten and Axaph,
19:26. And Elmelech and Amaad and Messal: and it reacheth to Carmel by the sea and Sihor and Labanath,
19:27. And it returneth towards the east to Bethdagon: and passeth along to Zabulon and to the valley of Jephthael towards the north to Bethemec and Nehiel. And it goeth out to the left side of Cabul,
19:28. And to Abaran and Rohob and Hamon and Cana, as far as the great Sidon.
19:29. And it returneth to Horma to the strong city of Tyre, and to Hosa: and the outgoings thereof shall be at the sea from the portion of Achziba:
19:30. And Amma and Aphec and Rohob: twenty-two cities, and their villages.
19:31. This is the possession of the children of Aser by their kindreds, and the cities and their villages.
19:32. The sixth lot came out to the sons of Nephtali by their families:
19:33. And the border began from Heleph and Elon to Saananim, and Adami, which is Neceb, and Jebnael even to Lecum:
19:34. And the border returneth westward to Azanotthabor, and goeth out from thence to Hucuca, and passeth along to Zabulon southward, and to Aser westward, and to Juda upon the Jordan towards the rising of the sun.
19:35. And the strong cities are Assedim, Ser, and Emath, and Reccath and Cenereth,
19:36. And Edema and Arama, Asor,
19:37. And Cedes and Edri, Enhasor,
19:38. And Jeron and Magdalel, Horem, and Bethanath and Bethsames: nineteen cities, and their villages.
19:39. This is the possession of the tribe of the children of Nephtali by their kindreds, the cities and their villages.
19:40. The seventh lot came out to the tribe of the children of Dan by their families,
19:41. And the border of their possession was Saraa and Esthaol, and Hirsemes, that is, the city of the sun,
19:42. Selebin and Aialon and Jethela,
19:43. Elon and Themna and Acron,
19:44. Elthece, Gebbethon and Balaath,
19:45. And Juda and Bane and Barach and Gethremmon:
19:46. And Mejarcon and Arecon, with the border that looketh towards Joppe,
19:47. And is terminated there. And the children of Dan went up and fought against Lesem, and took it: and they put it to the sword, and possessed it, and dwelt in it, calling the name of it Lesem Dan, by the name of Dan their father.

19:48. This is the possession of the tribe of the sons of Dan, by their kindreds, the cities and their villages.
19:49. And when he had made an end of dividing the land by lot to each one by their tribes, the children of Israel gave a possession to Josue the son of Nun in the midst of them,
19:50. According to the commandment of the Lord, the city which he asked for, Thamnath Saraa, in mount Ephraim: and he built up the city, and dwelt in it.
19:51. These are the possessions which Eleazar the priest, and Josue the son of Nun, and the princes of the families, and of the tribes of the children of Israel, distributed by lot in Silo, before the Lord at the door of the tabernacle of the testimony, and they divided the land.

Josue Chapter 20

The cities of refuge are appointed for casual manslaughter.

20:1. And the Lord spoke to Josue, saying: Speak to children of Israel and say to them:
20:2. Appoint cities of refuge, of which I spoke to you by the hand of Moses:
20:3. That whosoever shall kill a person unawares may flee to them, and may escape the wrath of the kinsman, who is the avenger of blood.
20:4. And when he shall flee to one of these cities: he shall stand before the gate of the city, and shall speak to the ancients of that city, such things as prove him innocent: and so shall they receive him, and give him a place to dwell in.
20:5. And when the avenger of blood shall pursue him, they shall not deliver him into his hands, because he slew his neighbour unawares, and is not proved to have been his enemy two or three days before,
20:6. And he shall dwell in that city, till he stand before judgment to give an account of his fact, and till the death of the high priest, who shall be at that time: then shall the manslayer return, and go into his own city and house from whence he fled.
20:7. And they appointed Cedes in Galilee of mount Nephtali, and Sichem in mount Ephraim, and Cariath-Arbe, the same is Hebron in the mountain of Juda.
20:8. And beyond the Jordan to the east of Jericho, they appointed Bosor, which is upon the plain of the wilderness of the tribe of Ruben, and Ramoth in Galaad of the tribe of Gad, and Gaulon in Basan of the tribe of Manasses.
20:9. These cities were appointed for all the children of Israel, and for the

strangers, that dwelt among them, that whosoever had killed a person unawares might flee to them, and not die by the hand of the kinsman, coveting to revenge the blood that was shed, until he should stand before the people to lay open his cause.

Josue Chapter 21

Cities with their suburbs are assigned for the priests and Levites.

21:1. Then the princes of the families of Levi came to Eleazar the priest, and to Josue the son of Nun, and to the princes of the kindreds of all the tribes of the children of Israel.
21:2. And they spoke to them in Silo in the land of Chanaan, and said: The Lord commanded by the hand of Moses, that cities should be given us to dwell in, and their suburbs to feed our cattle.
21:3. And the children of Israel gave out of their possessions according to the commandment of the Lord, cities and their suburbs.
21:4. And the lot came out for the family of Caath of the children of Aaron the priest out of the tribes of Juda, and of Simeon, and of Benjamin, thirteen cities.
21:5. And to the rest of the children of Caath, that is, to thee Levites, who remained, out of the tribes of Ephraim, and of Dan, and the half tribe of Manasses, ten cities.
21:6. And the lot came out to children of Gerson, that they should take of the tribes of Issachar and of Aser and of Nephtali, and of the half tribe of Manasses in Basan, thirteen cities.
21:7. And to the sons of Merari by their kindreds, of the tribes of Ruben and of Gad and of Zabulon, twelve cities.
21:8. And the children of Israel gave to the Levites the cities and their suburbs, as the Lord commanded by the hand of Moses, giving to every one by lot.
21:9. Of the tribes of the children of Juda and of Simeon Josue gave cities: whose names are these,
21:10. To the sons of Aaron, of the families of Caath of the race of Levi (for the first lot came out for them)
21:11. The city of Arbe the father of Enac, which is called Hebron, in the mountain of Juda, and the suburbs thereof round about.
21:12. But the fields and the villages thereof he had given to Caleb the son of Jephone for his possession.
21:13. He gave therefore to the children of Aaron the priest, Hebron a city of refuge, and the suburbs thereof, and Lebna with the suburbs thereof,
21:14. And Jether and Estemo,

21:15. And Holon, and Dabir,
21:16. And Ain, and Jeta, and Bethsames, with their suburbs: nine cities out of the two tribes, as hath been said.
21:17. And out of the tribe of the children of Benjamin, Gabaon, and Gabae,
21:18. And Anathoth and Almon, with, their suburbs: four cities.
21:19. All the cities together of the children of Aaron the priest, were thirteen, with their suburbs,
21:20. And to the rest of the families of the children of Caath of the race of Levi was given this possession.
21:21. Of the tribe of Ephraim, Sichem one of the cities of refuge, with the suburbs thereof in mount Ephraim, and Gazer,
21:22. And Cibsaim, and Beth-horon, with their suburbs, four cities.
21:23. And of he tribe of Dan, Eltheco and Gabathon,
21:24. And Aialon and Gethremmon, with their suburbs, four cities.
21:25. And of the half tribe of Manasses, Thanac and Gethremmon, with their suburbs, two cities.
21:26. All the cities were ten, with their suburbs, which were given to the children of Caath, of the inferior degree.
21:27. To the children of Gerson also of the race of Levi out of the half tribe of Manasses, Gaulon in Basan, one of the cities of refuge, and Bosra, with their suburbs, two cities.
21:28. And of the tribe of Issachar, Cesion, and Dabereth,
21:29. And Jaramoth, and Engannim, with their suburbs, four cities.
21:30. And of the tribe of Aser, Masal and Abdon,
21:31. And Helcath, and Rohob, with their suburbs, four cities.
21:32. Of the tribe also of Nephtali, Cedes in Galilee, one of the cities of refuge: and Hammoth Dor, and Carthan, with their suburbs, three cities.
21:33. All the cities of the families of Gerson, were thirteen, with their suburbs.
21:34. And to the children of Merari, Levites of the inferior degree, by their families were given of the tribe of Zabulon, Jecnam and Cartha,
21:35. And Damna and Naalol, four cities with their suburbs.
21:36. Of the tribe of Ruben beyond the Jordan over against Jericho, Bosor in the wilderness, one of the cities of refuge, Misor and Jaser and Jethson and Mephaath, four cities with their suburbs.
Four cities... There are no more, though there be five names: for Misor is the same city as Bosor, which is to be observed in some other places, where the number of names exceeds the number of cities.
21:37. Of the tribe of Gad, Ramoth in Galaad, one of the cities of refuge, and Manaim and Hesebon and Jaser, four cities with their suburbs,
21:38. All the cities of the children of Merari by their families and kindreds, were twelve.

21:39. So all the cities of the Levites within the possession of the children of Israel were forty-eight,
21:40. With their suburbs, each distributed by the families.
21:41. And the Lord God gave to Israel all the land that he had sworn to give to their fathers: and they possessed it, and dwelt in it.
21:42. And he gave them peace from all nations round about: and none of their enemies durst stand against them, but were brought under their dominion.
21:43. Not so much as one word, which he had promised to perform unto them, was made void, but all came to pass.

Josue Chapter 22

The tribes of Ruben and Gad, and half the tribe of Manasses return to their possessions. They build an altar by the side of the Jordan, which alarms the other tribes. An embassage is sent to them, to which they give a satisfactory answer.

22:1. At the same time Josue called the Rubenites, and the Gadites, and the half tribe of Manasses,
22:2. And said to them: You have done all that Moses the servant of the Lord commanded you: you have also obeyed me in all things,
22:3. Neither have you left your brethren this long time, until this present day, keeping the commandment of the Lord your God.
22:4. Therefore as the Lord your God hath given your brethren rest and peace, as he promised: return, and go to your dwellings, and to the land of your possession, which Moses the servant of the Lord gave you beyond the Jordan:
22:5. Yet so that you observe attentively, and in work fulfil the commandment and the law which Moses the servant of the Lord commanded you: that you love the Lord your God, and walk in all his ways, and keep all his commandments, and cleave to him, and serve him with all your heart, and with all your soul.
22:6. And Josue blessed them, and sent them away, and they returned to their dwellings.
22:7. Now to half the tribe of Manasses, Moses had given a possession in Basan: and therefore to the half that remained, Josue gave a lot among the rest of their brethren beyond the Jordan to the west. And when he sent them away to their dwellings and had blessed them,
22:8. He said to them: With much substance and riches, you return to your settlements, with silver and gold, brass and iron, and variety of raiment: divide the prey of your enemies with your brethren.

22:9. So the children of Ruben, and the children of Gad, and the half tribe of Manasses returned, and parted from the children of Israel in Silo, which is in Chanaan, to go into Galaad the land of their possession, which they had obtained according to the commandment of the Lord by the hand of Moses.
22:10. And when they were come to banks of the Jordan, in the land of Chanaan, they built an altar immensely great near the Jordan.
22:11. And when the children of Israel had heard of it, and certain messengers brought them an account that the children of Ruben, and of Gad, and the half tribe of Manasses had built an altar in the land of Chanaan, upon the banks of the Jordan, over against the children of Israel:
22:12. They all assembled in Silo, to go up and fight against them.
22:13. And in the mean time they sent to them into the land of Galaad, Phinees the son of Eleazar the priest,
22:14. And ten princes with him, one of every tribe.
22:15. Who came to the children of Ruben, and of Gad, and the half tribe of Manasses, into the land of Galaad, and said to them:
22:16. Thus saith all the people of the Lord: What meaneth this transgression? Why have you forsaken the Lord the God of Israel, building a sacrilegious altar, and revolting from the worship of him?
22:17. Is it a small thing to you that you sinned with Beelphegor, and the stain of that crime remaineth in us to this day? and many of the people perished.
22:18. And you have forsaken the Lord to day, and to morrow his wrath will rage against all Israel.
22:19. But if you think the land of your possession to be unclean, pass over to the land wherein is the tabernacle of the Lord, and dwell among us: only depart not from the Lord, and from our society, by building an altar beside the altar of the Lord our God.
22:20. Did not Achan the son of Zare transgress the commandment of the Lord, and his wrath lay upon all the people of Israel? And he was but one man, and would to God he alone had perished in his wickedness.
22:21. And the children of Ruben, and of Gad, and of the half tribe of Manasses answered the princes of the embassage of Israel:
22:22. The Lord the most mighty God, the Lord the most mighty God, he knoweth, and Israel also shall understand: If with the design of transgression we have set up this altar, let him not save us, but punish us immediately:
22:23. And if we did it with that mind, that we might lay upon it holocausts, and sacrifice, and victims of peace offerings, let him require and judge:
22:24. And not rather with this thought and design, that we should say: To morrow your children will say to our children: What have you to do with the Lord the God of Israel?

22:25. The Lord hath put the river Jordan for a border between us and you, O ye children of Ruben, and ye children of Gad: and therefore you have no part in the Lord. And by this occasion your children shall turn away our children from the fear of the Lord. We therefore thought it best,
22:26. And said: Let us build us an altar, not for holocausts, nor to offer victims,
22:27. But for a testimony between us and you, and our posterity and yours, that we may serve the Lord, and that we may have a right to offer both holocausts, and victims and sacrifices of peace offerings: and that your children to morrow may not say to our children: You have no part in the Lord.
22:28. And if they will say so, they shall answer them: Behold the altar of the Lord, which our fathers made, not for holocausts, nor for sacrifice, but for a testimony between us and you.
22:29. God keep us from any such wickedness that we should revolt from the Lord, and leave off following his steps, by building an altar to offer holocausts, and sacrifices, and victims, beside the altar of the Lord our God, which is erected before his tabernacle.
22:30. And when Phinees the priest, and the princes of the embassage, who were with him, had heard this, they were satisfied: and they admitted most willingly the words of the children of Ruben, and Gad, and of the half tribe of Manasses,
22:31. And Phinees the priest the son of Eleazar said to them: Now we know that the Lord is with us, because you are not guilty of this revolt, and you have delivered the children of Israel from the hand of the Lord.
22:32. And he returned with the princes from the children of Ruben and Gad, out of the land of Galaad, into the land of Chanaan, to the children of Israel, and brought them word again.
22:33. And the saying pleased all that heard it. And the children of Israel praised God, and they no longer said that they would go up against them, and fight, and destroy the land of their possession.
22:34. And the children of Ruben, and the children of Gad called the altar which they had built, Our testimony, that the Lord is God,

Josue Chapter 23

Josue being old admonisheth the people to keep God's commandments: and to avoid marriages and all society with the Gentiles for fear of being brought to idolatry.

23:1. And when a long time was passed, after that the Lord had given peace to Israel, all the nations round about being subdued and Josue being now

old, and far advanced in years:
23:2. Josue called for all Israel, and for the elders, and for the princes, and for the judges, and for the masters, and said to them: I am old, and far advanced in years,
23:3. And you see all that the Lord your God hath done to all the nations round about, how he himself hath fought for you:
23:4. And now since he hath divided to you by lot all the land, from the east of the Jordan unto the great sea, ant many nations yet remain:
23:5. The Lord your God will destroy them, and take them away from before your face, and you shall possess the land as he hath promised you.
23:6. Only take courage, and be careful to observe all things that are written in the book of the law of Moses: and turn not aside from them neither to the right hand nor to the left:
23:7. Lest after that you are come in among the Gentiles, who will remain among you, you should swear by the name of their gods, and serve them, and adore them:
23:8. But cleave ye unto the Lord your God, as you have done until this day.
23:9. And then the Lord God will take away before your eyes nations that are great and very strong, and no man shall be able to resist you.
23:10. One of you shall chase a thousand men of the enemies: because the Lord your God himself will fight for you, as he hath promised.
23:11. This only take care of with all diligence, that you love the Lord your God.
23:12. But if you will embrace the errors of these nations that dwell among you, and make marriages with them, and join friendships:
23:13. Know ye for a certainty that the Lord your God will not destroy them before your face, but they shall be a pit and a snare in your way, and a stumbling-block at your side, and stakes in your eyes, till he take you away and destroy you from off this excellent land, which he hath given you.
23:14. Behold this day I am going into the way of all the earth, and you shall know with all your mind that of all the words which the Lord promised to perform for you, not one hath failed,
23:15. Therefore as he hath fulfilled in deed, what he promised, and all things prosperous have come: so will he bring upon you all the evils he hath threatened, till he take you away and destroy you from off this excellent land, which he hath given you,
23:16. When you shall have transgressed the covenant of the Lord your God, which he hath made with you, and shall have served strange gods, and adored them: then shall the indignation of the Lord rise up quickly and speedily against you, and you shall be taken away from this excellent land, which he hath delivered to you.

Josue Chapter 24

Josue assembleth the people, and reneweth the covenant between them and God. His death and burial.

24:1. And Josue gathered together all the tribes of Israel in Sichem, and called for the ancients, and the princes and the judges, and the masters: and they stood in the sight of the Lord:
24:2. And he spoke thus to the people: Thus saith the Lord the God of Israel: Your fathers dwelt of old on the other side of the river, Thare the father of Abraham, and Nachor: and they served strange gods.
Of the river... The Euphrates.
24:3. And I took your father Abraham from the borders of Mesopotamia: and brought him into the land of Chanaan: and I multiplied his seed,
24:4. And gave him Isaac: and to him again I gave Jacob and Esau. And I gave to Esau mount Seir for his possession: but Jacob and his children went down into Egypt.
24:5. And I sent Moses and Aaron, and I struck Egypt with many signs and wonders.
24:6. And I brought you and your fathers out of Egypt, and you came to the sea: and the Egyptians pursued your fathers with chariots and horsemen, as far as the Red Sea.
24:7. And the children of Israel cried to the Lord: and he put darkness between you and the Egyptians, and brought the sea upon them, and covered them. Your eyes saw all that I did in Egypt, and you dwelt in the wilderness a long time.
24:8. And I brought you into the land of the Amorrhite, who dwelt beyond the Jordan. And when they fought against you, I delivered them into your hands, and you possessed their land, and slew them.
24:9. And Balac son of Sephor king of Moab arose and fought against Israel. And he sent and called for Balaam son of Beor, to curse you:
24:10. And I would not hear him, but on the contrary I blessed you by him, and I delivered you out of his hand.
24:11. And you passed over the Jordan, and you came to Jericho. And the men of that city fought against you, the Amorrhite, and the Pherezite, and the Chanaanite, and the Hethite, and the Gergesite, and the Hevite, and the Jebusite: and I delivered them into your hands.
24:12. And I sent before you and I drove them out from their places, the two kings of the Amorrhites, not with thy sword nor with thy bow,
24:13. And I gave you a land, in which you had not laboured, and cities to dwell in which you built not, vineyards and oliveyards, which you planted not.

24:14. Now therefore fear the Lord, and serve him with a perfect and most sincere heart: and put away the gods which your fathers served in Mesopotamia and in Egypt, and serve the Lord.
24:15. But if it seem evil to you to serve the Lord, you have your choice: choose this day that which pleaseth you, whom you would rather serve, whether the gods which your fathers served in Mesopotamia, or the gods of the Amorrhites, in whose land you dwell: but as for me and my house we will serve thee Lord,
24:16. And the people answered, and said, God forbid we should leave the Lord, and serve strange gods.
24:17. The Lord our God he brought us and our fathers out of the land of Egypt, out of the house of bondage: and did very great signs in our sight, and preserved us in all the way by which we journeyed, and among all the people through whom we passed.
24:18. And he hath cast out all the nations, the Amorrhite the inhabitant of the land into which we are come. Therefore we will serve the Lord, for he is our God.
24:19. And Josue said to the people: You will not be able to serve the Lord: for he is a holy God, and mighty and jealous, and will not forgive your wickedness and sins.
You will not be able to serve the Lord, etc... This was not said by way of discouraging them; but rather to make them more earnest and resolute, by setting before them the greatness of the undertaking, and the courage and constancy necessary to go through with it.
24:20. If you leave the Lord, and serve strange gods, he will turn, and will afflict you, and will destroy you after all the good he hath done you.
24:21. And the people said to Josue: No, it shall not be so as thou sayest, but we will serve the Lord.
24:22. And Josue said to the people, You are witnesses, that you yourselves have chosen you the Lord to serve him. And they answered: We are witnesses.
24:23. Now therefore, said he, put away strange gods from among you, and incline your hearts to the Lord the God of Israel.
24:24. And the people said to Josue: We will serve the Lord our God, and we will be obedient to his commandments.
24:25. Josue therefore on that day made a covenant, and set before the people commandments and judgments in Sichem.
24:26. And he wrote all these things in the volume of the law of the Lord: and he took a great stone, and set it under the oak that was in the sanctuary of the Lord.
24:27. And he said to all the people: Behold this stone shall be a testimony unto you, that it hath heard all the words of the Lord, which he hath spoken to you: lest perhaps hereafter you will deny it, and lie to the Lord

your God.
It hath heard... This is a figure of speech, by which sensation is attributed to inanimate things; and they are called upon, as it were, to bear witness in favour of the great Creator, whom they on their part constantly obey.
24:28. And he sent the people away every one to their own possession,
24:29. And after these things Josue the son of Nun the servant of the Lord died, being a hundred and ten years old:
And after, etc... If Josue wrote this book, as is commonly believed, these last verses were added by Samuel, or some other prophet.
24:30. And they buried him in the border of his possession in Thamnathsare, which is situate in mount Ephraim, on the north side of mount Gaas.
24:31. And Israel served the Lord all the days of Josue, and of the ancients that lived a long time after Josue, and that had known all the works of the Lord which he had done in Israel.
24:32. And the bones of Joseph which the children of Israel had taken out of Egypt, they buried in Sichem, in that part of the field which Jacob had bought of the sons of Hemor the father of Sichem, for a hundred young ewes, and it was in the possession of the sons of Joseph.
24:33. Eleazar also the son of Aaron died: and they buried him in Gabaath that belongeth to Phinees his son, which was given him in mount Ephraim.

THE BOOK OF JOSHUA

AMERICAN STANDARD VERSION

Chapter 1

1 Now it came to pass after the death of Moses the servant of Jehovah, that
Jehovah spake unto Joshua the son of Nun, Moses' minister, saying,
2 Moses my servant is dead; now therefore arise, go over this Jordan, thou,
and all this people, unto the land which I do give to them, even to the
children of Israel.
3 Every place that the sole of your foot shall tread upon, to you have I
given it, as I spake unto Moses.
4 From the wilderness, and this Lebanon, even unto the great river, the
river Euphrates, all the land of the Hittites, and unto the great sea toward
the going down of the sun, shall be your border.
5 There shall not any man be able to stand before thee all the days of thy
life. as I was with Moses, so I will be with thee; I will not fail thee, nor
forsake thee.
6 Be strong and of good courage; for thou shalt cause this people to inherit
the land which I sware unto their fathers to give them.
7 Only be strong and very courageous, to observe to do according to all the
law, which Moses my servant commanded thee: turn not from it to the right
hand or to the left, that thou mayest have good success whithersoever thou
goest.
8 This book of the law shall not depart out of thy mouth, but thou shalt
meditate thereon day and night, that thou mayest observe to do according
to all that is written therein: for then thou shalt make thy way prosperous,
and then thou shalt have good success.

9 Have not I commanded thee? Be strong and of good courage; be not
affrighted, neither be thou dismayed: for Jehovah thy God is with thee
whithersoever thou goest.
10 Then Joshua commanded the officers of the people, saying,
11 Pass through the midst of the camp, and command the people, saying,
Prepare you victuals; for within three days ye are to pass over this Jordan, to
go in to possess the land, which Jehovah your God giveth you to possess it.
12 And to the Reubenites, and to the Gadites, and to the half-tribe of
Manasseh, spake Joshua, saying,
13 Remember the word which Moses the servant of Jehovah commanded
you, saying, Jehovah your God giveth you rest, and will give you this land.
14 Your wives, your little ones, and your cattle, shall abide in the land which
Moses gave you beyond the Jordan; but ye shall pass over before your
brethren armed, all the mighty men of valor, and shall help them;
15 until Jehovah have given your brethren rest, as [he hath given] you, and
they also have possessed the land which Jehovah your God giveth them:
then ye shall return unto the land of your possession, and possess it, which
Moses the servant of Jehovah gave you beyond the Jordan toward the
sunrising.
16 And they answered Joshua, saying, All that thou hast commanded us we
will do, and whithersoever thou sendest us we will go.
17 According as we hearkened unto Moses in all things, so will we hearken
unto thee: only Jehovah thy God be with thee, as he was with Moses.
18 Whosoever he be that shall rebel against thy commandment, and shall
not hearken unto thy words in all that thou commandest him, he shall be
put to death: only be strong and of good courage.

Chapter 2

1 And Joshua the son of Nun sent out of Shittim two men as spies secretly,
saying, Go, view the land, and Jericho. And they went and came into the
house of a harlot whose name was Rahab, and lay there.
2 And it was told the king of Jericho, saying, Behold, there came men in
hither to-night of the children of Israel to search out the land.
3 And the king of Jericho sent unto Rahab, saying, Bring forth the men that
are come to thee, that are entered into thy house; for they are come to
search out all the land.
4 And the woman took the two men, and hid them; and she said, Yea, the
men came unto me, but I knew not whence they were:
5 and it came to pass about the time of the shutting of the gate, when it was
dark, that the men went out; whither the men went I know not: pursue after
them quickly; for ye will overtake them.

6 But she had brought them up to the roof, and hid them with the stalks of
flax, which she had laid in order upon the roof.
7 And the men pursued after them the way to the Jordan unto the fords:
and as soon as they that pursued after them were gone out, they shut the
gate.
8 And before they were laid down, she came up unto them upon the roof;
9 and she said unto the men, I know that Jehovah hath given you the land,
and that the fear of you is fallen upon us, and that all the inhabitants of the
land melt away before you.
10 For we have heard how Jehovah dried up the water of the Red Sea
before you, when ye came out of Egypt; and what ye did unto the two kings
of the Amorites, that were beyond the Jordan, unto Sihon and to Og,
whom ye utterly destroyed.
11 And as soon as we had heard it, our hearts did melt, neither did there
remain any more spirit in any man, because of you: for Jehovah your God,
he is God in heaven above, and on earth beneath.
12 Now therefore, I pray you, swear unto me by Jehovah, since I have dealt
kindly with you, that ye also will deal kindly with my father's house, and
give me a true token;
13 and that ye will save alive my father, and my mother, and my brethren,
and my sisters, and all that they have, and will deliver our lives from death.
14 And the men said unto her, Our life for yours, if ye utter not this our
business; and it shall be, when Jehovah giveth us the land, that we will deal
kindly and truly with thee.
15 Then she let them down by a cord through the window: for her house
was upon the side of the wall, and she dwelt upon the wall.
16 And she said unto them, Get you to the mountain, lest the pursuers light
upon you; and hide yourselves there three days, until the pursuers be
returned: and afterward may ye go your way.
17 And the men said unto her, We will be guiltless of this thine oath which
thou hast made us to swear.
18 Behold, when we come into the land, thou shalt bind this line of scarlet
thread in the window which thou didst let us down by: and thou shalt
gather unto thee into the house thy father, and thy mother, and thy
brethren, and all thy father's household.
19 And it shall be, that whosoever shall go out of the doors of thy house
into the street, his blood shall be upon his head, and we shall be guiltless:
and whosoever shall be with thee in the house, his blood shall be on our
head, if any hand be upon him.
20 But if thou utter this our business, then we shall be guiltless of thine
oath which thou hast made us to swear.
21 And she said, According unto your words, so be it. And she sent them
away, and they departed: and she bound the scarlet line in the window.

22 And they went, and came unto the mountain, and abode there three
days, until the pursuers were returned: and the pursuers sought them
throughout all the way, but found them not.
23 Then the two men returned, and descended from the mountain, and
passed over, and came to Joshua the son of Nun; and they told him all that
had befallen them.
24 And they said unto Joshua, Truly Jehovah hath delivered into our hands
all the land; and moreover all the inhabitants of the land do melt away
before us.

Chapter 3

1 And Joshua rose up early in the morning; and they removed from Shittim,
and came to the Jordan, he and all the children of Israel; and they lodged
there before they passed over.
2 And it came to pass after three days, that the officers went through the
midst of the camp;
3 and they commanded the people, saying, When ye see the ark of the
covenant of Jehovah your God, and the priests the Levites bearing it, then
ye shall remove from your place, and go after it.
4 Yet there shall be a space between you and it, about two thousand cubits
by measure: come not near unto it, that ye may know the way by which ye
must go; for ye have not passed this way heretofore.
5 And Joshua said unto the people, Sanctify yourselves; for tomorrow
Jehovah will do wonders among you.
6 And Joshua spake unto the priests, saying, Take up the ark of the
covenant, and pass over before the people. And they took up the ark of the
covenant, and went before the people.
7 And Jehovah said unto Joshua, This day will I begin to magnify thee in
the sight of all Israel, that they may know that, as I was with Moses, so I
will be with thee.
8 And thou shalt command the priests that bear the ark of the covenant,
saying, When ye are come to the brink of the waters of the Jordan, ye shall
stand still in the Jordan.
9 And Joshua said unto the children of Israel, Come hither, and hear the
words of Jehovah your God.
10 And Joshua said, Hereby ye shall know that the living God is among
you, and that he will without fail drive out from before you the Canaanite,
and the Hittite, and the Hivite, and the Perizzite, and the Girgashite, and
the Amorite, and the Jebusite.
11 Behold, the ark of the covenant of the Lord of all the earth passeth over
before you into the Jordan.

12 Now therefore take you twelve men out of the tribes of Israel, for every tribe a man.
13 And it shall come to pass, when the soles of the feet of the priests that bear the ark of Jehovah, the Lord of all the earth, shall rest in the waters of the Jordan, that the waters of the Jordan shall be cut off, even the waters that come down from above; and they shall stand in one heap.
14 And it came to pass, when the people removed from their tents, to pass over the Jordan, the priests that bare the ark of the covenant being before the people;
15 and when they that bare the ark were come unto the Jordan, and the feet of the priests that bare the ark were dipped in the brink of the water (for the Jordan overfloweth all its banks all the time of harvest,)
16 that the waters which came down from above stood, and rose up in one heap, a great way off, at Adam, the city that is beside Zarethan; and those that went down toward the sea of the Arabah, even the Salt Sea, were wholly cut off: and the people passed over right against Jericho.
17 And the priests that bare the ark of the covenant of Jehovah stood firm on dry ground in the midst of the Jordan; and all Israel passed over on dry ground, until all the nation were passed clean over the Jordan.

Chapter 4

1 And it came to pass, when all the nation were clean passed over the Jordan, that Jehovah spake unto Joshua, saying,
2 Take you twelve men out of the people, out of every tribe a man,
3 and command ye them, saying, Take you hence out of the midst of the Jordan, out of the place where the priests' feet stood firm, twelve stones, and carry them over with you, and lay them down in the lodging-place, where ye shall lodge this night.
4 Then Joshua called the twelve men, whom he had prepared of the children of Israel, out of every tribe a man:
5 and Joshua said unto them, Pass over before the ark of Jehovah your God into the midst of the Jordan, and take you up every man of you a stone upon his shoulder, according unto the number of the tribes of the children of Israel;
6 that this may be a sign among you, that, when your children ask in time to come, saying, What mean ye by these stones?
7 then ye shall say unto them, Because the waters of the Jordan were cut off before the ark of the covenant of Jehovah; when it passed over the Jordan, the waters of the Jordan were cut off: and these stones shall be for a memorial unto the children of Israel for ever.
8 And the children of Israel did so as Joshua commanded, and took up

twelve stones out of the midst of the Jordan, as Jehovah spake unto Joshua, according to the number of the tribes of the children of Israel; and they carried them over with them unto the place where they lodged, and laid them down there.
9 And Joshua set up twelve stones in the midst of the Jordan, in the place where the feet of the priests that bare the ark of the covenant stood: and they are there unto this day.
10 For the priests that bare the ark stood in the midst of the Jordan, until everything was finished that Jehovah commanded Joshua to speak unto the people, according to all that Moses commanded Joshua: and the people hasted and passed over.
11 And it came to pass, when all the people were clean passed over, that the ark of Jehovah passed over, and the priests, in the presence of the people.
12 And the children of Reuben, and the children of Gad, and the half-tribe of Manasseh, passed over armed before the children of Israel, as Moses spake unto them:
13 about forty thousand ready armed for war passed over before Jehovah unto battle, to the plains of Jericho.
14 On that day Jehovah magnified Joshua in the sight of all Israel; and they feared him, as they feared Moses, all the days of his life.
15 And Jehovah spake unto Joshua, saying,
16 Command the priests that bear the ark of the testimony, that they come up out of the Jordan.
17 Joshua therefore commanded the priests, saying, Come ye up out of the Jordan.
18 And it came to pass, when the priests that bare the ark of the covenant of Jehovah were come up out of the midst of the Jordan, and the soles of the priests' feet were lifted up unto the dry ground, that the waters of the Jordan returned unto their place, and went over all its banks, as aforetime.
19 And the people came up out of the Jordan on the tenth day of the first month, and encamped in Gilgal, on the east border of Jericho.
20 And those twelve stones, which they took out of the Jordan, did Joshua set up in Gilgal.
21 And he spake unto the children of Israel, saying, When your children shall ask their fathers in time to come, saying, What mean these stones?
22 Then ye shall let your children know, saying, Israel came over this Jordan on dry land.
23 For Jehovah your God dried up the waters of the Jordan from before you, until ye were passed over, as Jehovah your God did to the Red Sea, which he dried up from before us, until we were passed over;
24 that all the peoples of the earth may know the hand of Jehovah, that it is mighty; that ye may fear Jehovah your God for ever.

Chapter 5

1 And it came to pass, when all the kings of the Amorites, that were beyond
the Jordan westward, and all the kings of the Canaanites, that were by the
sea, heard how that Jehovah had dried up the waters of the Jordan from
before the children of Israel, until we were passed over, that their heart
melted, neither was there spirit in them any more, because of the children
of Israel.
2 At that time Jehovah said unto Joshua, Make thee knives of flint, and
circumcise again the children of Israel the second time.
3 And Joshua made him knives of lint, and circumcised the children of
Israel at the hill of the foreskins.
4 And this is the cause why Joshua did circumcise: all the people that came
forth out of Egypt, that were males, even all the men of war, died in the
wilderness by the way, after they came forth out of Egypt.
5 For all the people that came out were circumcised; but all the people that
were born in the wilderness by the way as they came forth out of Egypt,
they had not circumcised.
6 For the children of Israel walked forty years in the wilderness, till all the
nation, even the men of war that came forth out of Egypt, were consumed,
because they hearkened not unto the voice of Jehovah: unto whom Jehovah
sware that he would not let them see the land which Jehovah sware unto
their fathers that he would give us, a land flowing with milk and honey.
7 And their children, whom he raised up in their stead, them did Joshua
circumcise: for they were uncircumcised, because they had not circumcised
them by the way.
8 And it came to pass, when they had done circumcising all the nation, that
they abode in their places in the camp, till they were whole.
9 And Jehovah said unto Joshua, This day have I rolled away the reproach
of Egypt from off you. Wherefore the name of that place was called Gilgal,
unto this day.
10 And the children of Israel encamped in Gilgal; and they kept the
passover on the fourteenth day of the month at even in the plains of
Jericho.
11 And they did eat of the produce of the land on the morrow after the
passover, unleavened cakes and parched grain, in the selfsame day.
12 And the manna ceased on the morrow, after they had eaten of the
produce of the land; neither had the children of Israel manna any more; but
they did eat of the fruit of the land of Canaan that year.
13 And it came to pass, when Joshua was by Jericho, that he lifted up his
eyes and looked, and, behold, there stood a man over against him with his
sword drawn in his hand: and Joshua went unto him, and said unto him,

Art thou for us, or for our adversaries?
14 And he said, Nay; but [as] prince of the host of Jehovah am I now come. And Joshua fell on his face to the earth, and did worship, and said unto him, What saith my lord unto his servant?
15 And the prince of Jehovah's host said unto Joshua, Put off thy shoe from off thy foot; for the place whereon thou standest is holy. And Joshua did so.

Chapter 6

1 Now Jericho was straitly shut up because of the children of Israel: none went out, and none came in.
2 And Jehovah said unto Joshua, See, I have given into thy hand Jericho, and the king thereof, and the mighty men of valor.
3 And ye shall compass the city, all the men of war, going about the city once. Thus shalt thou do six days.
4 And seven priests shall bear seven trumpets of rams' horns before the ark: and the seventh day ye shall compass the city seven times, and the priests shall blow the trumpets.
5 And it shall be, that, when they make a long blast with the ram's horn, and when ye hear the sound of the trumpet, all the people shall shout with a great shout; and the wall of the city shall fall down flat, and the people shall go up every man straight before him.
6 And Joshua the son of Nun called the priests, and said unto them, Take up the ark of the covenant, and let seven priests bear seven trumpets of rams' horns before the ark of Jehovah.
7 And they said unto the people, Pass on, and compass the city, and let the armed men pass on before the ark of Jehovah.
8 And it was so, that, when Joshua had spoken unto the people, the seven priests bearing the seven trumpets of rams' horns before Jehovah passed on, and blew the trumpets: and the ark of the covenant of Jehovah followed them.
9 And the armed men went before the priests that blew the trumpets, and the rearward went after the ark, [the priests] blowing the trumpets as they went.
10 And Joshua commanded the people, saying, Ye shall not shout, nor let your voice be heard, neither shall any word proceed out of your mouth, until the day I bid you shout; then shall ye shout.
11 So he caused the ark of Jehovah to compass the city, going about it once: and they came into the camp, and lodged in the camp.
12 And Joshua rose early in the morning, and the priests took up the ark of Jehovah.

13 And the seven priests bearing the seven trumpets of rams' horns before
the ark of Jehovah went on continually, and blew the trumpets: and the
armed men went before them; and the rearward came after the ark of
Jehovah, [the priests] blowing the trumpets as they went.
14 And the second day they compassed the city once, and returned into the
camp: so they did six days.
15 And it came to pass on the seventh day, that they rose early at the
dawning of the day, and compassed the city after the same manner seven
times: only on the day they compassed the city seven times.
16 And it came to pass at the seventh time, when the priests blew the
trumpets, Joshua said unto the people, Shout; for Jehovah hath given you
the city.
17 And the city shall be devoted, even it and all that is therein, to Jehovah:
only Rahab the harlot shall live, she and all that are with her in the house,
because she hid the messengers that we sent.
18 But as for you, only keep yourselves from the devoted thing, lest when
ye have devoted it, ye take of the devoted thing; so would ye make the
camp of Israel accursed, and trouble it.
19 But all the silver, and gold, and vessels of brass and iron, are holy unto
Jehovah: they shall come into the treasury of Jehovah.
20 So the people shouted, and [the priests] blew the trumpets; and it came
to pass, when the people heard the sound of the trumpet, that the people
shouted with a great shout, and the wall fell down flat, so that the people
went up into the city, every man straight before him, and they took the city.
21 And they utterly destroyed all that was in the city, both man and woman,
both young and old, and ox, and sheep, and ass, with the edge of the sword.
22 And Joshua said unto the two men that had spied out the land, Go into
the harlot's house, and bring out thence the woman, and all that she hath, as
ye sware unto her.
23 And the young men the spies went in, and brought out Rahab, and her
father, and her mother, and her brethren, and all that she had; all her
kindred also they brought out; and they set them without the camp of
Israel.
24 And they burnt the city with fire, and all that was therein; only the silver,
and the gold, and the vessels of brass and of iron, they put into the treasury
of the house of Jehovah.
25 But Rahab the harlot, and her father's household, and all that she had,
did Joshua save alive; and she dwelt in the midst of Israel unto this day,
because she hid the messengers, whom Joshua sent to spy out Jericho.
26 And Joshua charged them with an oath at that time, saying, Cursed be
the man before Jehovah, that riseth up and buildeth this city Jericho: with
the loss of his first-born shall he lay the foundation thereof, and with the
loss of his youngest son shall he set up the gates of it.

27 So Jehovah was with Joshua; and his fame was in all the land.

Chapter 7

1 But the children of Israel committed a trespass in the devoted thing; for
Achan, the son of Carmi, the son of Zabdi, the son of Zerah, of the tribe of
Judah, took of the devoted thing: and the anger of Jehovah was kindled
against the children of Israel.
2 And Joshua sent men from Jericho to Ai, which is beside Beth-aven, on
the east side of Beth-el, and spake unto them, saying, Go up and spy out
the land. And the men went up and spied out Ai.
3 And they returned to Joshua, and said unto him, Let not all the people go
up; but let about two or three thousand men go up and smite Ai; make not
all the people to toil thither; for they are but few.
4 So there went up thither of the people about three thousand men: and
they fled before the men of Ai.
5 And the men of Ai smote of them about thirty and six men; and they
chased them [from] before the gate even unto Shebarim, and smote them at
the descent; and the hearts of the people melted, and became as water.
6 And Joshua rent his clothes, and fell to the earth upon his face before the
ark of Jehovah until the evening, he and the elders of Israel; and they put
dust upon their heads.
7 And Joshua said, Alas, O Lord Jehovah, wherefore hast thou at all
brought this people over the Jordan, to deliver us into the hand of the
Amorites, to cause us to perish? would that we had been content and dwelt
beyond the Jordan!
8 Oh, Lord, what shall I say, after that Israel hath turned their backs before
their enemies!
9 For the Canaanites and all the inhabitants of the land will hear of it, and
will compass us round, and cut off our name from the earth: and what wilt
thou do for thy great name?
10 And Jehovah said unto Joshua, Get thee up; wherefore art thou thus
fallen upon thy face?
11 Israel hath sinned; yea, they have even transgressed my covenant which I
commanded them: yea, they have even taken of the devoted thing, and have
also stolen, and dissembled also; and they have even put it among their own
stuff.
12 Therefore the children of Israel cannot stand before their enemies; they
turn their backs before their enemies, because they are become accursed: I
will not be with you any more, except ye destroy the devoted thing from
among you.
13 Up, sanctify the people, and say, Sanctify yourselves against tomorrow:

for thus saith Jehovah, the God of Israel, There is a devoted thing in the
midst of thee, O Israel; thou canst not stand before thine enemies, until ye
take away the devoted thing from among you.
14 In the morning therefore ye shall be brought near by your tribes: and it
shall be, that the tribe which Jehovah taketh shall come near by families;
and the family which Jehovah shall take shall come near by households; and
the household which Jehovah shall take shall come near man by man.
15 And it shall be, that he that is taken with the devoted thing shall be burnt
with fire, he and all that he hath; because he hath transgressed the covenant
of Jehovah, and because he hath wrought folly in Israel.
16 So Joshua rose up early in the morning, and brought Israel near by their
tribes; and the tribe of Judah was taken:
17 and he brought near the family of Judah; and he took the family of the
Zerahites: and he brought near the family of the Zerahites man by man; and
Zabdi was taken:
18 and he brought near his household man by man; and Achan, the son of
Carmi, the son of Zabdi, the son of Zerah, of the tribe of Judah, was taken.
19 And Joshua said unto Achan, My son, give, I pray thee, glory to Jehovah,
the God of Israel, and make confession unto him; and tell me now what
thou hast done; hide it not from me.
20 And Achan answered Joshua, and said, Of a truth I have sinned against
Jehovah, the God of Israel, and thus and thus have I done:
21 when I saw among the spoil a goodly Babylonish mantle, and two
hundred shekels of silver, and a wedge of gold of fifty shekels weight, then
I coveted them, and took them; and, behold, they are hid in the earth in the
midst of my tent, and the silver under it.
22 So Joshua sent messengers, and they ran unto the tent; and, behold, it
was hid in his tent, and the silver under it.
23 And they took them from the midst of the tent, and brought them unto
Joshua, and unto all the children of Israel; and they laid them down before
Jehovah.
24 And Joshua, and all Israel with him, took Achan the son of Zerah, and
the silver, and the mantle, and the wedge of gold, and his sons, and his
daughters, and his oxen, and his asses, and his sheep, and his tent, and all
that he had: and they brought them up unto the valley of Achor.
25 And Joshua said, Why hast thou troubled us? Jehovah shall trouble thee
this day. And all Israel stoned him with stones; and they burned them with
fire, and stoned them with stones.
26 And they raised over him a great heap of stones, unto this day; and
Jehovah turned from the fierceness of his anger. Wherefore the name of
that place was called, The valley of Achor, unto this day.

Chapter 8

1 And Jehovah said unto Joshua, Fear not, neither be thou dismayed: take all the people of war with thee, and arise, go up to Ai; see, I have given into thy hand the king of Ai, and his people, and his city, and his land;
2 And thou shalt do to Ai and her king as thou didst unto Jericho and her king: only the spoil thereof, and the cattle thereof, shall ye take for a prey unto yourselves: set thee an ambush for the city behind it.
3 So Joshua arose, and all the people of war, to go up to Ai: and Joshua chose out thirty thousand men, the mighty men of valor, and sent them forth by night.
4 And he commanded them, saying, Behold, ye shall lie in ambush against the city, behind the city; go not very far from the city, but be ye all ready:
5 and I, and all the people that are with me, will approach unto the city. And it shall come to pass, when they come out against us, as at the first, that we will flee before them;
6 and they will come out after us, till we have drawn them away from the city; for they will say, They flee before us, as at the first: so we will flee before them;
7 and ye shall rise up from the ambush, and take possession of the city: for Jehovah your God will deliver it into your hand.
8 And it shall be, when ye have seized upon the city, that ye shall set the city on fire; according to the word of Jehovah shall ye do: see, I have commanded you.
9 And Joshua sent them forth; and they went to the ambushment, and abode between Beth-el and Ai, on the west side of Ai: but Joshua lodged that night among the people.
10 And Joshua arose up early in the morning, and mustered the people, and went up, he and the elders of Israel, before the people to Ai.
11 And all the people, [even] the [men of] war that were with him, went up, and drew nigh, and came before the city, and encamped on the north side of Ai: now there was a valley between him and Ai.
12 And he took about five thousand men, and set them in ambush between Beth-el and Ai, on the west side of the city.
13 So they set the people, even all the host that was on the north of the city, and their liers-in-wait that were on the west of the city; and Joshua went that night into the midst of the valley.
14 And it came to pass, when the king of Ai saw it, that they hasted and rose up early, and the men of the city went out against Israel to battle, he and all his people, at the time appointed, before the Arabah; but he knew not that there was an ambush against him behind the city.
15 And Joshua and all Israel made as if they were beaten before them, and fled by the way of the wilderness.

16 And all the people that were in the city were called together to pursue
after them: and they pursued after Joshua, and were drawn away from the
city.
17 And there was not a man left in Ai or Beth-el, that went not out after
Israel: and they left the city open, and pursued after Israel.
18 And Jehovah said unto Joshua, Stretch out the javelin that is in thy hand
toward Ai; for I will give it into thy hand. And Joshua stretched out the
javelin that was in his hand toward the city.
19 And the ambush arose quickly out of their place, and they ran as soon as
he had stretched out his hand, and entered into the city, and took it; and
they hasted and set the city on fire.
20 And when the men of Ai looked behind them, they saw, and, behold, the
smoke of the city ascended up to heaven, and they had no power to flee
this way or that way: and the people that fled to the wilderness turned back
upon the pursuers.
21 And when Joshua and all Israel saw that the ambush had taken the city,
and that the smoke of the city ascended, then they turned again, and slew
the men of Ai.
22 And the others came forth out of the city against them; so they were in
the midst of Israel, some on this side, and some on that side: and they
smote them, so that they let none of them remain or escape.
23 And the king of Ai they took alive, and brought him to Joshua.
24 And it came to pass, when Israel had made an end of slaying all the
inhabitants of Ai in the field, in the wilderness wherein they pursued them,
and they were all fallen by the edge of the sword, until they were consumed,
that all Israel returned unto Ai, and smote it with the edge of the sword.
25 And all that fell that day, both of men and women, were twelve
thousand, even all the men of Ai.
26 For Joshua drew not back his hand, wherewith he stretched out the
javelin, until he had utterly destroyed all the inhabitants of Ai.
27 Only the cattle and the spoil of that city Israel took for prey unto
themselves, according unto the word of Jehovah which he commanded
Joshua.
28 So Joshua burnt Ai, and made it a heap for ever, even a desolation, unto
this day.
29 And the king of Ai he hanged on a tree until the eventide: and at the
going down of the sun Joshua commanded, and they took his body down
from the tree, and cast it at the entrance of the gate of the city, and raised
thereon a great heap of stones, unto this day.
30 Then Joshua built an altar unto Jehovah, the God of Israel, in mount
Ebal,
31 as Moses the servant of Jehovah commanded the children of Israel, as it
is written in the book of the law of Moses, an altar of unhewn stones, upon

which no man had lifted up any iron: and they offered thereon burnt-offerings unto Jehovah, and sacrificed peace-offerings.
32 And he wrote there upon the stones a copy of the law of Moses, which he wrote, in the presence of the children of Israel.
33 And all Israel, and their elders and officers, and their judges, stood on this side of the ark and on that side before the priests the Levites, that bare the ark of the covenant of Jehovah, as well the sojourner as the homeborn; half of them in front of mount Gerizim, and half of them in front of mount Ebal; as Moses the servant of Jehovah had commanded at the first, that they should bless the people of Israel.
34 And afterward he read all the words of the law, the blessing and the curse, according to all that is written in the book of the law.
35 There was not a word of all that Moses commanded, which Joshua read not before all the assembly of Israel, and the women, and the little ones, and the sojourners that were among them.

Chapter 9

1 And it came to pass, when all the kings that were beyond the Jordan, in the hill-country, and in the lowland, and on all the shore of the great sea in front of Lebanon, the Hittite, and the Amorite, the Canaanite, the Perizzite, the Hivite, and the Jebusite, heard thereof;
2 that they gathered themselves together, to fight with Joshua and with Israel, with one accord.
3 But when the inhabitants of Gibeon heard what Joshua had done unto Jericho and to Ai,
4 they also did work wilily, and went and made as if they had been ambassadors, and took old sacks upon their asses, and wine-skins, old and rent and bound up,
5 and old and patched shoes upon their feet, and old garments upon them; and all the bread of their provision was dry and was become mouldy.
6 And they went to Joshua unto the camp at Gilgal, and said unto him, and to the men of Israel, We are come from a far country: now therefore make ye a covenant with us.
7 And the men of Israel said unto the Hivites, Peradventure ye dwell among us; and how shall we make a covenant with you?
8 And they said unto Joshua, We are thy servants. And Joshua said unto them, Who are ye? and from whence come ye?
9 And they said unto him, From a very far country thy servants are come because of the name of Jehovah thy God: for we have heard the fame of him, and all that he did in Egypt,
10 and all that he did to the two kings of the Amorites, that were beyond

the Jordan, to Sihon king of Heshbon, and to Og king of Bashan, who was
at Ashtaroth.
11 And our elders and all the inhabitants of our country spake to us, saying,
Take provision in your hand for the journey, and go to meet them, and say
unto them, We are your servants: and now make ye a covenant with us.
12 This our bread we took hot for our provision out of our houses on the
day we came forth to go unto you; but now, behold, it is dry, and is become
mouldy:
13 and these wine-skins, which we filled, were new; and, behold, they are
rent: and these our garments and our shoes are become old by reason of the
very long journey.
14 And the men took of their provision, and asked not counsel at the
mouth of Jehovah.
15 And Joshua made peace with them, and made a covenant with them, to
let them live: and the princes of the congregation sware unto them.
16 And it came to pass at the end of three days after they had made a
covenant with them, that they heard that they were their neighbors, and that
they dwelt among them.
17 And the children of Israel journeyed, and came unto their cities on the
third day. Now their cities were Gibeon, and Chephirah, and Beeroth, and
Kiriath-jearim.
18 And the children of Israel smote them not, because the princes of the
congregation had sworn unto them by Jehovah, the God of Israel. And all
the congregation murmured against the princes.
19 But all the princes said unto all the congregation, We have sworn unto
them by Jehovah, the God of Israel: now therefore we may not touch them.
20 This we will do to them, and let them live; lest wrath be upon us,
because of the oath which we sware unto them.
21 And the princes said unto them, Let them live: so they became hewers of
wood and drawers of water unto all the congregation, as the princes had
spoken unto them.
22 And Joshua called for them, and he spake unto them, saying, Wherefore
have ye beguiled us, saying, We are very far from you; when ye dwell among
us?
23 Now therefore ye are cursed, and there shall never fail to be of you
bondmen, both hewers of wood and drawers of water for the house of my
God.
24 And they answered Joshua, and said, Because it was certainly told thy
servants, how that Jehovah thy God commanded his servant Moses to give
you all the land, and to destroy all the inhabitants of the land from before
you; therefore we were sore afraid for our lives because of you, and have
done this thing.
25 And now, behold, we are in thy hand: as it seemeth good and right unto

thee to do unto us, do.
26 And so did he unto them, and delivered them out of the hand of the
children of Israel, that they slew them not.
27 And Joshua made them that day hewers of wood and drawers of water
for the congregation, and for the altar of Jehovah, unto this day, in the
place which he should choose.

Chapter 10

1 Now it came to pass, when Adoni-zedek king of Jerusalem heard how
Joshua had taken Ai, and had utterly destroyed it; as he had done to Jericho
and her king, so he had done to Ai and her king; and how the inhabitants of
Gibeon had made peace with Israel, and were among them;
2 that they feared greatly, because Gibeon was a great city, as one of the
royal cities, and because it was greater than Ai, and all the men thereof were
mighty.
3 Wherefore Adoni-zedek king of Jerusalem sent unto Hoham king of
Hebron, and unto Piram king of Jarmuth, and unto Japhia king of Lachish,
and unto Debir king of Eglon, saying,
4 Come up unto me, and help me, and let us smite Gibeon; for it hath made
peace with Joshua and with the children of Israel.
5 Therefore the five kings of the Amorites, the king of Jerusalem, the king
of Hebron, the king of Jarmuth, the king of Lachish, the king of Eglon,
gathered themselves together, and went up, they and all their hosts, and
encamped against Gibeon, and made war against it.
6 And the men of Gibeon sent unto Joshua to the camp to Gilgal, saying,
Slack not thy hand from thy servants; come up to us quickly, and save us,
and help us: for all the kings of the Amorites that dwell in the hill-country
are gathered together against us.
7 So Joshua went up from Gilgal, he, and all the people of war with him,
and all the mighty men of valor.
8 And Jehovah said unto Joshua, Fear them not: for I have delivered them
into thy hands; there shall not a man of them stand before thee.
9 Joshua therefore came upon them suddenly; [for] he went up from Gilgal
all the night.
10 And Jehovah discomfited them before Israel, and he slew them with a
great slaughter at Gibeon, and chased them by the way of the ascent of
Beth-horon, and smote them to Azekah, and unto Makkedah.
11 And it came to pass, as they fled from before Israel, while they were at
the descent of Beth-horon, that Jehovah cast down great stones from
heaven upon them unto Azekah, and they died: they were more who died
with the hailstones than they whom the children of Israel slew with the

sword.
12 Then spake Joshua to Jehovah in the day when Jehovah delivered up the Amorites before the children of Israel; and he said in the sight of Israel, Sun, stand thou still upon Gibeon; And thou, Moon, in the valley of Aijalon.
13 And the sun stood still, and the moon stayed, Until the nation had avenged themselves of their enemies. Is not this written in the book of Jashar? And the sun stayed in the midst of heaven, and hasted not to go down about a whole day.
14 And there was no day like that before it or after it, that Jehovah hearkened unto the voice of a man: for Jehovah fought for Israel.
15 And Joshua returned, and all Israel with him, unto the camp to Gilgal.
16 And these five kings fled, and hid themselves in the cave at Makkedah.
17 And it was told Joshua, saying, The five kings are found, hidden in the cave at Makkedah.
18 And Joshua said, Roll great stones unto the mouth of the cave, and set men by it to keep them:
19 but stay not ye; pursue after your enemies, and smite the hindmost of them; suffer them not to enter into their cities: for Jehovah your God hath delivered them into your hand.
20 And it came to pass, when Joshua and the children of Israel had made an end of slaying them with a very great slaughter, till they were consumed, and the remnant which remained of them had entered into the fortified cities,
21 that all the people returned to the camp to Joshua at Makkedah in peace: none moved his tongue against any of the children of Israel.
22 Then said Joshua, Open the mouth of the cave, and bring forth those five kings unto me out of the cave.
23 And they did so, and brought forth those five kings unto him out of the cave, the king of Jerusalem, the king of Hebron, the king of Jarmuth, the king of Lachish, the king of Eglon.
24 And it came to pass, when they brought forth those kings unto Joshua, that Joshua called for all the men of Israel, and said unto the chiefs of the men of war that went with him, Come near, put your feet upon the necks of these kings. And they came near, and put their feet upon the necks of them.
25 And Joshua said unto them, Fear not, nor be dismayed; be strong and of good courage: for thus shall Jehovah do to all your enemies against whom ye fight.
26 And afterward Joshua smote them, and put them to death, and hanged them on five trees: and they were hanging upon the trees until the evening.
27 And it came to pass at the time of the going down of the sun, that Joshua commanded, and they took them down off the trees, and cast them into the cave wherein they had hidden themselves, and laid great stones on

the mouth of the cave, unto this very day.
28 And Joshua took Makkedah on that day, and smote it with the edge of the sword, and the king thereof: he utterly destroyed them and all the souls that were therein; he left none remaining; and he did to the king of Makkedah as he had done unto the king of Jericho.
29 And Joshua passed from Makkedah, and all Israel with him, unto Libnah, and fought against Libnah:
30 and Jehovah delivered it also, and the king thereof, into the hand of Israel; and he smote it with the edge of the sword, and all the souls that were therein; he left none remaining in it; and he did unto the king thereof as he had done unto the king of Jericho.
31 And Joshua passed from Libnah, and all Israel with him, unto Lachish, and encamped against it, and fought against it:
32 and Jehovah delivered Lachish into the hand of Israel; and he took it on the second day, and smote it with the edge of the sword, and all the souls that were therein, according to all that he had done to Libnah.
33 Then Horam king of Gezer came up to help Lachish; and Joshua smote him and his people, until he had left him none remaining.
34 And Joshua passed from Lachish, and all Israel with him, unto Eglon; and they encamped against it, and fought against it;
35 and they took it on that day, and smote it with the edge of the sword; and all the souls that were therein he utterly destroyed that day, according to all that he had done to Lachish.
36 And Joshua went up from Eglon, and all Israel with him, unto Hebron; and they fought against it:
37 and they took it, and smote it with the edge of the sword, and the king thereof, and all the cities thereof, and all the souls that were therein; he left none remaining, according to all that he had done to Eglon; but he utterly destroyed it, and all the souls that were therein.
38 And Joshua returned, and all Israel with him, to Debir, and fought against it:
39 and he took it, and the king thereof, and all the cities thereof; and they smote them with the edge of the sword, and utterly destroyed all the souls that were therein; he left none remaining: as he had done to Hebron, so he did to Debir, and to the king thereof; as he had done also to Libnah, and to the king thereof.
40 So Joshua smote all the land, the hill-country, and the South, and the lowland, and the slopes, and all their kings: he left none remaining, but he utterly destroyed all that breathed, as Jehovah, the God of Israel, commanded.
41 And Joshua smote them from Kadesh-barnea even unto Gaza, and all the country of Goshen, even unto Gibeon.
42 And all these kings and their land did Joshua take at one time, because

Jehovah, the God of Israel, fought for Israel.
43 And Joshua returned, and all Israel with him, unto the camp to Gilgal.

Chapter 11

1 And it came to pass, when Jabin king of Hazor heard thereof, that he sent to Jobab king of Madon, and to the king of Shimron, and to the king of Achshaph,
2 and to the kings that were on the north, in the hill-country, and in the Arabah south of Chinneroth, and in the lowland, and in the heights of Dor on the west,
3 to the Canaanite on the east and on the west, and the Amorite, and the Hittite, and the Perizzite, and the Jebusite in the hill-country, and the Hivite under Hermon in the land of Mizpah.
4 And they went out, they and all their hosts with them, much people, even as the sand that is upon the sea-shore in multitude, with horses and chariots very many.
5 And all these kings met together; and they came and encamped together at the waters of Merom, to fight with Israel.
6 And Jehovah said unto Joshua, Be not afraid because of them; for to-morrow at this time will I deliver them up all slain before Israel: thou shalt hock their horses, and burn their chariots with fire.
7 So Joshua came, and all the people of war with him, against them by the waters of Merom suddenly, and fell upon them.
8 And Jehovah delivered them into the hand of Israel, and they smote them, and chased them unto great Sidon, and unto Misrephoth-maim, and unto the valley of Mizpeh eastward; and they smote them, until they left them none remaining.
9 And Joshua did unto them as Jehovah bade him: he hocked their horses, and burnt their chariots with fire.
10 And Joshua turned back at that time, and took Hazor, and smote the king thereof with the sword: for Hazor beforetime was the head of all those kingdoms.
11 And they smote all the souls that were therein with the edge of the sword, utterly destroying them; there was none left that breathed: and he burnt Hazor with fire.
12 And all the cities of those kings, and all the kings of them, did Joshua take, and he smote them with the edge of the sword, and utterly destroyed them; as Moses the servant of Jehovah commanded.
13 But as for the cities that stood on their mounds, Israel burned none of them, save Hazor only; that did Joshua burn.
14 And all the spoil of these cities, and the cattle, the children of Israel took

for a prey unto themselves; but every man they smote with the edge of the sword, until they had destroyed them, neither left they any that breathed.
15 As Jehovah commanded Moses his servant, so did Moses command Joshua: and so did Joshua; he left nothing undone of all that Jehovah commanded Moses.
16 So Joshua took all that land, the hill-country, and all the South, and all the land of Goshen, and the lowland, and the Arabah, and the hill-country of Israel, and the lowland of the same;
17 from mount Halak, that goeth up to Seir, even unto Baal-gad in the valley of Lebanon under mount Hermon: and all their kings he took, and smote them, and put them to death.
18 Joshua made war a long time with all those kings.
19 There was not a city that made peace with the children of Israel, save the Hivites the inhabitants of Gibeon: they took all in battle.
20 For it was of Jehovah to harden their hearts, to come against Israel in battle, that he might utterly destroy them, that they might have no favor, but that he might destroy them, as Jehovah commanded Moses.
21 And Joshua came at that time, and cut off the Anakim from the hill-country, from Hebron, from Debir, from Anab, and from all the hill-country of Judah, and from all the hill-country of Israel: Joshua utterly destroyed them with their cities.
22 There was none of the Anakim left in the land of the children of Israel: only in Gaza, in Gath, and in Ashdod, did some remain.
23 So Joshua took the whole land, according to all that Jehovah spake unto Moses; and Joshua gave it for an inheritance unto Israel according to their divisions by their tribes. And the land had rest from war.

Chapter 12

1 Now these are the kings of the land, whom the children of Israel smote, and possessed their land beyond the Jordan toward the sunrising, from the valley of the Arnon unto mount Hermon, and all the Arabah eastward:
2 Sihon king of the Amorites, who dwelt in Heshbon, and ruled from Aroer, which is on the edge of the valley of the Arnon, and [the city that is in] the middle of the valley, and half Gilead, even unto the river Jabbok, the border of the children of Ammon;
3 and the Arabah unto the sea of Chinneroth, eastward, and unto the sea of the Arabah, even the Salt Sea, eastward, the way to Beth-jeshimoth; and on the south, under the slopes of Pisgah:
4 and the border of Og king of Bashan, of the remnant of the Rephaim, who dwelt at Ashtaroth and at Edrei,
5 and ruled in mount Hermon, and in Salecah, and in all Bashan, unto the

border of the Geshurites and the Maacathites, and half Gilead, the border of Sihon king of Heshbon.
6 Moses the servant of Jehovah and the children of Israel smote them: and Moses the servant of Jehovah gave it for a possession unto the Reubenites, and the Gadites, and the half-tribe of Manasseh.
7 And these are the kings of the land whom Joshua and the children of Israel smote beyond the Jordan westward, from Baal-gad in the valley of Lebanon even unto mount Halak, that goeth up to Seir; and Joshua gave it unto the tribes of Israel for a possession according to their divisions;
8 in the hill-country, and in the lowland, and in the Arabah, and in the slopes, and in the wilderness, and in the South; the Hittite, the Amorite, and the Canaanite, the Perizzite, the Hivite, and the Jebusite:
9 the king of Jericho, one; the king of Ai, which is beside Bethel, one;
10 the king of Jerusalem, one; the king of Hebron, one;
11 the king of Jarmuth, one; the king of Lachish, one;
12 the king of Eglon, one; the king of Gezer, one;
13 the king of Debir, one; the king of Geder, one;
14 the king of Hormah, one; the king of Arad, one;
15 the king of Libnah, one; the king of Adullam, one;
16 the king of Makkedah, one; the king of Bethel, one;
17 the king of Tappuah, one; the king of Hepher, one;
18 the king of Aphek, one; the king of Lassharon, one;
19 the king of Madon, one; the king of Hazor, one;
20 the king of Shimron-meron, one; the king of Achshaph, one;
21 the king of Taanach, one; the king of Megiddo, one;
22 the king of Kedesh, one; the king of Jokneam in Carmel, one;
23 the king of Dor in the height of Dor, one; the king of Goiim in Gilgal, one;
24 the king of Tirzah, one: all the kings thirty and one.

Chapter 13

1 Now Joshua was old and well stricken in years; and Jehovah said unto him, Thou art old and well stricken in years, and there remaineth yet very much land to be possessed.
2 This is the land that yet remaineth: all the regions of the Philistines, and all the Geshurites;
3 from the Shihor, which is before Egypt, even unto the border of Ekron northward, [which] is reckoned to the Canaanites; the five lords of the Philistines; the Gazites, and the Ashdodites, the Ashkelonites, the Gittites, and the Ekronites; also the Avvim,
4 on the south; all the land of the Canaanites, and Mearah that belongeth to

the Sidonians, unto Aphek, to the border of the Amorites;
5 and the land of the Gebalites, and all Lebanon, toward the sunrising, from
Baal-gad under mount Hermon unto the entrance of Hamath;
6 all the inhabitants of the hill-country from Lebanon unto Misrephoth-maim, even all the Sidonians; them will I drive out from before the children of Israel: only allot thou it unto Israel for an inheritance, as I have commanded thee.
7 Now therefore divide this land for an inheritance unto the nine tribes, and the half-tribe of Manasseh.
8 With him the Reubenites and the Gadites received their inheritance, which Moses gave them, beyond the Jordan eastward, even as Moses the servant of Jehovah gave them:
9 from Aroer, that is on the edge of the valley of the Arnon, and the city that is in the middle of the valley, and all the plain of Medeba unto Dibon;
10 and all the cities of Sihon king of the Amorites, who reigned in Heshbon, unto the border of the children of Ammon;
11 and Gilead, and the border of the Geshurites and Maacathites, and all mount Hermon, and all Bashan unto Salecah;
12 all the kingdom of Og in Bashan, who reigned in Ashtaroth and in Edrei (the same was left of the remnant of the Rephaim); for these did Moses smite, and drove them out.
13 Nevertheless the children of Israel drove not out the Geshurites, nor the Maacathites: but Geshur and Maacath dwell in the midst of Israel unto this day.
14 Only unto the tribe of Levi he gave no inheritance; the offerings of Jehovah, the God of Israel, made by fire are his inheritance, as he spake unto him.
15 And Moses gave unto the tribe of the children of Reuben according to their families.
16 And their border was from Aroer, that is on the edge of the valley of the Arnon, and the city that is in the middle of the valley, and all the plain by Medeba;
17 Heshbon, and all its cities that are in the plain; Dibon, and Bamoth-baal, and Beth-baal-meon,
18 and Jahaz, and Kedemoth, and Mephaath,
19 and Kiriathaim, and Sibmah, and Zereth-shahar in the mount of the valley,
20 and Beth-peor, and the slopes of Pisgah, and Beth-jeshimoth,
21 and all the cities of the plain, and all the kingdom of Sihon king of the Amorites, who reigned in Heshbon, whom Moses smote with the chiefs of Midian, Evi, and Rekem, and Zur, and Hur, and Reba, the princes of Sihon, that dwelt in the land.
22 Balaam also the son of Beor, the soothsayer, did the children of Israel

slay with the sword among the rest of their slain.
23 And the border of the children of Reuben was the Jordan, and the border [thereof]. This was the inheritance of the children of Reuben according to their families, the cities and the villages thereof.
24 And Moses gave unto the tribe of Gad, unto the children of Gad, according to their families.
25 And their border was Jazer, and all the cities of Gilead, and half the land of the children of Ammon, unto Aroer that is before Rabbah;
26 and from Heshbon unto Ramath-mizpeh, and Betonim; and from Mahanaim unto the border of Debir;
27 and in the valley, Beth-haram, and Beth-nimrah, and Succoth, and Zaphon, the rest of the kingdom of Sihon king of Heshbon, the Jordan and the border [thereof], unto the uttermost part of the sea of Chinnereth beyond the Jordan eastward.
28 This is the inheritance of the children of Gad according to their families, the cities and the villages thereof.
29 And Moses gave [inheritance] unto the half-tribe of Manasseh: and it was for the half-tribe of the children of Manasseh according to their families.
30 And their border was from Mahanaim, all Bashan, all the kingdom of Og king of Bashan, and all the towns of Jair, which are in Bashan, threescore cities:
31 and half Gilead, and Ashtaroth, and Edrei, the cities of the kingdom of Og in Bashan, were for the children of Machir the son of Manasseh, even for the half of the children of Machir according to their families.
32 These are the inheritances which Moses distributed in the plains of Moab, beyond the Jordan at Jericho, eastward.
33 But unto the tribe of Levi Moses gave no inheritance: Jehovah, the God of Israel, is their inheritance, as he spake unto them.

Chapter 14

1 And these are the inheritances which the children of Israel took in the land of Canaan, which Eleazar the priest, and Joshua the son of Nun, and the heads of the fathers' [houses] of the tribes of the children of Israel, distributed unto them,
2 by the lot of their inheritance, as Jehovah commanded by Moses, for the nine tribes, and for the half-tribe.
3 For Moses had given the inheritance of the two tribes and the half-tribe beyond the Jordan: but unto the Levites he gave no inheritance among them.
4 For the children of Joseph were two tribes, Manasseh and Ephraim: and

they gave no portion unto the Levites in the land, save cities to dwell in, with the suburbs thereof for their cattle and for their substance.
5 As Jehovah commanded Moses, so the children of Israel did; and they divided the land.
6 Then the children of Judah drew nigh unto Joshua in Gilgal: and Caleb the son of Jephunneh the Kenizzite said unto him, Thou knowest the thing that Jehovah spake unto Moses the man of God concerning me and concerning thee in Kadesh-barnea.
7 Forty years old was I when Moses the servant of Jehovah sent me from Kadesh-barnea to spy out the land; and I brought him word again as it was in my heart.
8 Nevertheless my brethren that went up with me made the heart of the people melt; but I wholly followed Jehovah my God.
9 And Moses sware on that day, saying, Surely the land whereon thy foot hath trodden shall be an inheritance to thee and to thy children for ever, because thou hast wholly followed Jehovah my God.
10 And now, behold, Jehovah hath kept me alive, as he spake, these forty and five years, from the time that Jehovah spake this word unto Moses, while Israel walked in the wilderness: and now, lo, I am this day fourscore and five years old.
11 As yet I am as strong this day as I as in the day that Moses sent me: as my strength was then, even so is my strength now, for war, and to go out and to come in.
12 Now therefore give me this hill-country, whereof Jehovah spake in that day; for thou heardest in that day how the Anakim were there, and cities great and fortified: it may be that Jehovah will be with me, and I shall drive them out, as Jehovah spake.
13 And Joshua blessed him; and he gave Hebron unto Caleb the son of Jephunneh for an inheritance.
14 Therefore Hebron became the inheritance of Caleb the son of Jephunneh the Kenizzite unto this day; because that he wholly followed Jehovah, the God of Israel.
15 Now the name of Hebron beforetime was Kiriath-arba; [which Arba was] the greatest man among the Anakim. And the land had rest from war.

Chapter 15

1 And the lot for the tribe of the children of Judah according to their families was unto the border of Edom, even to the wilderness of Zin southward, at the uttermost part of the south.
2 And their south border was from the uttermost part of the Salt Sea, from the bay that looketh southward;

3 and it went out southward of the ascent of Akrabbim, and passed along to
Zin, and went up by the south of Kadesh-barnea, and passed along by
Hezron, and went up to Addar, and turned about to Karka;
4 and it passed along to Azmon, and went out at the brook of Egypt; and
the goings out of the border were at the sea: this shall be your south border.
5 And the east border was the Salt Sea, even unto the end of the Jordan.
And the border of the north quarter was from the bay of the sea at the end
of the Jordan;
6 and the border went up to Beth-hoglah, and passed along by the north of
Beth-arabah; and the border went up to the stone of Bohan the son of
Reuben;
7 and the border went up to Debir from the valley of Achor, and so
northward, looking toward Gilgal, that is over against the ascent of
Adummim, which is on the south side of the river; and the border passed
along to the waters of En-shemesh, and the goings out thereof were at En-rogel;
8 and the border went up by the valley of the son of Hinnom unto the side
of the Jebusite southward (the same is Jerusalem); and the border went up
to the top of the mountain that lieth before the valley of Hinnom westward,
which is at the uttermost part of the vale of Rephaim northward;
9 and the border extended from the top of the mountain unto the fountain
of the waters of Nephtoah, and went out to the cities of mount Ephron;
and the border extended to Baalah (the same is Kiriath-jearim);
10 and the border turned about from Baalah westward unto mount Seir,
and passed along unto the side of mount Jearim on the north (the same is
Chesalon), and went down to Beth-shemesh, and passed along by Timnah;
11 and the border went out unto the side of Ekron northward; and the
border extended to Shikkeron, and passed along to mount Baalah, and went
out at Jabneel; and the goings out of the border were at the sea.
12 And the west border was to the great sea, and the border [thereof]. This
is the border of the children of Judah round about according to their
families.
13 And unto Caleb the son of Jephunneh he gave a portion among the
children of Judah, according to the commandment of Jehovah to Joshua,
even Kiriath-arba, [which Arba was] the father of Anak (the same is
Hebron).
14 And Caleb drove out thence the three sons of Anak: Sheshai, and
Ahiman, and Talmai, the children of Anak.
15 And he went up thence against the inhabitants of Debir: now the name
of Debir beforetime was Kiriath-sepher.
16 And Caleb said, He that smiteth Kiriath-sepher, and taketh it, to him will
I give Achsah my daughter to wife.
17 And Othniel the son of Kenaz, the brother of Caleb, took it: and he

gave him Achsah his daughter to wife.
18 And it came to pass, when she came [unto him], that she moved him to ask of her father a field: and she alighted from off her ass; and Caleb said, What wouldest thou?
19 And she said, Give me a blessing; for that thou hast set me in the land of the South, give me also springs of water. And he gave her the upper springs and the nether springs.
20 This is the inheritance of the tribe of the children of Judah according to their families.
21 And the uttermost cities of the tribe of the children of Judah toward the border of Edom in the South were Kabzeel, and Eder, and Jagur,
22 and Kinah, and Dimonah, and Adadah,
23 and Kedesh, and Hazor, and Ithnan,
24 Ziph, and Telem, and Bealoth,
25 and Hazor-hadattah, and Kerioth-hezron (the same is Hazor),
26 Amam, and Shema, and Moladah,
27 and Hazar-gaddah, and Heshmon, and Beth-pelet,
28 and Hazar-shual, and Beer-sheba, and Biziothiah,
29 Baalah, and Iim, and Ezem,
30 and Eltolad, and Chesil, and Hormah,
31 and Ziklag, and Madmannah, and Sansannah,
32 and Lebaoth, and Shilhim, and Ain, and Rimmon: all the cities are twenty and nine, with their villages.
33 In the lowland, Eshtaol, and Zorah, and Ashnah,
34 and Zanoah, and En-gannim, Tappuah, and Enam,
35 Jarmuth, and Adullam, Socoh, and Azekah,
36 and Shaaraim, and Adithaim, and Gederah, and Gederothaim; fourteen cities with their villages.
37 Zenan, and Hadashah, and Migdal-gad,
38 and Dilean, and Mizpeh, and Joktheel,
39 Lachish, and Bozkath, and Eglon,
40 and Cabbon, and Lahmam, and Chitlish,
41 and Gederoth, Beth-dagon, and Naamah, and Makkedah; sixteen cities with their villages.
42 Libnah, and Ether, and Ashan,
43 and Iphtah, and Ashnah, and Nezib,
44 and Keilah, and Achzib, and Mareshah; nine cities with their villages.
45 Ekron, with its towns and its villages;
46 from Ekron even unto the sea, all that were by the side of Ashdod, with their villages.
47 Ashdod, its towns and its villages; Gaza, its towns and its villages; unto the brook of Egypt, and the great sea, and the border [thereof].
48 And in the hill-country, Shamir, and Jattir, and Socoh,

49 and Dannah, and Kiriath-sannah (the same is Debir),
50 and Anab, and Eshtemoh, and Anim,
51 and Goshen, and Holon, and Giloh; eleven cities with their villages.
52 Arab, and Dumah, and Eshan,
53 and Janim, and Beth-tappuah, and Aphekah,
54 and Humtah, and Kiriath-arba (the same is Hebron), and Zior; nine cities with their villages.
55 Maon, Carmel, and Ziph, and Jutah,
56 and Jezreel, and Jokdeam, and Zanoah,
57 Kain, Gibeah, and Timnah; ten cities with their villages.
58 Halhul, Beth-zur, and Gedor,
59 and Maarath, and Beth-anoth, and Eltekon; six cities with their villages.
60 Kiriath-baal (the same is Kiriath-jearim), and Rabbah; two cities with their villages.
61 In the wilderness, Beth-arabah, Middin, and Secacah,
62 and Nibshan, and the City of Salt, and En-gedi; six cities with their villages.
63 And as for the Jebusites, the inhabitants of Jerusalem, the children of Judah could not drive them out: but the Jebusites dwell with the children of Judah at Jerusalem unto this day.

Chapter 16

1 And the lot came out for the children of Joseph from the Jordan at Jericho, at the waters of Jericho on the east, even the wilderness, going up from Jericho through the hill-country to Beth-el;
2 and it went out from Beth-el to Luz, and passed along unto the border of the Archites to Ataroth;
3 and it went down westward to the border of the Japhletites, unto the border of Beth-horon the nether, even unto Gezer; and the goings out thereof were at the sea.
4 And the children of Joseph, Manasseh and Ephraim, took their inheritance.
5 And the border of the children of Ephraim according to their families was [thus]: the border of their inheritance eastward was Ataroth-addar, unto Beth-horon the upper;
6 and the border went out westward at Michmethath on the north; and the border turned about eastward unto Taanath-shiloh, and passed along it on the east of Janoah;
7 and it went down from Janoah to Ataroth, and to Naarah, and reached unto Jericho, and went out at the Jordan.
8 From Tappuah the border went along westward to the brook of Kanah;

and the goings out thereof were at the sea. This is the inheritance of the tribe of the children of Ephraim according to their families;
9 together with the cities which were set apart for the children of Ephraim in the midst of the inheritance of the children of Manasseh, all the cities with their villages.
10 And they drove not out the Canaanites that dwelt in Gezer: but the Canaanites dwell in the midst of Ephraim unto this day, and are become servants to do taskwork.

Chapter 17

1 And [this] was the lot for the tribe of Manasseh; for he was the first-born of Joseph. As for Machir the first-born of Manasseh, the father of Gilead, because he was a man of war, therefore he had Gilead and Bashan.
2 So [the lot] was for the rest of the children of Manasseh according to their families: for the children of Abiezer, and for the children of Helek, and for the children of Asriel, and for the children of Shechem, and for the children of Hepher, and for the children of Shemida: these were the male children of Manasseh the son of Joseph according to their families.
3 But Zelophehad, the son of Hepher, the son of Gilead, the son of Machir, the son of Manasseh, had no sons, but daughters: and these are the names of his daughters: Mahlah, and Noah, Hoglah, Milcah, and Tirzah.
4 And they came near before Eleazar the priest, and before Joshua the son of Nun, and before the princes, saying, Jehovah commanded Moses to give us an inheritance among our brethren: therefore according to the commandment of Jehovah he gave them an inheritance among the brethren of their father.
5 And there fell ten parts to Manasseh, besides the land of Gilead and Bashan, which is beyond the Jordan;
6 because the daughters of Manasseh had an inheritance among his sons. And the land of Gilead belonged unto the rest of the sons of Manasseh.
7 And the border of Manasseh was from Asher to Michmethath, which is before Shechem; and the border went along to the right hand, unto the inhabitants of En-tappuah.
8 The land of Tappuah belonged to Manasseh; but Tappuah on the border of Manasseh belonged to the children of Ephraim.
9 And the border went down unto the brook of Kanah, southward of the brook: these cities belonged to Ephraim among the cities of Manasseh: and the border of Manasseh was on the north side of the brook, and the goings out thereof were at the sea:
10 southward it was Ephraim's, and northward it was Manasseh's, and the sea was his border; and they reached to Asher on the north, and to Issachar

on the east.
11 And Manasseh had in Issachar and in Asher Beth-shean and its towns,
and Ibleam and its towns, and the inhabitants of Dor and its towns, and the
inhabitants of En-dor and its towns, and the inhabitants of Taanach and its
towns, and the inhabitants of Megiddo and its towns, even the three
heights.
12 Yet the children of Manasseh could not drive out [the inhabitants of]
those cities; but the Canaanites would dwell in that land.
13 And it came to pass, when the children of Israel were waxed strong, that
they put the Canaanites to taskwork, and did not utterly drive them out.
14 And the children of Joseph spake unto Joshua, saying, Why hast thou
given me but one lot and one part for an inheritance, seeing I am a great
people, forasmuch as hitherto Jehovah hath blessed me?
15 And Joshua said unto them, If thou be a great people, get thee up to the
forest, and cut down for thyself there in the land of the Perizzites and of
the Rephaim; since the hill-country of Ephraim is too narrow for thee.
16 And the children of Joseph said, The hill-country is not enough for us:
and all the Canaanites that dwell in the land of the valley have chariots of
iron, both they who are in Beth-shean and its towns, and they who are in
the valley of Jezreel.
17 And Joshua spake unto the house of Joseph, even to Ephraim and to
Manasseh, saying, Thou art a great people, and hast great power; thou shalt
not have one lot only:
18 but the hill-country shall be thine; for though it is a forest, thou shalt cut
it down, and the goings out thereof shall be thine; for thou shalt drive out
the Canaanites, though they have chariots of iron, and though they are
strong.

Chapter 18

1 And the whole congregation of the children of Israel assembled
themselves together at Shiloh, and set up the tent of meeting there: and the
land was subdued before them.
2 And there remained among the children of Israel seven tribes, which had
not yet divided their inheritance.
3 And Joshua said unto the children of Israel, How long are ye slack to go
in to possess the land, which Jehovah, the God of your fathers, hath given
you?
4 Appoint for you three men of each tribe: and I will send them, and they
shall arise, and walk through the land, and describe it according to their
inheritance; and they shall come unto me.
5 And they shall divide it into seven portions: Judah shall abide in his

border on the south, and the house of Joseph shall abide in their border on the north.

6 And ye shall describe the land into seven portions, and bring [the description] hither to me; and I will cast lots for you here before Jehovah our God.

7 For the Levites have no portion among you; for the priesthood of Jehovah is their inheritance: and Gad and Reuben and the half-tribe of Manasseh have received their inheritance beyond the Jordan eastward, which Moses the servant of Jehovah gave them.

8 And the men arose, and went: and Joshua charged them that went to describe the land, saying, Go and walk through the land, and describe it, and come again to me; and I will cast lots for you here before Jehovah in Shiloh.

9 And the men went and passed through the land, and described it by cities into seven portions in a book; and they came to Joshua unto the camp at Shiloh.

10 And Joshua cast lots for them in Shiloh before Jehovah: and there Joshua divided the land unto the children of Israel according to their divisions.

11 And the lot of the tribe of the children of Benjamin came up according to their families: and the border of their lot went out between the children of Judah and the children of Joseph.

12 And their border on the north quarter was from the Jordan; and the border went up to the side of Jericho on the north, and went up through the hill-country westward; and the goings out thereof were at the wilderness of Beth-aven.

13 And the border passed along from thence to Luz, to the side of Luz (the same is Beth-el), southward; and the border went down to Ataroth-addar, by the mountain that lieth on the south of Beth-horon the nether.

14 And the border extended [thence], and turned about on the west quarter southward, from the mountain that lieth before Beth-horon southward; and the goings out thereof were at Kiriath-baal (the same is Kiriath-jearim), a city of the children of Judah: this was the west quarter.

15 And the south quarter was from the uttermost part of Kiriath-jearim; and the border went out westward, and went out to the fountain of the waters of Nephtoah;

16 and the border went down to the uttermost part of the mountain that lieth before the valley of the son of Hinnom, which is in the vale of Rephaim northward; and it went down to the valley of Hinnom, to the side of the Jebusite southward, and went down to En-rogel;

17 and it extended northward, and went out at En-shemesh, and went out to Geliloth, which is over against the ascent of Adummim; and it went down to the stone of Bohan the son of Reuben;

18 and it passed along to the side over against the Arabah northward, and
went down unto the Arabah;
19 and the border passed along to the side of Beth-hoglah northward; and
the goings out of the border were at the north bay of the Salt Sea, at the
south end of the Jordan: this was the south border.
20 And the Jordan was the border of it on the east quarter. This was the
inheritance of the children of Benjamin, by the borders thereof round
about, according to their families.
21 Now the cities of the tribe of the children of Benjamin according to their
families were Jericho, and Beth-hoglah, and Emek-keziz,
22 and Beth-arabah, and Zemaraim, and Beth-el,
23 and Avvim, and Parah, and Ophrah,
24 and Chephar-ammoni, and Ophni, and Geba; twelve cities with their
villages:
25 Gibeon, and Ramah, and Beeroth,
26 and Mizpeh, and Chephirah, and Mozah,
27 and Rekem, and Irpeel, and Taralah,
28 and Zelah, Eleph, and the Jebusite (the same is Jerusalem), Gibeath,
[and] Kiriath; fourteen cities with their villages. This is the inheritance of
the children of Benjamin according to their families.

Chapter 19

1 And the second lot came out for Simeon, even for the tribe of the
children of Simeon according to their families: and their inheritance was in
the midst of the inheritance of the children of Judah.
2 And they had for their inheritance Beer-sheba, or Sheba, and Moladah,
3 and Hazar-shual, and Balah, and Ezem,
4 and Eltolad, and Bethul, and Hormah,
5 and Ziklag, and Beth-marcaboth, and Hazar-susah,
6 and Beth-lebaoth, and Sharuhen; thirteen cities with their villages:
7 Ain, Rimmon, and Ether, and Ashan; four cities with their villages:
8 and all the villages that were round about these cities to Baalath-beer,
Ramah of the South. This is the inheritance of the tribe of the children of
Simeon according to their families.
9 Out of the part of the children of Judah was the inheritance of the
children of Simeon; for the portion of the children of Judah was too much
for them: therefore the children of Simeon had inheritance in the midst of
their inheritance.
10 And the third lot came up for the children of Zebulun according to their
families; and the border of their inheritance was unto Sarid;
11 and their border went up westward, even to Maralah, and reached to

Dabbesheth; and it reached to the brook that is before Jokneam;
12 and it turned from Sarid eastward toward the sunrising unto the border of Chisloth-tabor; and it went out to Daberath, and went up to Japhia;
13 and from thence it passed along eastward to Gath-hepher, to Eth-kazin; and it went out at Rimmon which stretcheth unto Neah;
14 and the border turned about it on the north to Hannathon; and the goings out thereof were at the valley of Iphtah-el;
15 and Kattath, and Nahalal, and Shimron, and Idalah, and Bethlehem: twelve cities with their villages.
16 This is the inheritance of the children of Zebulun according to their families, these cities with their villages.
17 The fourth lot came out for Issachar, even for the children of Issachar according to their families.
18 And their border was unto Jezreel, and Chesulloth, and Shunem,
19 and Hapharaim, and Shion, and Anaharath,
20 and Rabbith, and Kishion, and Ebez,
21 and Remeth, and Engannim, and En-haddah, and Beth-pazzez,
22 and the border reached to Tabor, and Shahazumah, and Beth-shemesh; and the goings out of their border were at the Jordan: sixteen cities with their villages.
23 This is the inheritance of the tribe of the children of Issachar according to their families, the cities with their villages.
24 And the fifth lot came out for the tribe of the children of Asher according to their families.
25 And their border was Helkath, and Hali, and Beten, and Achshaph,
26 and Allammelech, and Amad, and Mishal; and it reached to Carmel westward, and to Shihor-libnath;
27 and it turned toward the sunrising to Beth-dagon, and reached to Zebulun, and to the valley of Iphtah-el northward to Beth-emek and Neiel; and it went out to Cabul on the left hand,
28 and Ebron, and Rehob, and Hammon, and Kanah, even unto great Sidon;
29 and the border turned to Ramah, and to the fortified city of Tyre; and the border turned to Hosah; and the goings out thereof were at the sea by the region of Achzib;
30 Ummah also, and Aphek, and Rehob: twenty and two cities with their villages.
31 This is the inheritance of the tribe of the children of Asher according to their families, these cities with their villages.
32 The sixth lot came out for the children of Naphtali, even for the children of Naphtali according to their families.
33 And their border was from Heleph, from the oak in Zaanannim, and Adaminekeb, and Jabneel, unto Lakkum; and the goings out thereof were at

the Jordan;
34 and the border turned westward to Aznoth-tabor, and went out from
thence to Hukkok; and it reached to Zebulun on the south, and reached to
Asher on the west, and to Judah at the Jordan toward the sunrising.
35 And the fortified cities were Ziddim, Zer, and Hammath, Rakkath, and
Chinnereth,
36 and Adamah, and Ramah, and Hazor,
37 and Kedesh, and Edrei, and En-hazor,
38 And Iron, and Migdal-el, Horem, and Beth-anath, and Beth-shemesh;
nineteen cities with their villages.
39 This is the inheritance of the tribe of the children of Naphtali according
to their families, the cities with their villages.
40 The seventh lot came out for the tribe of the children of Dan according
to their families.
41 And the border of their inheritance was Zorah, and Eshtaol, and Ir-
shemesh,
42 and Shaalabbin, and Aijalon, and Ithlah,
43 and Elon, and Timnah, and Ekron,
44 and Eltekeh, and Gibbethon, and Baalath,
45 and Jehud, and Bene-berak, and Gath-rimmon,
46 and Me-jarkon, and Rakkon, with the border over against Joppa.
47 And the border of the children of Dan went out beyond them; for the
children of Dan went up and fought against Leshem, and took it, and smote
it with the edge of the sword, and possessed it, and dwelt therein, and called
Leshem, Dan, after the name of Dan their father.
48 This is the inheritance of the tribe of the children of Dan according to
their families, these cities with their villages.
49 So they made an end of distributing the land for inheritance by the
borders thereof; and the children of Israel gave an inheritance to Joshua the
son of Nun in the midst of them:
50 according to the commandment of Jehovah they gave him the city which
he asked, even Timnath-serah in the hill-country of Ephraim; and he built
the city, and dwelt therein.
51 These are the inheritances, which Eleazar the priest, and Joshua the son
of Nun, and the heads of the fathers' [houses] of the tribes of the children
of Israel, distributed for inheritance by lot in Shiloh before Jehovah, at the
door of the tent of meeting. So they made an end of dividing the land.

Chapter 20

1 And Jehovah spake unto Joshua, saying,
2 Speak to the children of Israel, saying, Assign you the cities of refuge,

whereof I spake unto you by Moses,
3 that the manslayer that killeth any person unwittingly [and] unawares may flee thither: and they shall be unto you for a refuge from the avenger of blood.
4 And he shall flee unto one of those cities, and shall stand at the entrance of the gate of the city, and declare his cause in the ears of the elders of that city; and they shall take him into the city unto them, and give him a place, that he may dwell among them.
5 And if the avenger of blood pursue after him, then they shall not deliver up the manslayer into his hand; because he smote his neighbor unawares, and hated him not beforetime.
6 And he shall dwell in that city, until he stand before the congregation for judgment, until the death of the high priest that shall be in those days: then shall the manslayer return, and come unto his own city, and unto his own house, unto the city from whence he fled.
7 And they set apart Kedesh in Galilee in the hill-country of Naphtali, and Shechem in the hill-country of Ephraim, and Kiriath-arba (the same is Hebron) in the hill-country of Judah.
8 And beyond the Jordan at Jericho eastward, they assigned Bezer in the wilderness in the plain out of the tribe of Reuben, and Ramoth in Gilead out of the tribe of Gad, and Golan in Bashan out of the tribe of Manasseh.
9 These were the appointed cities for all the children of Israel, and for the stranger that sojourneth among them, that whosoever killeth any person unwittingly might flee thither, and not die by the hand of the avenger of blood, until he stood before the congregation.

Chapter 21

1 Then came near the heads of fathers' [houses] of the Levites unto Eleazar the priest, and unto Joshua the son of Nun, and unto the heads of fathers' [houses] of the tribes of the children of Israel;
2 and they spake unto them at Shiloh in the land of Canaan, saying, Jehovah commanded Moses to give us cities to dwell in, with the suburbs thereof for our cattle.
3 And the children of Israel gave unto the Levites out of their inheritance, according to the commandment of Jehovah, these cities with their suburbs.
4 And the lot came out for the families of the Kohathites: and the children of Aaron the priest, who were of the Levites, had by lot out of the tribe of Judah, and out of the tribe of the Simeonites, and out of the tribe of Benjamin, thirteen cities.
5 And the rest of the children of Kohath had by lot out of the families of the tribe of Ephraim, and out of the tribe of Dan, and out of the half-tribe

of Manasseh, ten cities.
6 And the children of Gershon had by lot out of the families of the tribe of Issachar, and out of the tribe of Asher, and out of the tribe of Naphtali, and out of the half-tribe of Manasseh in Bashan, thirteen cities.
7 The children of Merari according to their families had out of the tribe of Reuben, and out of the tribe of Gad, and out of the tribe of Zebulun, twelve cities.
8 And the children of Israel gave by lot unto the Levites these cities with their suburbs, as Jehovah commanded by Moses.
9 And they gave out of the tribe of the children of Judah, and out of the tribe of the children of Simeon, these cities which are [here] mentioned by name:
10 and they were for the children of Aaron, of the families of the Kohathites, who were of the children of Levi; for theirs was the first lot.
11 And they gave them Kiriath-arba, [which Arba was] the father of Anak (the same is Hebron), in the hill-country of Judah, with the suburbs thereof round about it.
12 But the fields of the city, and the villages thereof, gave they to Caleb the son of Jephunneh for his possession.
13 And unto the children of Aaron the priest they gave Hebron with its suburbs, the city of refuge for the manslayer, and Libnah with its suburbs,
14 and Jattir with its suburbs, and Eshtemoa with its suburbs,
15 and Holon with its suburbs, and Debir with its suburbs,
16 and Ain with its suburbs, and Juttah with its suburbs, [and] Beth-shemesh with its suburbs; nine cities out of those two tribes.
17 And out of the tribe of Benjamin, Gibeon with its suburbs, Geba with its suburbs,
18 Anathoth with its suburbs, and Almon with its suburbs; four cities.
19 All the cities of the children of Aaron, the priests, were thirteen cities with their suburbs.
20 And the families of the children of Kohath, the Levites, even the rest of the children of Kohath, they had the cities of their lot out of the tribe of Ephraim.
21 And they gave them Shechem with its suburbs in the hill-country of Ephraim, the city of refuge for the manslayer, and Gezer with its suburbs,
22 and Kibzaim with its suburbs, and Beth-horon with its suburbs; four cities.
23 And out of the tribe of Dan, Elteke with its suburbs, Gibbethon with its suburbs,
24 Aijalon with its suburbs, Gath-rimmon with its suburbs; four cities.
25 And out of the half-tribe of Manasseh, Taanach with its suburbs, and Gath-rimmon with its suburbs; two cities.
26 All the cities of the families of the rest of the children of Kohath were

ten with their suburbs.
27 And unto the children of Gershon, of the families of the Levites, out of
the half-tribe of Manasseh [they gave] Golan in Bashan with its suburbs, the
city of refuge for the manslayer, and Be-eshterah with its suburbs; two
cities.
28 And out of the tribe of Issachar, Kishion with its suburbs, Daberath
with its suburbs,
29 Jarmuth with its suburbs, En-gannim with its suburbs; four cities.
30 And out of the tribe of Asher, Mishal with its suburbs, Abdon with its
suburbs,
31 Helkath with its suburbs, and Rehob with its suburbs; four cities.
32 And out of the tribe of Naphtali, Kedesh in Galilee with its suburbs, the
city of refuge for the manslayer, and Hammoth-dor with its suburbs, and
Kartan with its suburbs; three cities.
33 All the cities of the Gershonites according to their families were thirteen
cities with their suburbs.
34 And unto the families of the children of Merari, the rest of the Levites,
out of the tribe of Zebulun, Jokneam with its suburbs, and Kartah with its
suburbs,
35 Dimnah with its suburbs, Nahalal with its suburbs; four cities.
36 And out of the tribe of Reuben, Bezer with its suburbs, and Jahaz with
its suburbs,
37 Kedemoth with its suburbs, and Mephaath with its suburbs; four cities.
38 And out of the tribe of Gad, Ramoth in Gilead with its suburbs, the city
of refuge for the manslayer, and Mahanaim with its suburbs,
39 Heshbon with its suburbs, Jazer with its suburbs; four cities in all.
40 All [these were] the cities of the children of Merari according to their
families, even the rest of the families of the Levites; and their lot was twelve
cities.
41 All the cities of the Levites in the midst of the possession of the children
of Israel were forty and eight cities with their suburbs.
42 These cities were every one with their suburbs round about them: thus it
was with all these cities.
43 So Jehovah gave unto Israel all the land which he sware to give unto
their fathers; and they possessed it, and dwelt therein.
44 And Jehovah gave them rest round about, according to all that he sware
unto their fathers: and there stood not a man of all their enemies before
them; Jehovah delivered all their enemies into their hand.
45 There failed not aught of any good thing which Jehovah had spoken
unto the house of Israel; all came to pass.

Chapter 22

1 Then Joshua called the Reubenites, and the Gadites, and the half-tribe of Manasseh,
2 and said unto them, Ye have kept all that Moses the servant of Jehovah commanded you, and have hearkened unto my voice in all that I commanded you:
3 ye have not left your brethren these many days unto this day, but have kept the charge of the commandment of Jehovah your God.
4 And now Jehovah your God hath given rest unto your brethren, as he spake unto them: therefore now turn ye, and get you unto your tents, unto the land of your possession, which Moses the servant of Jehovah gave you beyond the Jordan.
5 Only take diligent heed to do the commandment and the law which Moses the servant of Jehovah commanded you, to love Jehovah your God, and to walk in all his ways, and to keep his commandments, and to cleave unto him, and to serve him with all your heart and with all your soul.
6 So Joshua blessed them, and sent them away; and they went unto their tents.
7 Now to the one half-tribe of Manasseh Moses had given [inheritance] in Bashan; but unto the other half gave Joshua among their brethren beyond the Jordan westward; moreover when Joshua sent them away unto their tents, he blessed them,
8 and spake unto them, saying, Return with much wealth unto your tents, and with very much cattle, with silver, and with gold, and with brass, and with iron, and with very much raiment: divide the spoil of your enemies with your brethren.
9 And the children of Reuben and the children of Gad and the half-tribe of Manasseh returned, and departed from the children of Israel out of Shiloh, which is in the land of Canaan, to go unto the land of Gilead, to the land of their possession, whereof they were possessed, according to the commandment of Jehovah by Moses.
10 And when they came unto the region about the Jordan, that is in the land of Canaan, the children of Reuben and the children of Gad and the half-tribe of Manasseh built there an altar by the Jordan, a great altar to look upon.
11 And the children of Israel heard say, Behold, the children of Reuben and the children of Gad and the half-tribe of Manasseh have built an altar in the forefront of the land of Canaan, in the region about the Jordan, on the side that pertaineth to the children of Israel.
12 And when the children of Israel heard of it, the whole congregation of the children of Israel gathered themselves together at Shiloh, to go up against them to war.
13 And the children of Israel sent unto the children of Reuben, and to the

children of Gad, and to the half-tribe of Manasseh, into the land of Gilead, Phinehas the son of Eleazar the priest,
14 and with him ten princes, one prince of a fathers' house for each of the tribes of Israel; and they were every one of them head of their fathers' houses among the thousands of Israel.
15 And they came unto the children of Reuben, and to the children of Gad, and to the half-tribe of Manasseh, unto the land of Gilead, and they spake with them, saying,
16 Thus saith the whole congregation of Jehovah, What trespass is this that ye have committed against the God of Israel, to turn away this day from following Jehovah, in that ye have builded you an altar, to rebel this day against Jehovah?
17 Is the iniquity of Peor too little for us, from which we have not cleansed ourselves unto this day, although there came a plague upon the congregation of Jehovah,
18 that ye must turn away this day from following Jehovah? and it will be, seeing ye rebel to-day against Jehovah, that to-morrow he will be wroth with the whole congregation of Israel.
19 Howbeit, if the land of your possession be unclean, then pass ye over unto the land of the possession of Jehovah, wherein Jehovah's tabernacle dwelleth, and take possession among us: but rebel not against Jehovah, nor rebel against us, in building you an altar besides the altar of Jehovah our God.
20 Did not Achan the son of Zerah commit a trespass in the devoted thing, and wrath fell upon all the congregation of Israel? and that man perished not alone in his iniquity.
21 Then the children of Reuben and the children of Gad and the half-tribe of Manasseh answered, and spake unto the heads of the thousands of Israel,
22 The Mighty One, God, Jehovah, the Mighty One, God, Jehovah, he knoweth; and Israel he shall know: if it be in rebellion, or if in trespass against Jehovah (save thou us not this day,)
23 that we have built us an altar to turn away from following Jehovah; or if to offer thereon burnt-offering or meal-offering, or if to offer sacrifices of peace-offerings thereon, let Jehovah himself require it;
24 and if we have not [rather] out of carefulness done this, [and] of purpose, saying, In time to come your children might speak unto our children, saying, What have ye to do with Jehovah, the God of Israel?
25 for Jehovah hath made the Jordan a border between us and you, ye children of Reuben and children of Gad; ye have no portion in Jehovah: so might your children make our children cease from fearing Jehovah.
26 Therefore we said, Let us now prepare to build us an altar, not for burnt-offering, nor for sacrifice:
27 but it shall be a witness between us and you, and between our

generations after us, that we may do the service of Jehovah before him with
our burnt-offerings, and with our sacrifices, and with our peace-offerings;
that your children may not say to our children in time to come, Ye have no
portion in Jehovah.
28 Therefore said we, It shall be, when they so say to us or to our
generations in time to come, that we shall say, Behold the pattern of the
altar of Jehovah, which our fathers made, not for burnt-offering, nor for
sacrifice; but it is a witness between us and you.
29 Far be it from us that we should rebel against Jehovah, and turn away
this day from following Jehovah, to build an altar for burnt-offering, for
meal-offering, or for sacrifice, besides the altar of Jehovah our God that is
before his tabernacle.
30 And when Phinehas the priest, and the princes of the congregation, even
the heads of the thousands of Israel that were with him, heard the words
that the children of Reuben and the children of Gad and the children of
Manasseh spake, it pleased them well.
31 And Phinehas the son of Eleazar the priest said unto the children of
Reuben, and to the children of Gad, and to the children of Manasseh, This
day we know that Jehovah is in the midst of us, because ye have not
committed this trespass against Jehovah: now have ye delivered the children
of Israel out of the hand of Jehovah.
32 And Phinehas the son of Eleazar the priest, and the princes, returned
from the children of Reuben, and from the children of Gad, out of the land
of Gilead, unto the land of Canaan, to the children of Israel, and brought
them word again.
33 And the thing pleased the children of Israel; and the children of Israel
blessed God, and spake no more of going up against them to war, to
destroy the land wherein the children of Reuben and the children of Gad
dwelt.
34 And the children of Reuben and the children of Gad called the altar
[Ed]: For, [said they], it is a witness between us that Jehovah is God.

Chapter 23

1 And it came to pass after many days, when Jehovah had given rest unto
Israel from all their enemies round about, and Joshua was old and well
stricken in years;
2 that Joshua called for all Israel, for their elders and for their heads, and
for their judges and for their officers, and said unto them, I am old and well
stricken in years:
3 and ye have seen all that Jehovah your God hath done unto all these
nations because of you; for Jehovah your God, he it is that hath fought for

you.
4 Behold, I have allotted unto you these nations that remain, to be an
inheritance for your tribes, from the Jordan, with all the nations that I have
cut off, even unto the great sea toward the going down of the sun.
5 And Jehovah your God, he will thrust them out from before you, and
drive them from out of your sight; and ye shall possess their land, as
Jehovah your God spake unto you.
6 Therefore be ye very courageous to keep and to do all that is written in
the book of the law of Moses, that ye turn not aside therefrom to the right
hand or to the left;
7 that ye come not among these nations, these that remain among you;
neither make mention of the name of their gods, nor cause to swear [by
them], neither serve them, nor bow down yourselves unto them;
8 but cleave unto Jehovah your God, as ye have done unto this day.
9 For Jehovah hath driven out from before you great nations and strong:
but as for you, no man hath stood before you unto this day.
10 One man of you shall chase a thousand; for Jehovah your God, he it is
that fighteth for you, as he spake unto you.
11 Take good heed therefore unto yourselves, that ye love Jehovah your
God.
12 Else if ye do at all go back, and cleave unto the remnant of these nations,
even these that remain among you, and make marriages with them, and go
in unto them, and they to you;
13 know for a certainty that Jehovah your God will no more drive these
nations from out of your sight; but they shall be a snare and a trap unto
you, and a scourge in your sides, and thorns in your eyes, until ye perish
from off this good land which Jehovah your God hath given you.
14 And, behold, this day I am going the way of all the earth: and ye know in
all your hearts and in all your souls, that not one thing hath failed of all the
good things which Jehovah your God spake concerning you; all are come to
pass unto you, not one thing hath failed thereof.
15 And it shall come to pass, that as all the good things are come upon you
of which Jehovah your God spake unto you, so will Jehovah bring upon
you all the evil things, until he have destroyed you from off this good land
which Jehovah your God hath given you.
16 When ye transgress the covenant of Jehovah your God, which he
commanded you, and go and serve other gods, and bow down yourselves to
them; then will the anger of Jehovah be kindled against you, and ye shall
perish quickly from off the good land which he hath given unto you.

Chapter 24

1 And Joshua gathered all the tribes of Israel to Shechem, and called for the elders of Israel, and for their heads, and for their judges, and for their officers; and they presented themselves before God.
2 And Joshua said unto all the people, Thus saith Jehovah, the God of Israel, Your fathers dwelt of old time beyond the River, even Terah, the father of Abraham, and the father of Nahor: and they served other gods.
3 And I took your father Abraham from beyond the River, and led him throughout all the land of Canaan, and multiplied his seed, and gave him Isaac.
4 And I gave unto Isaac Jacob and Esau: and I gave unto Esau mount Seir, to possess it: and Jacob and his children went down into Egypt.
5 And I sent Moses and Aaron, and I plagued Egypt, according to that which I did in the midst thereof: and afterward I brought you out.
6 And I brought your fathers out of Egypt: and ye came unto the sea; and the Egyptians pursued after your fathers with chariots and with horsemen unto the Red Sea.
7 And when they cried out unto Jehovah, he put darkness between you and the Egyptians, and brought the sea upon them, and covered them; and your eyes saw what I did in Egypt: and ye dwelt in the wilderness many days.
8 And I brought you into the land of the Amorites, that dwelt beyond the Jordan: and they fought with you; and I gave them into your hand, and ye possessed their land; and I destroyed them from before you.
9 Then Balak the son of Zippor, king of Moab, arose and fought against Israel: and he sent and called Balaam the son of Beor to curse you;
10 but I would not hearken unto Balaam; therefore he blessed you still: so I delivered you out of his hand.
11 And ye went over the Jordan, and came unto Jericho: and the men of Jericho fought against you, the Amorite, and the Perizzite, and the Canaanite, and the Hittite, and the Girgashite, the Hivite, and the Jebusite; and I delivered them into your hand.
12 And I sent the hornet before you, which drove them out from before you, even the two kings of the Amorites; not with thy sword, nor with thy bow.
13 And I gave you a land whereon thou hadst not labored, and cities which ye built not, and ye dwell therein; of vineyards and oliveyards which ye planted not do ye eat.
14 Now therefore fear Jehovah, and serve him in sincerity and in truth; and put away the gods which your fathers served beyond the River, and in Egypt; and serve ye Jehovah.
15 And if it seem evil unto you to serve Jehovah, choose you this day whom ye will serve; whether the gods which your fathers served that were beyond the River, or the gods of the Amorites, in whose land ye dwell: but as for me and my house, we will serve Jehovah.

16 And the people answered and said, Far be it from us that we should
forsake Jehovah, to serve other gods;
17 for Jehovah our God, he it is that brought us and our fathers up out of
the land of Egypt, from the house of bondage, and that did those great
signs in our sight, and preserved us in all the way wherein we went, and
among all the peoples through the midst of whom we passed;
18 and Jehovah drove out from before us all the peoples, even the
Amorites that dwelt in the land: therefore we also will serve Jehovah; for he
is our God.
19 And Joshua said unto the people, Ye cannot serve Jehovah; for he is a
holy God; he is a jealous God; he will not forgive your transgression nor
your sins.
20 If ye forsake Jehovah, and serve foreign gods, then he will turn and do
you evil, and consume you, after that he hath done you good.
21 And the people said unto Joshua, Nay; but we will serve Jehovah.
22 And Joshua said unto the people, Ye are witnesses against yourselves
that ye have chosen you Jehovah, to serve him. And they said, We are
witnesses.
23 Now therefore put away, [said he], the foreign gods which are among
you, and incline your heart unto Jehovah, the God of Israel.
24 And the people said unto Joshua, Jehovah our God will we serve, and
unto his voice will we hearken.
25 So Joshua made a covenant with the people that day, and set them a
statute and an ordinance in Shechem.
26 And Joshua wrote these words in the book of the law of God; and he
took a great stone, and set it up there under the oak that was by the
sanctuary of Jehovah.
27 And Joshua said unto all the people, Behold, this stone shall be a witness
against us; for it hath heard all the words of Jehovah which he spake unto
us: it shall be therefore a witness against you, lest ye deny your God.
28 So Joshua sent the people away, every man unto his inheritance.
29 And it came to pass after these things, that Joshua the son of Nun, the
servant of Jehovah, died, being a hundred and ten years old.
30 And they buried him in the border of his inheritance in Timnathserah,
which is in the hill-country of Ephraim, on the north of the mountain of
Gaash.
31 And Israel served Jehovah all the days of Joshua, and all the days of the
elders that outlived Joshua, and had known all the work of Jehovah, that he
had wrought for Israel.
32 And the bones of Joseph, which the children of Israel brought up out of
Egypt, buried they in Shechem, in the parcel of ground which Jacob bought
of the sons of Hamor the father of Shechem for a hundred pieces of
money: and they became the inheritance of the children of Joseph.

33 And Eleazar the son of Aaron died; and they buried him in the hill of
Phinehas his son, which was given him in the hill-country of Ephraim.

BOOK OF JOSHUA

BIBLE IN BASIC ENGLISH

1

1 Now after the death of Moses, the servant of the Lord, the word of the
Lord came to Joshua, the son of Nun, Moses' helper, saying, 2 Moses my
servant is dead; so now get up! Go over Jordan, you and all this people, into
the land which I am giving to them, to the children of Israel. 3 Every place
on which you put your foot I have given to you, as I said to Moses. 4 From
the waste land and this mountain Lebanon, as far as the great river, the river
Euphrates, and all the land of the Hittites to the Great Sea, in the west, will
be your country. 5 While you are living, all will give way before you: as I
was with Moses, so I will be with you; I will not take away my help from
you or give you up. 6 Take heart and be strong; for you will give to this
people for their heritage the land which I gave by an oath to their fathers. 7
Only take heart and be very strong; take care to do all the law which Moses
my servant gave you, not turning from it to the right hand or to the left, so
that you may do well in all your undertakings. 8 Let this book of the law be
ever on your lips and in your thoughts day and night, so that you may keep
with care everything in it; then a blessing will be on all your way, and you
will do well. 9 Have I not given you your orders? Take heart and be strong;
have no fear and do not be troubled; for the Lord your God is with you
wherever you go, 10Then Joshua gave their orders to those who were in
authority over the people, saying, 11 Go through the tents and give orders
to the people, saying, Get ready a store of food; for in three days you are to
go over this river Jordan and take for your heritage the land which the Lord
your God is giving you. 12 And to the Reubenites and the Gadites and the

half-tribe of Manasseh, Joshua said, 13 Keep in mind what Moses, the servant of the Lord, said to you, The Lord your God is sending you rest and will give you this land. 14Your wives, your little ones, and your cattle will be kept here in the land which Moses gave you on this side of Jordan; but you, the fighting-men, are to go over before your brothers, armed, to give them help; 15 Till the Lord has given your brothers rest, as he has given it to you, and they have taken their heritage in the land which the Lord your God is giving them: then you will go back to the land of your heritage which Moses, the servant of the Lord, gave you on the east side of Jordan. 16 Then they said to Joshua in answer, Whatever you say to us we will do, and wherever you send us we will go. 17 As we gave attention to Moses in all things, so we will give attention to you: and may the Lord your God be with you as he was with Moses. 18 Whoever goes against your orders, and does not give attention to all your words, will be put to death: only take heart and be strong.

2

1 Then Joshua, the son of Nun, sent two men from Shittim secretly, with the purpose of searching out the land, and Jericho. So they went and came to the house of a loose woman of the town, named Rahab, where they took their rest for the night. 2 And it was said to the king of Jericho, See, some men have come here tonight from the children of Israel with the purpose of searching out the land. 3 Then the king of Jericho sent to Rahab, saying, Send out the men who have come to you and are in your house; for they have come with the purpose of searching out all the land. 4 And the woman took the two men and put them in a secret place; then she said, Yes, the men came to me, but I had no idea where they came from; 5 And when it was the time for shutting the doors at dark, they went out; I have no idea where the men went: but if you go after them quickly, you will overtake them. 6 But she had taken them up to the roof, covering them with the stems of flax which she had put out in order there. 7 So the men went after them on the road to Jordan as far as the river-crossing: and when they had gone out after them, the door into the town was shut. 8 And before the men went to rest, she came up to them on the roof, 9 And said to them, It is clear to me that the Lord has given you the land, and that the fear of you has come on us; 10 For we have had news of how the Lord made the Red Sea dry before you when you came out of Egypt; and what you did to the two kings of the Amorites, on the other side of Jordan, to Sihon and Og, whom you gave up to the curse. 11 And because of this news, our hearts became like water, and there was no more spirit in any of us because of you; for the Lord your God is God in heaven on high and here on earth. 12 So

now, will you give me your oath by the Lord, that, because I have been kind
to you, you will be kind to my father's house, 13 And that you will keep safe
my father and mother and my brothers and sisters and all they have, so that
death may not come on us? 14 And the men said to her, Our life for yours
if you keep our business secret; and when the Lord has given us the land,
we will keep faith and be kind to you.15 Then she let them down from the
window by a cord, for the house where she was living was on the town wall.
16 And she said to them, Get away into the hill-country, or the men who
have gone after you will overtake you; keep yourselves safe there for three
days, till the searchers have come back, and then go on your way. 17 And
the men said to her, We will only be responsible for this oath which you
have made us take, 18 If, when we come into the land, you put this cord of
bright red thread in the window from which you let us down; and get your
father and mother and your brothers and all your family into the house; 19
Then if anyone goes out of your house into the street, his blood will be on
his head, we will not be responsible; but if any damage comes to anyone in
the house, his blood will be on our heads. 20 But if you say anything about
our business here, then we will be free from the oath you have made us
take. 21 And she said, Let it be as you say. Then she sent them away, and
they went; and she put the bright red cord in the window. 22 And they went
into the hill-country and were there three days, till the men who had gone
after them had come back; and those who went after them were searching
for them everywhere without coming across them. 23 Then the two men
came down from the hill-country and went over and came back to Joshua,
the son of Nun; and they gave him a complete account of what had taken
place. 24 And they said to Joshua, Truly, the Lord has given all the land into
our hands; and all the people of the land have become like water because of
us.

3

1 Then Joshua got up early in the morning, and, moving on from Shittim,
he and all the children of Israel came to Jordan and were there for the night
before going over. 2 And at the end of three days, the men in authority over
the people went through the tents, 3 Giving the people their orders, and
saying, When you see the ark of the agreement of the Lord your God lifted
up by the priests, the Levites, then get up from your places and go after it; 4
But let there be a space between you and it of about two thousand cubits:
come no nearer to it, so that you may see the way you have to go, for you
have not been over this way before. 5 And Joshua said to the people, Make
yourselves holy, for tomorrow the Lord will do works of wonder among
you. 6 Then Joshua said to the priests, Take up the ark of the agreement

and go over in front of the people. So they took up the ark of the
agreement and went in front of the people. 7 And the Lord said to Joshua,
From now on I will give you glory in the eyes of all Israel, so that they may
see that, as I was with Moses, so I will be with you. 8 And you are to give
orders to the priests who take up the ark of the agreement, and say, When
you come to the edge of the waters of Jordan, go no further. 9 And Joshua
said to the children of Israel, Come to me here: and give ear to the words of
the Lord your God.10 And Joshua said, By this you will see that the living
God is among you, and that he will certainly send out from before you the
Canaanite and the Hittite and the Hivite and the Perizzite and the
Girgashite and the Amorite and the Jebusite. 11 See, the ark of the
agreement of the Lord of all the earth is going over before you into Jordan.
12 So take twelve men out of the tribes of Israel, a man from every tribe. 13
And when the feet of the priests who take up the ark of the Lord, the Lord
of all the earth, come to rest in the waters of Jordan, the waters of Jordan
will be cut off, all the waters flowing down from higher up, and will come
together in a mass. 14 So when the people went out from their tents to go
over Jordan, the priests who took up the ark of the agreement were in front
of the people; 15 And when those who took up the ark came to Jordan, and
the feet of the priests who took up the ark were touching the edge of the
water (for the waters of Jordan are overflowing all through the time of the
grain-cutting), 16 Then the waters flowing down from higher up were
stopped and came together in a mass a long way back at Adam, a town near
Zarethan; and the waters flowing down to the sea of the Arabah, the Salt
Sea, were cut off: and the people went across opposite Jericho. 17 And the
priests who took up the ark of the agreement of the Lord kept their places,
with their feet on dry land in the middle of Jordan, while all Israel went
over on dry land, till all the nation had gone over Jordan.

4

1 Now when all the nation had come to the other side of Jordan, the Lord
said to Joshua, 2 Take twelve men from the people, a man for every tribe, 3
And say to them, Take up from the middle of Jordan, from the place where
the feet of the priests were resting, twelve stones, and take them over with
you and put them down in the place where you take your rest tonight. 4 So
Joshua sent for the twelve men, whom he had ready, one man out of every
tribe of the children of Israel, 5 And he said to them, Go over before the
ark of the Lord your God into the middle of Jordan, and let every one of
you take up a stone on his back, one for every tribe of the children of Israel:
6 So that this may be a sign among you; when your children say to you in
time to come, What is the reason for these stones? 7 Then you will say to

them, Because the waters of Jordan were cut off before the ark of the
Lord's agreement; when it went over Jordan the waters of Jordan were cut
off: and these stones will be a sign for the children of Israel, keeping it in
their memory for ever. 8 So the children of Israel did as Joshua gave them
orders, and took twelve stones from the middle of Jordan, as the Lord had
said to Joshua, one for every tribe of the children of Israel; these they took
across with them to their night's resting-place and put them down there. 9
And Joshua put up twelve stones in the middle of Jordan, where the feet of
the priests who took up the ark of the agreement had been placed: and
there they are to this day. 10 For the priests who took up the ark kept there
in the middle of Jordan till all the orders given to Joshua by Moses from the
Lord had been done: then the people went over quickly. 11 And when all
the people had come to the other side, the ark of the Lord went over, and
the priests, before the eyes of the people. 12 And the children of Reuben
and the children of Gad and the half-tribe of Manasseh went over armed
before the children of Israel as Moses had said to them: 13 About forty
thousand armed for war went over before the Lord to the fight, to the
lowlands of Jericho. 14 That day the Lord made Joshua great in the eyes of
all Israel; and all the days of his life they went in fear of him, as they had
gone in fear of Moses. 15 Then the Lord said to Joshua, 16 Give orders to
the priests who take up the ark of witness, to come up out of Jordan. 17 So
Joshua gave orders to the priests, saying, Come up now out of Jordan. 18
And when the priests who took up the ark of the Lord's agreement came up
out of Jordan and their feet came out on to dry land, the waters of Jordan
went back to their place, overflowing its edges as before. 19 So on the tenth
day of the first month the people came up out of Jordan, and put up their
tents in Gilgal, on the east side of Jericho. 20 And the twelve stones which
they took out of Jordan, Joshua put up in Gilgal. 21 And he said to the
children of Israel, When your children say to their fathers in time to come,
What is the reason for these stones? 22 Then give your children the story,
and say, Israel came over this river Jordan on dry land. 23 For the Lord
your God made the waters of Jordan dry before you till you had gone
across, as he did to the Red Sea, drying it up before us till we had gone
across: 24 So that all the peoples of the earth may see that the hand of the
Lord is strong; and that they may go in fear of the Lord your God for ever.

5

1 Now when the news came to all the kings of the Amorites on the west
side of Jordan, and all the kings of the Canaanites living by the sea, how the
Lord had made the waters of Jordan dry before the children of Israel, till
they had gone across, their hearts became like water, and there was no more

spirit in them, because of the children of Israel. 2 At that time the Lord said
to Joshua, Make yourself stone knives and give the children of Israel
circumcision a second time. 3 So Joshua made stone knives and gave the
children of Israel circumcision at Gibeath-ha-araloth. 4 And this is the
reason why Joshua did so: all the males of the people who came out of
Egypt, all the fighting-men, had been overtaken by death in the waste land
on the way, after they came out of Egypt. 5 All the people who came out
had undergone circumcision; but all the people whose birth had taken place
in the waste land on their journey from Egypt had not. 6 For the children
of Israel were wandering in the waste land for forty years, till all the nation,
that is, all the fighting-men, who had come out of Egypt, were dead,
because they did not give ear to the voice of the Lord: to whom the Lord
said, with an oath, that he would not let them see the land which the Lord
had given his word to their fathers to give us, a land flowing with milk and
honey. 7 And their children, who came up in their place, now underwent
circumcision by the hands of Joshua, not having had it before: for there had
been no circumcision on the journey. 8 So when all the nation had
undergone circumcision, they kept in their tents till they were well again. 9
And the Lord said to Joshua, Today the shame of Egypt has been rolled
away from you. So that place was named Gilgal, to this day. 10 So the
children of Israel put up their tents in Gilgal; and they kept the Passover on
the fourteenth day of the month, in the evening, in the lowlands of Jericho.
11 And on the day after the Passover, they had for their food the produce
of the land, unleavened cakes and dry grain on the same day. 12 And there
was no more manna from the day after they had for their food the produce
of the land; the children of Israel had manna no longer, but that year the
produce of the land of Canaan was their food. 13 Now when Joshua was
near Jericho, lifting up his eyes he saw a man in front of him, with his
sword uncovered in his hand: and Joshua went up to him and said, Are you
for us or against us? 14 And he said, No; but I have come as captain of the
armies of the Lord. Then Joshua, falling down with his face to the earth in
worship, said, What has my lord to say to his servant? 15 And the captain of
the Lord's army said to Joshua, Take off your shoes from your feet, for the
place where you are is holy. And Joshua did so.

6

1 (Now Jericho was all shut up because of the children of Israel: there was
no going out or coming in.) 2And the Lord said to Joshua, See, I have given
into your hands Jericho with its king and all its men of war.3 Now let all
your fighting-men make a circle round the town, going all round it once.
Do this for six days.4 And let seven priests go before the ark with seven

loud-sounding horns in their hands: on the seventh day you are to go round
the town seven times, the priests blowing their horns. 5 And at the sound
of a long note on the horns, let all the people give a loud cry; and the wall
of the town will come down flat, and all the people are to go straight
forward. 6 Then Joshua, the son of Nun, sent for the priests and said to
them, Take up the ark of the agreement, and let seven priests take seven
horns in their hands and go before the ark of the Lord. 7 And he said to the
people, Go forward, circling the town, and let the armed men go before the
ark of the Lord. 8 So after Joshua had said this to the people, the seven
priests with their seven horns went forward before the Lord, blowing on
their horns: and the ark of the Lord's agreement went after them. 9 And the
armed men went before the priests who were blowing the horns, and the
mass of the people went after the ark, blowing their horns. 10 And to the
people Joshua gave an order, saying, You will give no cry, and make no
sound, and let no word go out of your mouth till the day when I say, Give a
loud cry; then give a loud cry. 11 So he made the ark of the Lord go all
round the town once: then they went back to the tents for the night. 12
And early in the morning Joshua got up, and the priests took up the ark of
the Lord. 13 And the seven priests with their seven horns went on before
the ark of the Lord, blowing their horns: the armed men went before them,
and the mass of the people went after the ark of the Lord, blowing their
horns. 14 The second day they went all round the town once, and then
went back to their tents: and so they did for six days. 15 Then on the
seventh day they got up early, at the dawn of the day, and went round the
town in the same way, but that day they went round it seven times.16 And
the seventh time, at the sound of the priests' horns, Joshua said to the
people, Now give a loud cry; for the Lord has given you the town. 17 And
the town will be put to the curse, and everything in it will be given to the
Lord: only Rahab, the loose woman, and all who are in the house with her,
will be kept safe, because she kept secret the men we sent. 18 And as for
you, keep yourselves from the cursed thing, for fear that you may get a
desire for it and take some of it for yourselves, and so be the cause of a
curse and great trouble on the tents of Israel. 19 But all the silver and gold
and the vessels of brass and iron are holy to the Lord: they are to come into
the store-house of the Lord. 20 So the people gave a loud cry, and the
horns were sounded; and on hearing the horns the people gave a loud cry,
and the wall came down flat, so that the people went up into the town,
every man going straight before him, and they took the town. 21 And they
put everything in the town to the curse; men and women, young and old, ox
and sheep and ass, they put to death without mercy. 22 Then Joshua said to
the two men who had been sent to make a search through the land, Go into
the house of the loose woman, and get her out, and all who are with her, as
you gave her your oath. 23 So the searchers went in and got out Rahab and

her father and mother and her brothers and all she had, and they got out all
her family; and they took them outside the tents of Israel. 24 Then, after
burning up the town and everything in it, they put the silver and gold and
the vessels of brass and iron into the store-house of the Lord's house. 25
But Joshua kept Rahab, the loose woman, and her father's family and all she
had, from death, and so she got a living-place among the children of Israel
to this day; because she kept safe the men whom Joshua had sent to make a
search through the land. 26 Then Joshua gave the people orders with an
oath, saying, Let that man be cursed before the Lord who puts his hand to
the building up of this town: with the loss of his first son will he put the
first stone of it in place, and with the loss of his youngest son he will put up
its doors. 27 So the Lord was with Joshua; and news of him went through
all the land.

7

1 But the children of Israel did wrong about the cursed thing: for Achan,
the son of Carmi, the son of Zabdi, the son of Zerah, of the family of
Judah, took of the cursed thing, moving the Lord to wrath against the
children of Israel. 2 Now Joshua sent men from Jericho to Ai, which is by
the side of Beth-aven, on the east side of Beth-el, and said to them, Go up
and make a search through the land. And the men went up and saw how Ai
was placed. 3 Then they came back to Joshua and said to him, Do not send
all the people up, but let about two or three thousand men go up and make
an attack on Ai; there is no need for all the people to be tired with the
journey there, for it is only a small town. 4 So about three thousand of the
people went up, and were sent in flight by the men of Ai. 5 The men of Ai
put to death about thirty-six of them, driving them from before the town as
far as the stoneworks, and overcoming them on the way down: and the
hearts of the people became like water. 6 Then Joshua, in great grief, went
down on the earth before the ark of the Lord till the evening, and all the
chiefs of Israel with him, and they put dust on their heads. 7 And Joshua
said, O Lord God, why have you taken us over Jordan only to give us up
into the hands of the Amorites for our destruction? If only it had been
enough for us to keep on the other side of Jordan! 8 O Lord, what am I to
say now that Israel have given way before their attackers? 9 For when the
news comes to the Canaanites and all the people of the land, they will come
up, shutting us in and cutting off our name from the earth: and what will
you do for the honour of your great name? 10 Then the Lord said to
Joshua, Get up; what are you doing with your face to the earth? 11 Israel
has done wrong, sinning against the agreement which I made with them:
they have even taken of the cursed thing; acting falsely like thieves they

have put it among their goods. 12 For this reason the children of Israel
have given way, turning their backs in flight before their attackers, because
they are cursed: I will no longer be with you, if you do not put the cursed
thing away from among you. 13 Up! make the people holy; say to them,
Make yourselves holy before tomorrow, for the Lord, the God of Israel, has
said, There is a cursed thing among you, O Israel, and you will give way
before your attackers in the fight till the cursed thing has been taken away
from among you. 14 So in the morning you are to come near, tribe by tribe;
and the tribe marked out by the Lord is to come near, family by family; and
the family marked out by the Lord is to come near, house by house; and the
house marked out by the Lord is to come near, man by man. 15 Then the
man who is taken with the cursed thing is to be burned, with everything
which is his; because he has gone against the agreement of the Lord and has
done an act of shame in Israel. 16 So Joshua got up early in the morning,
and made Israel come before him by their tribes; and the tribe of Judah was
taken; 17 Then he made Judah come forward, and the family of the
Zerahites was taken; and he made the family of the Zerahites come forward
man by man; and Zabdi was taken; 18 Then the house of Zabdi came
forward man by man, and Achan, the son of Carmi, the son of Zabdi, the
son of Zerah, of the tribe of Judah, was taken. 19 And Joshua said to
Achan, My son, give glory and praise to the Lord, the God of Israel; give
me word now of what you have done, and keep nothing back from me. 20
And Achan, answering, said to Joshua, Truly I have done wrong against the
Lord, the God of Israel, and this is what I have done: 21 When I saw
among their goods a fair robe of Babylon and two hundred shekels of
silver, and a mass of gold, fifty shekels in weight, I was overcome by desire
and took them; and they are put away in the earth in my tent, and the silver
is under it. 22 So Joshua sent men quickly, and looking in his tent, they saw
where the robe had been put away secretly with the silver under it. 23 And
they took them from the tent and came back with them to Joshua and the
children of Israel, and put them before the Lord. 24 Then Joshua and all
Israel took Achan, the son of Zerah, and the silver and the robe and the
mass of gold, and his sons and his daughters and his oxen and his asses and
his sheep and his tent and everything he had; and they took them up into
the valley of Achor. 25 And Joshua said, Why have you been a cause of
trouble to us? Today the Lord will send trouble on you. And all Israel took
part in stoning him; they had him stoned to death and then burned with
fire. 26 And over him they put a great mass of stones, which is there to this
day; then the heat of the Lord's wrath was turned away. So that place was
named, The Valley of Achor, to this day.

8

1 Then the Lord said to Joshua, Have no fear and do not be troubled: take with you all the fighting-men and go up against Ai: for I have given into your hands the king of Ai and his people and his town and his land: 2 And you are to do to Ai and its king as you did to Jericho and its king: but their goods and their cattle you may take for yourselves: let a secret force be stationed to make a surprise attack on the town from the back. 3 So Joshua and the fighting-men got ready to go up against Ai; and Joshua took thirty thousand men of war, and sent them out by night. 4 And he gave them their orders, saying, Go and take up your position secretly at the back of the town: do not go very far away, and let all of you be ready: 5And I and all the people with me will come near the town, and when they come out against us as they did before, we will go in flight from them; 6 And they will come out after us, till we have got them away from the town; for they will say, They have gone in flight from us as before; so we will go in flight before them; 7 Then you will get up from your secret position and take the town, for the Lord your God will give it up into your hands. 8 And when you have taken the town, put fire to it, as the Lord has said: see, I have given you your orders. 9 So Joshua sent them out: and they took up a secret position between Beth-el and Ai, on the west side of Ai: but Joshua kept with the people that night. 10 And early in the morning Joshua got up, and put the people in order, and he and the chiefs of Israel went up before the people to Ai. 11 And all the fighting-men who were with him went up and came near the town, and took up a position on the north side of Ai facing the town, with a valley between him and the town. 12 And taking about five thousand men, he put them in position for a surprise attack on the west side of Ai, between Beth-el and Ai. 13 So all the people were in their places, the army on the north side of the town and the secret force on the west; and that night Joshua went down into the valley. 14 Now when the king of Ai saw it, he got up quickly and went out to war against Israel, he and all his people, to the slope going down to the valley; but he had no idea that a secret force was waiting at the back of the town. 15 Then Joshua and all Israel, acting as if they were overcome before them, went in flight by way of the waste land. 16 And all the people in Ai came together to go after them; and they went after Joshua, moving away from the town. 17 There was not a man in Ai and Beth-el who did not go out after Israel; and the town was open and unwatched while they went after Israel. 18 And the Lord said to Joshua, Let your spear be stretched out against Ai; for I will give it into your hands. So Joshua took up his spear, stretching it out in the direction of the town. 19 Then the secret force came quickly from their place, and running forward when they saw his hand stretched out, went into the town and took it, and put fire to it straight away. 20 Then the men of Ai, looking back, saw the smoke of the town going up to heaven, and were unable to go this way

or that: and the people who had gone in flight to the waste land were turned back on those who were coming after them. 21 And when Joshua and all Israel saw that the town had been taken by the surprise attack, and that the smoke of the town had gone up, turning round they overcame the men of Ai. 22 Then the other force came out of the town against them, so that they were being attacked on this side and on that: and Israel overcame them and let not one of them get away with his life. 23 But the king of Ai they made prisoner, and took him to Joshua. 24 Then, after the destruction of all the people of Ai in the field and in the waste land where they went after them, and when all the people had been put to death without mercy, all Israel went back to Ai, and put to death all who were in it without mercy. 25 On that day twelve thousand were put to death, men and women, all the people of Ai. 26 For Joshua did not take back his hand with the outstretched spear till the destruction of the people of Ai was complete. 27 But the cattle and the goods from that town, Israel took for themselves, as the Lord had given orders to Joshua. 28 So Joshua gave Ai to the flames, and made it a waste mass of stones for ever, as it is to this day. 29 And he put the king of Ai to death, hanging him on a tree till evening: and when the sun went down, Joshua gave them orders to take his body down from the tree, and put it in the public place of the town, covering it with a great mass of stones, which is there to this day. 30 Then Joshua put up an altar to the Lord, the God of Israel, in Mount Ebal, 31 In the way ordered by Moses, the servant of the Lord, as it is recorded in the book of the law of Moses, an altar of uncut stones, untouched by any iron instrument: and on it they made burned offerings and peace-offerings to the Lord. 32 And he made there on the stones a copy of the law of Moses, writing it before the eyes of the children of Israel. 33 And all Israel, those who were Israelites by birth, as well as the men from other lands living with them, and their responsible men and their overseers and judges, took their places round the ark, in front of the priests, the Levites, whose work it was to take up the ark of the Lord's agreement; half of them were stationed in front of Mount Gerizim and half in front of Mount Ebal, in agreement with the orders for the blessing of the children of Israel which Moses, the servant of the Lord, had given. 34 And after, he gave them all the words of the law, the blessing and the curse, as it is all recorded in the book of the law; 35 Reading to all the meeting of Israel, with the women and the children and the men from other lands who were living among them, every word of the orders which Moses had given.

9

1 Now on hearing the news of these things, all the kings on the west side of

Jordan, in the hill-country and the lowlands and by the Great Sea in front of
Lebanon, the Hittites and the Amorites, the Canaanites, the Perizzites, the
Hivites, and the Jebusites, 2 Came together with one purpose, to make war
against Joshua and Israel. 3 And the men of Gibeon, hearing what Joshua
had done to Jericho and Ai, 4 Acting with deceit, got food together as if for
a long journey; and took old food-bags for their asses, and old and cracked
wine-skins kept together with cord; 5 And put old stitched-up shoes on
their feet, and old clothing on their backs; and all the food they had with
them was dry and broken up. 6 And they came to Joshua to the tent-circle
at Gilgal, and said to him and to the men of Israel, We have come from a
far country: so now make an agreement with us. 7 And the men of Israel
said to the Hivites, It may be that you are living among us; how then may
we make an agreement with you? 8 And they said to Joshua, We are your
servants. Then Joshua said to them, Who are you and where do you come
from? 9 And they said to him, Your servants have come from a very far
country, because of the name of the Lord your God: for the story of his
great name, and of all he did in Egypt has come to our ears, 10 And what
he did to the two kings of the Amorites east of Jordan, to Sihon, king of
Heshbon, and to Og, king of Bashan, at Ashtaroth. 11 So the responsible
men and all the people of our country said to us, Take food with you for
the journey and go to them, and say to them, We are your servants: so now
make an agreement with us. 12 This bread which we have with us for our
food, we took warm and new from our houses when starting on our
journey to you; but now see, it has become dry and broken up. 13 And
these wine-skins were new when we put the wine in them, and now they are
cracked as you see; and our clothing and our shoes have become old
because of our very long journey here. 14 And the men took some of their
food, without requesting directions from the Lord. 15 So Joshua made
peace with them, and made an agreement with them that they were not to
be put to death: and the chiefs of the people took an oath to them. 16 Now
three days after, when they had made this agreement with them, they had
word that these men were their neighbours, living near them. 17 And the
children of Israel went forward on their journey, and on the third day came
to their towns. Now their towns were Gibeon and Chephirah and Beeroth
and Kiriath-jearim. 18And the children of Israel did not put them to death,
because the chiefs of the people had taken an oath to them by the Lord, the
God of Israel. And all the people made an outcry against the chiefs. 19 But
all the chiefs said to the people, We have taken an oath to them by the
Lord, the God of Israel, and so we may not put our hands on them. 20 This
is what we will do to them: we will not put them to death, for fear that
wrath may come on us because of our oath to them. 21 Keep them living,
and let them be servants, cutting wood and getting water for all the people.
And all the people did as the chiefs had said to them. 22Then Joshua sent

for them, and said to them, Why have you been false to us, saying, We are very far from you, when you are living among us? 23 Now because of this you are cursed, and you will for ever be our servants, cutting wood and getting water for the house of my God. 24 And, answering Joshua, they said, Because it came to the ears of your servants that the Lord your God had given orders to his servant Moses to give you all this land, and to send destruction on all the people living in it, because of you; so, fearing greatly for our lives because of you, we have done this. 25 And now we are in your hands: do to us whatever seems good and right to you. 26 So he kept them safe from the children of Israel, and did not let them be put to death. 27 And that day Joshua made them servants, cutting wood and getting water for the people and for the altar of the Lord, in the place marked out by him, to this day.

10

1 Now when it came to the ears of Adoni-zedek, king of Jerusalem, that Joshua had taken Ai, and had given it up to the curse (for as he had done to Jericho and its king, so he had done to Ai and its king); and that the people of Gibeon had made peace with Israel and were living among them; 2 He was in great fear, because Gibeon was a great town, like one of the king's towns, greater than Ai, and all the men in it were men of war. 3 So Adoni-zedek, king of Jerusalem, sent to Hoham, king of Hebron, and to Piram, king of Jarmuth, and to Japhia, king of Lachish, and to Debir, king of Eglon, saying, 4 Come up to me and give me help, and let us make an attack on Gibeon: for they have made peace with Joshua and the children of Israel. 5 So the five kings of the Amorites, the king of Jerusalem, the king of Hebron, the king of Jarmuth, the king of Lachish, and the king of Eglon, were banded together, and went up with all their armies and took up their position before Gibeon and made war against it. 6 And the men of Gibeon sent to Joshua to the tent-circle at Gilgal, saying, Be not slow to send help to your servants; come up quickly to our support and keep us safe: for all the kings of the Amorites from the hill-country have come together against us. 7 So Joshua went up from Gilgal with all his army and all his men of war. 8 And the Lord said to Joshua, Have no fear of them, for I have given them into your hands; they will all give way before you. 9 So Joshua, having come up from Gilgal all night, made a sudden attack on them. 10 And the Lord made them full of fear before Israel, and they put great numbers of them to death at Gibeon, and went after them by the way going up to Beth-horon, driving them back to Azekah and Makkedah 11 And in their flight before Israel, on the way down from Beth-horon, the Lord sent down great stones from heaven on them all the way to Azekah,

causing their death: those whose death was caused by the stones were more than those whom the children of Israel put to death with the sword. 12 It was on the day when the Lord gave up the Amorites into the hands of the children of Israel that Joshua said to the Lord, before the eyes of Israel, Sun, be at rest over Gibeon; and you, O moon, in the valley of Aijalon. 13 And the sun was at rest and the moon kept its place till the nation had given punishment to their attackers. (Is it not recorded in the book of Jashar?) So the sun kept its place in the middle of the heavens, and was waiting, and did not go down, for the space of a day. 14 And there was no day like that, before it or after it, when the Lord gave ear to the voice of a man; for the Lord was fighting for Israel. 15 And Joshua, with all Israel, went back to the tent-circle at Gilgal. 16 But these five kings went in flight secretly to a hole in the rock at Makkedah. 17 And word was given to Joshua that the five kings had been taken in a hole in the rock at Makkedah. 18And Joshua said, Let great stones be rolled against the mouth of the hole, and let men keep watch by it:19 But do you, without waiting, go after their army, attacking them from the back; do not let them get into their towns, for the Lord your God has given them into your hands. 20 Now when Joshua and the children of Israel had come to the end of their war of complete destruction, and had put to death all but a small band who had got safely into the walled towns, 21 All the people went back to Joshua to the tent-circle at Makkedah in peace: and no one said a word against the children of Israel. 22 Then Joshua said, Take away the stones from the mouth of the hole in the rock, and make those five kings come out to me. 23And they did so, and made those five kings come out of the hole to him, the king of Jerusalem, the king of Hebron, the king of Jarmuth, the king of Lachish, and the king of Eglon. 24 And when they had made those kings come out to Joshua, Joshua sent for all the men of Israel, and said to the chiefs of the men of war who had gone with him, Come near and put your feet on the necks of these kings. So they came near and put their feet on their necks. 25 And Joshua said to them, Have no fear and do not be troubled; be strong and take heart: for so will the Lord do to all against whom you make war. 26 Then Joshua had them put to death, hanging them on five trees, where they were till evening. 27 And when the sun went down, they were taken down from the trees, by Joshua's orders, and put into the hole where they had gone to be safe; and great stones were placed at the mouth of the hole, where they are to this day. 28That day Joshua took Makkedah, and put it and its king to the sword; every soul in it he gave up to the curse without mercy: and he did to the king of Makkedah as he had done to the king of Jericho. 29 Then Joshua and all Israel with him went on from Makkedah and came to Libnah, and made an attack on it; 30And again the Lord gave it and its king into the hands of Israel; and he put it and every person in it to the sword, till their destruction was complete; and he did to its king as he

had done to the king of Jericho. 31Then Joshua and all Israel with him went
on from Libnah to Lachish, and took up their position against it and made
an attack on it, 32 And the Lord gave Lachish into the hands of Israel, and
on the second day he took it, putting it and every person in it to the sword
without mercy, as he had done to Libnah. 33 Then Horam, king of Gezer,
came up to the help of Lachish; and Joshua overcame him and his people,
putting all of them to death. 34 And Joshua and all Israel with him went on
from Lachish to Eglon: and they took up their position against it and made
an attack on it; 35 And that day they took it, putting it and every person in
it to the sword, as he had done to Lachish. 36 And Joshua and all Israel
with him went up from Eglon to Hebron, and made an attack on it; 37 And
took it, overcoming it and putting it and its king and its towns and every
person in it to the sword: as he had done to Eglon, he put them all to death,
and gave it up to the curse with every person in it. 38 And Joshua and all
Israel with him went on to make an attack on Debir; 39 And he took it,
with its king and all its towns: and he put them to the sword, giving every
person in it to the curse; all were put to death: as he had done to Hebron,
so he did to Debir and its king. 40 So Joshua overcame all the land, the hill-
country and the South and the lowland and the mountain slopes, and all
their kings; all were put to death: and every living thing he gave up to the
curse, as the Lord, the God of Israel, had given him orders. 41 Joshua
overcame them from Kadesh-barnea to Gaza, and all the land of Goshen as
far as Gibeon. 42 And all these kings and their land Joshua took at the same
time, because the Lord, the God of Israel, was fighting for Israel. 43 Then
Joshua and all Israel with him went back to their tents at Gilgal.

11

1 Now Jabin, king of Hazor, hearing of these things, sent to Jobab, king of
Madon, and to the king of Shimron, and to the king of Achshaph, 2 And to
the kings on the north in the hill-country, and in the Arabah south of
Chinneroth, and in the lowland, and in the highlands of Dor on the west, 3
And to the Canaanites on the east and on the west, and to the Amorites and
the Hittites and the Perizzites, and the Jebusites in the hill-country, and the
Hivites under Hermon in the land of Mizpah. 4 And they went out, they
and all their armies with them, a great people, in number like the sand on
the seaside, with horses and war-carriages in great number. 5 And all these
kings came together, and put their forces in position at the waters of
Merom, to make war on Israel. 6 And the Lord said to Joshua, Have no fear
of them: for tomorrow at this time I will give them all up dead before
Israel; you are to have the leg-muscles of their horses cut and their war-
carriages burned with fire. 7 So Joshua and all the men of war with him

came against them suddenly at the waters of Merom, and made an attack on
them. 8 And the Lord gave them up into the hands of Israel, and they
overcame them driving them back to great Zidon and to Misrephoth-maim
and into the valley of Mizpeh to the east; and they put them all to death, no
man got away safely. 9 And Joshua did to them as the Lord had said to him;
he had the leg-muscles of their horses cut and their war-carriages burned
with fire. 10 At that time, Joshua went on to take Hazor and put its king to
the sword: for in earlier times Hazor was the chief of all those kingdoms. 11
And they put every person in it to death without mercy, giving every living
thing up to the curse, and burning Hazor. 12 And all the towns of these
kings, and all the kings, Joshua took, and put them to the sword: he gave
them up to the curse, as Moses, the servant of the Lord, had said. 13 As for
the towns made on hills of earth, not one was burned by Israel but Hazor,
which was burned by Joshua. 14 And all the goods taken from these towns,
and their cattle, the children of Israel kept for themselves; but every man
they put to death without mercy, till their destruction was complete, and
there was no one living. 15 As the Lord had given orders to Moses his
servant, so Moses gave orders to Joshua, and so Joshua did; every order
which the Lord had given to Moses was done. 16 So Joshua took all that
land, the hill-country and all the South, and all the land of Goshen, and the
lowland and the Arabah, the hill-country of Israel and its lowland; 17 From
Mount Halak, which goes up to Seir, as far as Baal-gad in the valley of
Lebanon under Mount Hermon: and all their kings he overcame and put to
death. 18 For a long time Joshua made war on all those kings. 19 Not one
town made peace with the children of Israel, but only the Hivites of
Gibeon: they took them all in war. 20 For the Lord made them strong in
heart to go to war against Israel, so that he might give them up to the curse
without mercy, and that destruction might come on them, as the Lord had
given orders to Moses. 21 And Joshua came at that time and put an end to
the Anakim in the hill-country, in Hebron, in Debir, in Anab, and in all the
hill-country of Judah and Israel: Joshua gave them and their towns to the
curse. 22 Not one of the Anakim was to be seen in the land of the children
of Israel: only in Gaza, in Gath, and in Ashdod, some were still living. 23 So
Joshua took all the land, as the Lord had said to Moses; and Joshua gave it
to the children of Israel as their heritage, making division of it among them
by their tribes. And the land had rest from war.

12

1 Now these are the kings of the land whom the children of Israel
overcame, taking as their heritage their land on the east side of Jordan, from
the valley of the Arnon to Mount Hermon, and all the Arabah to the east: 2

Sihon, king of the Amorites, who was living in Heshbon, ruling from Aroer, which is on the edge of the valley of the Arnon, and the town in the middle of the valley, and half Gilead, as far as the river Jabbok, the limits of the children of Ammon; 3 And the Arabah to the sea of Chinneroth, to the east, and to the sea of the Arabah, that is the Salt Sea, to the east, the way to Beth-jeshimoth; and on the south, under the slopes of Pisgah: 4 And the land of Og, king of Bashan, of the rest of the Rephaim, who was living at Ashtaroth and at Edrei, 5 Ruling in the mountain of Hermon, and in Salecah, and in all Bashan, as far as the limits of the Geshurites and the Maacathites, and half Gilead, to the land of Sihon, king of Heshbon. 6 Moses, the servant of the Lord, and the children of Israel overcame them; and Moses, the servant of the Lord, gave their land for a heritage to the Reubenites, and the Gadites, and the half-tribe of Manasseh. 7And these are the kings of the land whom Joshua and the children of Israel overcame on the west side of Jordan, from Baal-gad in the valley of Lebanon to Mount Halak, which goes up to Seir; and Joshua gave the land to the tribes of Israel for a heritage, in keeping with their divisions; 8 In the hill-country, and in the lowland, and in the Arabah, and on the mountain slopes, and in the waste land, and in the South; the Hittites, the Amorites, and the Canaanites, the Perizzites, the Hivites, and the Jebusites. 9 The king of Jericho, one; the king of Ai, which is near Beth-el, one; 10 The king of Jerusalem, one; the king of Hebron, one; 11 The king of Jarmuth, one; the king of Lachish, one; 12 The king of Eglon, one; the king of Gezer, one; 13 The king of Debir, one; the king of Geder, one; 14 The king of Hormah, one; the king of Arad, one;15 The king of Libnah, one; the king of Adullam, one; 16 The king of Makkedah, one; the king of Beth-el, one; 17 The king of Tappuah, one; the king of Hepher, one; 18 The king of Aphek, one; the king of Lassharon, one; 19 The king of Madon, one; the king of Hazor, one; 20 The king of Shimron-meron, one; the king of Achshaph, one; 21 The king of Taanach, one; the king of Megiddo, one; 22 The king of Kedesh, one; the king of Jokneam in Carmel, one; 23 The king of Dor on the hill of Dor, one; the king of Goiim in Gilgal, one; 24 The king of Tirzah, one; all the kings together were thirty-one.

13

1 Now Joshua was old and full of years; and the Lord said to him, You are old and full of years, and there is still very much land to be taken. 2 This is the land which is still to be taken: all the country of the Philistines, and all the Geshurites; 3 From the Shihor, which is before Egypt, to the edge of Ekron to the north, which is taken to be Canaanite property: the five chiefs of the Philistines; the Gazites, and the Ashdodites, the Ashkelonites, the

Gittites, and the Ekronites, as well as the Avvim; 4 On the south: all the
land of the Canaanites, and Mearah which is the property of the Zidonians,
to Aphek, as far as the limit of the Amorites: 5 And the land of the
Gebalites, and all Lebanon, looking east, from Baal-gad under Mount
Hermon as far as Hamath: 6 All the people of the hill-country from
Lebanon to Misrephoth-maim, all the Zidonians; them will I send out from
before the children of Israel: only make division of it to Israel for a heritage,
as I have given you orders to do. 7 So now make division of this land for a
heritage to the nine tribes, and the half-tribe of Manasseh. 8 With him the
Reubenites and the Gadites have been given their heritage, which Moses
gave them, on the east side of Jordan, as Moses, the servant of the Lord,
gave them; 9 From Aroer, on the edge of the valley of the Arnon, and the
town in the middle of the valley, and all the table-land from Medeba to
Dibon; 10 And all the towns of Sihon, king of the Amorites, who was
ruling in Heshbon, to the limits of the children of Ammon; 11 And Gilead,
and the land of the Geshurites and the Maacathites, and all Mount Hermon,
and all Bashan to Salecah; 12 All the kingdom of Og in Bashan, who was
ruling in Ashtaroth and in Edrei (he was one of the last of the Rephaim);
these did Moses overcome, driving them out of their country. 13 However,
the people of Israel did not send out the Geshurites, or the Maacathites: but
Geshur and Maacath are living among Israel to this day. 14 Only to the
tribe of Levi he gave no heritage; the offerings of the Lord, the God of
Israel, made by fire are his heritage, as he said to him. 15 And Moses gave
their heritage to the tribe of Reuben by their families. 16Their limit was
from Aroer, on the edge of the valley of the Arnon, and the town in the
middle of the valley, and all the table-land by Medeba; 17 Heshbon and all
her towns in the table-land; Dibon, and Bamoth-baal, and Beth-baal-meon;
18 And Jahaz, and Kedemoth, and Mephaath; 19 And Kiriathaim, and
Sibmah, and Zereth-shahar in the mountain of the valley; 20 And Beth-
peor, and the slopes of Pisgah, and Beth-jeshimoth; 21 And all the towns of
the table-land, and all the kingdom of Sihon, king of the Amorites, who was
ruling in Heshbon, whom Moses overcame, together with the chiefs of
Midian, Evi, and Rekem, and Zur, and Hur, and Reba, the chiefs of Sihon,
who were living in the land. 22 And Balaam, the son of Beor, the prophet,
the children of Israel put to death with the sword. 23 And the limit of the
children of Reuben was the edge of Jordan. This was the heritage of the
children of Reuben by their families, with its towns and its unwalled places.
24 And Moses gave their heritage to the tribe of Gad by their families. 25
And their limit was Jazer, and all the towns of Gilead, and half the land of
the children of Ammon, to Aroer before Rabbah; 26 And from Heshbon to
Ramath-mizpeh, and Betonim; and from Mahanaim to the edge of Debir;
27 And in the valley, Beth-haram, and Beth-nimrah, and Succoth, and
Zaphon, the rest of the kingdom of Sihon, king of Heshbon, having Jordan

for its limit, to the end of the sea of Chinnereth on the east side of Jordan. 28 This is the heritage of the children of Gad by their families, with its towns and its unwalled places 29 And Moses gave their heritage to the half-tribe of Manasseh by their families. 30 And their limit was from Mahanaim, all Bashan, all the kingdom of Og, king of Bashan, and all Havvoth-Jair, in Bashan, sixty towns; 31 And half Gilead, and Ashtaroth, and Edrei, towns of the kingdom of Og in Bashan, were for the children of Machir, the son of Manasseh, for half of the children of Machir by their families. 32 These are the heritages of which Moses made distribution in the lowlands of Moab, on the other side of Jordan in Jericho, to the east. 33 But to the tribe of Levi Moses gave no heritage: the Lord, the God of Israel, is their heritage, as he said to them.

14

1 And these are the heritages which the children of Israel took in the land of Canaan, which Eleazar, the priest, and Joshua, the son of Nun, and the heads of the tribes of the children of Israel, gave out to them;2 Their heritage by the Lord's decision, as he gave orders by Moses, for the nine tribes and the half-tribe.3 For Moses had given their heritage to the two tribes and the half-tribe on the other side of Jordan, but to the Levites he gave no heritage among them. 4 Because the children of Joseph were two tribes, Manasseh and Ephraim; and they gave the Levites no part in the land, only towns for their living-places, with the grass-lands for their cattle and for their property. 5 As the Lord had given orders to Moses, so the people of Israel did, and they made division of the land. 6 Then the children of Judah went to Joshua in Gilgal; and Caleb, the son of Jephunneh the Kenizzite, said to him, You have knowledge of what the Lord said to Moses, the man of God, about me and about you in Kadesh-barnea. 7 I was forty years old when Moses, the servant of the Lord, sent me from Kadesh-barnea to make a search through the land; and the account which I gave him was in keeping with his desire. 8 My brothers, however, who went up with me, made the heart of the people like water: but I was true to the Lord with all my heart. 9 And on that day Moses took an oath, saying, Truly the land where your feet have been placed will become a heritage for you and your children for ever, because you have been true to the Lord your God with all your heart. 10And now, as you see, the Lord has kept me safe these forty-five years, from the time when the Lord said this to Moses, while Israel was wandering in the waste land: and now I am eighty-five years old. 11 And still, I am as strong today as I was when Moses sent me out: as my strength was then, so is it now, for war and for all the business of life. 12 So now, give me this hill-country named by

the Lord at that time; for you had an account of it then, how the Anakim
were there, and great walled towns: it may be that the Lord will be with me,
and I will be able to take their land, as the Lord said. 13 And Joshua gave
him his blessing; and he gave Hebron to Caleb, the son of Jephunneh, for
his heritage. 14 So Hebron became the heritage of Caleb, the son of
Jephunneh the Kenizzite, to this day, because with all his heart he was true
to the Lord, the God of Israel. 15 In earlier times the name of Hebron had
been Kiriath-arba, named after Arba, the greatest of the Anakim. And the
land had rest from war.

15

1 Now the part of the land marked out for the children of Judah by
families, went up to the edge of Edom, as far as the waste land of Zin to
the south, to the farthest point of it on the south. 2 Their south limit was
from the farthest part of the Salt Sea, from the inlet looking to the south: 3
From there it goes south of the slope up to Akrabbim, and on to Zin, then
south past Kadesh-barnea, and on by Hezron and up to Addar, turning in
the direction of Karka: 4 Then on to Azmon, ending at the stream of
Egypt: and the end of the limit is at the sea; this will be your limit on the
south. 5 And the east limit is the Salt Sea as far as the end of Jordan. And
the limit of the north part of the land is from the inlet of the sea at the end
of Jordan: 6Then the line goes up to Beth-hoglah, past the north of Beth-
arabah, and up to the stone of Bohan, the son of Reuben; 7 Then the line
goes up to Debir from the valley of Achor, and so to the north, in the
direction of Gilgal, which is opposite the slope up to Adummim, on the
south side of the river: and the line goes on to the waters of En-shemesh,
ending at En-rogel: 8 Then the line goes up by the valley of the son of
Hinnom to the south side of the Jebusite (which is Jerusalem): then up to
the top of the mountain in front of the valley of Hinnom to the west, which
is at the farthest point of the valley of Rephaim on the north: 9 And the
limit is marked out from the top of the mountain to the fountain of the
waters of Nephtoah, and out to the towns of Mount Ephron, as far as
Baalah (which is Kiriath-jearim): 10 Then turning west, the line goes from
Baalah to Mount Seir, and on to the side of Mount Jearim (which is
Chesalon) on the north, then down to Beth-shemesh, and on past Timnah:
11 And out to the side of Ekron to the north: then it is marked out to
Shikkeron and on to Mount Baalah, ending at Jabneel; the end of the line is
at the sea. 12 And the limit on the west is the edge of the Great Sea. This is
the line going round the land marked out for the children of Judah, by their
families. 13 And to Caleb, the son of Jephunneh, he gave a part among the
children of Judah, as the Lord had given orders to Joshua, that is, Kiriath-

arba, named after Arba, the father of Anak which is Hebron. 14 And the
three sons of Anak, Sheshai and Ahiman and Talmai, the children of Anak,
were forced out from there by Caleb. 15 From there he went up against the
people of Debir: (now the name of Debir before that was Kiriath-sepher.)
16And Caleb said, I will give Achsah, my daughter, as wife to the man who
overcomes Kiriath-sepher and takes it. 17 And Othniel, the son of Kenaz,
Caleb's brother, took it: so he gave him his daughter Achsah for his wife. 18
Now when she came to him, he put into her mind the idea of requesting a
field from her father: and she got down from her ass; and Caleb said to her,
What is it? 19 And she said, Give me a blessing; because you have put me in
dry south-land, now give me springs of water. So he gave her the higher
spring and the lower spring. 20 This is the heritage of the tribe of Judah, by
their families. 21 The farthest towns of the tribe of Judah in the direction of
the limits of Edom to the south, were Kabzeel, and Eder, and Jagur; 22
And Kinah, and Dimonah, and Adadah; 23 And Kedesh, and Hazor, and
Ithnan; 24 Ziph, and Telem, and Bealoth; 25 And Hazor-hadattah, and
Kerioth-hezron (which is Hazor); 26 Amam, and Shema, and Moladah; 27
And Hazar-gaddah, and Heshmon, and Beth-pelet; 28 And Hazar-shual,
and Beer-sheba, and Biziothiah; 29 Baalah, and Iim, and Ezem; 30 And
Eltolad, and Chesil, and Hormah; 31 And Ziklag, and Madmannah, and
Sansannah; 32 And Lebaoth, and Shilhim, and Ain, and Rimmon; all the
towns are twenty-nine, with their unwalled places. 33 In the lowland,
Eshtaol, and Zorah, and Ashnah; 34 And Zanoah, and En-gannim,
Tappuah, and Enam; 35 Jarmuth, and Adullam, Socoh, and Azekah; 36 And
Shaaraim, and Adithaim, and Gederah, and Gederothaim; fourteen towns
with their unwalled places. 37 Zenan, and Hadashah, and Migdal-gad; 38
And Dilan, and Mizpeh, and Joktheel; 39 Lachish, and Bozkath, and Eglon;
40 And Cabbon, and Lahmas, and Chithlish; 41 And Gederoth, Beth-
dagon, and Naamah, and Makkedah; sixteen towns with their unwalled
places. 42 Libnah, and Ether, and Ashan; 43 And Iphtah, and Ashnah, and
Nezib; 44 And Keilah, and Achzib, and Mareshah; nine towns with their
unwalled places. 45 Ekron, with her daughter-towns and her unwalled
places; 46 From Ekron to the sea, all the towns by the side of Ashdod, with
their unwalled places. 47 Ashdod, with her daughter-towns and her
unwalled places; Gaza, with her daughter-towns and her unwalled places, to
the stream of Egypt, with the Great Sea as a limit. 48 And in the hill-
country, Shamir, and Jattir, and Socoh; 49 And Dannah, and Kiriath-sannah
(which is Debir); 50 And Anab, and Eshtemoh, and Anim; 51 And Goshen,
and Holon, and Giloh; eleven towns with their unwalled places. 52 Arab,
and Dumah, and Eshan; 53 And Janim, and Beth-tappuah, and Aphekah;
54 And Humtah, and Kiriath-arba (which is Hebron), and Zior; nine towns
with their unwalled places. 55 Maon, Carmel, and Ziph, and Jutah; 56 And
Jezreel, and Jokdeam, and Zanoah; 57 Kain, Gibeah, and Timnah; ten

towns with their unwalled places. 58 Halhul, Beth-zur, and Gedor; 59 And
Maarath, and Beth-anoth, and Eltekon; six towns with their unwalled
places. 60 Kiriath-baal (which is Kiriath-jearim), and Rabbah; two towns
with their unwalled places. 61 In the waste land, Beth-arabah, Middin, and
Secacah; 62 And Nibshan, and the Town of Salt, and En-gedi; six towns
with their unwalled places. 63 And as for the Jebusites living in Jerusalem,
the children of Judah were unable to make them go out; but the Jebusites
are living with the children of Judah at Jerusalem, to this day.

16

1 And the limit of the land marked out for the children of Joseph went out
from Jordan at Jericho, at the waters of Jericho on the east, in the waste
land, going up from Jericho through the hill-country to Beth-el;2 And it
goes out from Beth-el to Luz, and on as far as the limit of the Archites to
Ataroth; 3 And it goes down to the west to the limit of the Japhletites, to
the limit of Beth-horon the lower, as far as Gezer; ending at the sea. 4 And
the children of Joseph, Manasseh and Ephraim, took their heritage. 5 And
the limit of the land of the children of Ephraim by their families was
marked out in this way: the limit of their heritage to the east was Ataroth-
addar, to Beth-horon the higher; 6 The line goes out to the west at
Michmethath on the north; then turning to the east to Taanath-shiloh,
going past it on the east of Janoah; 7 And from Janoah down to Ataroth,
and to Naarah, and touching Jericho, it goes on to Jordan. 8 From Tappuah
the line goes on to the west to the river of Kanah; ending at the sea. This is
the heritage of the children of Ephraim by their families; 9 Together with
the towns marked out for the children of Ephraim in the heritage of
Manasseh, all the towns with their unwalled places. 10 And the Canaanites
who were living in Gezer were not forced out; but the Canaanites have
been living among Ephraim, to this day, as servants, doing forced work.

17

1 And this was the part marked out for the tribe of Manasseh, because he
was the oldest son of Joseph. As for Machir, the oldest son of Manasseh,
the father of Gilead, because he was a man of war he had Gilead and
Bashan. 2 And as for the rest of the children of Manasseh, their heritage
was given to them by families; for the children of Abiezer, and for the
children of Helek, and for the children of Asriel, and for the children of
Shechem, and for the children of Hepher, and for the children of Shemida:
these were the male children of Manasseh, the son of Joseph, by their

families. 3 But Zelophehad, the son of Hepher, the son of Gilead, the son
of Machir, the son of Manasseh, had no sons, but only daughters; and these
are the names of his daughters: Mahlah, and Noah, Hoglah, Milcah, and
Tirzah. 4 And they came before Eleazar the priest, and Joshua, the son of
Nun, and before the chiefs, saying, The Lord gave orders to Moses to give
us a heritage among our brothers: so in agreement with the orders of the
Lord he gave them a heritage among their father's brothers. 5 And ten parts
were given to Manasseh, in addition to the land of Gilead and Bashan,
which is on the other side of Jordan; 6 Because the daughters of Manasseh
had a heritage among his sons, and the land of Gilead was the property of
the other sons of Manasseh. 7 And the limit of Manasseh's land was from
Asher to Michmethath, which is before Shechem; the line goes on to the
right hand, to the people of En-tappuah. 8 The land of Tappuah was the
property of Manasseh; but Tappuah on the edge of Manasseh was the
property of the children of Ephraim. 9 And the limit goes down to the
stream Kanah, to the south of the stream: these towns were Ephraim's
among the towns of Manasseh; Manasseh's limit was on the north side of
the stream, ending at the sea: 10 To the south it is Ephraim's, and to the
north it is Manasseh's, and the sea is his limit; and they are touching Asher
on the north, and Issachar on the east. 11 In Issachar and Asher, Manasseh
had Beth-shean and its daughter-towns, and Ibleam and its daughter-towns,
and the people of Dor and its daughter-towns, and the people of En-dor
and its daughter-towns, and the people of Taanach and its daughter-towns,
and the people of Megiddo and its daughter-towns, that is, the three hills.
12 But the children of Manasseh were not able to make the people of those
towns go out; but the Canaanites would go on living in that land. 13 And
when the children of Israel had become strong, they put the Canaanites to
forced work, in place of driving them out. 14 Then the children of Joseph
said to Joshua, Why have you given me only one part and one stretch of
land for my heritage? For through the blessing given to me by the Lord up
to now, I am a great people. 15 Then Joshua said to them, If you are such a
great people, go up into the woodlands, clearing a place there for yourselves
in the land of the Perizzites and the Rephaim, if the hill-country of Ephraim
is not wide enough for you. 16 And the children of Joseph said, The hill-
country is not enough for us: and all the Canaanites living in the valley have
iron war-carriages, those in Beth-shean and its towns as well as those in the
valley of Jezreel. 17 Then Joshua said to the children of Joseph, to Ephraim
and Manasseh, You are a great people, and have great power: you are not to
have one property only, 18 For the hill-country of Gilead will be yours ...
the woodland and cut down ... its outskirts will be yours ... get the
Canaanites out, for they have iron war-carriages ... strong.

18

1 And all the meeting of the children of Israel came together at Shiloh and
put up the Tent of meeting there: and the land was crushed before them. 2
But there were still seven tribes among the children of Israel who had not
taken up their heritage. 3 Then Joshua said to the children of Israel, Why
are you so slow to go in and take up your heritage in the land which the
Lord, the God of your fathers, has given you? 4 Take from among you
three men from every tribe; and I will send them to go through the land and
make a record of it for distribution as their heritage; then let them come
back to me. 5 And let them make division of it into seven parts: let Judah
keep inside his limit on the south, and let the children of Joseph keep inside
their limit on the north. 6 And you are to have the land marked out in seven
parts, and come back to me with the record; and I will make the
distribution for you here by the decision of the Lord our God. 7 For the
Levites have no part among you; to be the Lord's priests is their heritage;
and Gad and Reuben and the half-tribe of Manasseh have had their heritage
on the east side of Jordan, given to them by Moses, the servant of the Lord.
8 So the men got up and went; and Joshua gave orders to those who went,
to make a record of the land, saying, Go up and down through the land,
and make a record of it and come back here to me, and I will make the
distribution for you here by the decision of the Lord in Shiloh. 9So the men
went, travelling through the land, and made a record of it by towns in seven
parts in a book, and came back to Joshua to the tent-circle at Shiloh. 10
And Joshua made the distribution for them in Shiloh by the decision of the
Lord, marking out the land for the children of Israel by their divisions. 11
And the first heritage came out for the tribe of Benjamin by their families:
and the limit of their heritage went between the children of Judah and the
children of Joseph. 12 And their limit on the north was from the Jordan,
and the line goes up to the side of Jericho on the north and through the
hill-country to the west, ending at the waste land of Beth-aven. 13 And
from there the line goes south to Luz, to the side of Luz (which is Beth-el),
then down to Ataroth-addar, by the mountain to the south of Beth-horon
the lower. 14 And the limit is marked as coming round to the south on the
west side from the mountain which is south of Beth-horon, and ending at
Kiriath-baal (which is Kiriath-jearim), a town of the children of Judah: this
is the west part. 15 And the south part is from the farthest point of Kiriath-
jearim, and the line goes out to the west to the fountain of the waters of
Nephtoah: 16 And the line goes down to the farthest part of the mountain
facing the valley of the son of Hinnom, which is on the north of the valley
of Rephaim: from there it goes down to the valley of Hinnom, to the side
of the Jebusite on the south as far as En-rogel; 17 And it goes to En-
shemesh and on to Geliloth, opposite the way up to Adummim, and it goes

down to the stone of Bohan, the son of Reuben; 18 And it goes on to the side facing the Arabah to the north, and down to the Arabah; 19 And on to the north side of Beth-hoglah, ending at the north inlet of the Salt Sea at the south end of Jordan; this is their limit on the south. 20 And the limit of the east part is the Jordan. This is the heritage of the children of Benjamin, marked out for their families by these limits on all sides. 21 And the towns of the children of Benjamin, given to them in the order of their families, are Jericho and Beth-hoglah and Emek-kezziz 22 And Beth-arabah and Zemaraim and Beth-el 23 And Avvim and Parah and Ophrah 24 And Chephar-Ammoni and Ophni and Geba; twelve towns with their unwalled places; 25 Gibeon and Ramah and Beeroth 26 And Mizpeh and Chephirah and Mozah 27 And Rekem and Irpeel and Taralah 28 And Zela, Eleph and the Jebusite (which is Jerusalem), Gibeath and Kiriath; fourteen towns with their unwalled places. This is the heritage of the children of Benjamin by their families.

19

1 And the second heritage came out for the tribe of Simeon by their families; and their heritage was in the middle of the heritage of the children of Judah. 2 And they had for their heritage Beer-sheba and Shema and Moladah 3 And Hazar-shual and Balah and Ezem 4 And Eltolad and Bethul and Hormah 5 And Ziklag and Beth-marcaboth and Hazar-susah 6 And Beth-lebaoth and Sharuhen; thirteen towns with their unwalled places; 7 Ain, Rimmon, and Ether and Ashan; four towns with their unwalled places; 8 And all the unwalled places round about these towns as far as Baalath-beer-ramah to the south. This is the heritage of the tribe of Simeon by their families. 9 The heritage of Simeon was taken out of Judah's stretch of land, for Judah's part was more than they had need of, so the heritage of the children of Simeon was inside their heritage. 10 And the third heritage came out for Zebulun by their families; the limit of their heritage was as far as Sarid; 11 And their limit goes up to the west to Maralah, stretching to Dabbesheth, and to the stream in front of Jokneam; 12 Then turning east from Sarid to the limit of Chisloth-tabor, it goes out to Daberath, and up to Japhia; 13 And from there it goes on east to Gath-hepher, to Eth-kazin; ending at Rimmon which goes as far as Neah; 14 And the line goes round it on the north to Hannathon, ending at the valley of Iphtah-el; 15 And Kattath and Nahalal and Shimron and Idalah and Beth-lehem; twelve towns with their unwalled places. 16 This is the heritage of the children of Zebulun by their families, these towns with their unwalled places. 17 For Issachar the fourth heritage came out, for the children of Issachar by their families; 18 And their limit was to Jezreel and Chesulloth and Shunem

19And Hapharaim and Shion and Anaharath 20 And Rabbith and Kishion
and Ebez 21 And Remeth and En-gannim and En-haddah and Beth-
pazzez; 22 And their limit goes as far as Tabor and Shahazimah and Beth-
shemesh, ending at Jordan; sixteen towns with their unwalled places. 23
This is the heritage of the tribe of the children of Issachar by their families,
these towns with their unwalled places. 24 And the fifth heritage came out
for the tribe of Asher by their families. 25 And their limit was Helkath and
Hali and Beten and Achshaph 26 And Alammelech and Amad and Mishal,
stretching to Carmel on the west and Shihor-libnath; 27 Turning to the east
to Beth-dagon and stretching to Zebulun and the valley of Iphtah-el as far
as Beth-emek and Neiel to the north; on the left it goes as far as Cabul 28
And Ebron and Rehob and Hammon and Kanah, to great Zidon; 29 And
the limit goes round to Ramah and the walled town of Tyre and Hosah,
ending at the sea by Heleb and Achzib; 30 And Ummah and Aphek and
Rehob; twenty-two towns with their unwalled places. 31 This is the heritage
of the tribe of the children of Asher by their families, these towns with their
unwalled places. 32 For the children of Naphtali the sixth heritage came
out, for the children of Naphtali by their families; 33 And their limit was
from Heleph, from the oak-tree in Zaanannim, and Adami-hannekeb and
Jabneel, as far as Lakkum, ending at Jordan; 34 And turning west to
Aznoth-tabor, the limit goes out from there to Hukkok, stretching to
Zebulun on the south, and Asher on the west, and Judah at Jordan on the
east. 35 And the walled towns are Ziddim, Zer, and Hammath, Rakkath,
and Chinnereth 36 And Adamah and Ramah and Hazor 37 And Kedesh
and Edrei and En-Hazor 38 And Iron and Migdal-el, Horem and Beth-
anath and Beth-shemesh; nineteen towns with their unwalled places. 39
This is the heritage of the tribe of the children of Naphtali by their families,
these towns with their unwalled places. 40 For the tribe of Dan by their
families the seventh heritage came out; 41 And the limit of their heritage
was Zorah and Eshtaol and Ir-shemesh 42 And Shaalabbin and Aijalon and
Ithlah 43 And Elon and Timnah and Ekron 44 And Eltekeh and
Gibbethon and Baalath 45 And Jehud and Bene-berak and Gath-rimmon;
46 And on the west was ... opposite Joppa. 47 (But the limit of the children
of Dan was not wide enough for them; so the children of Dan went up and
made war on Leshem and took it, putting it to the sword without mercy,
and they took it for their heritage and made a place for themselves there,
giving it the name of Leshem-dan, after the name of their father, Dan.) 48
This is the heritage of the tribe of the children of Dan by their families,
these towns with their unwalled places. 49 So the distribution of the land
and its limits was complete; and the children of Israel gave Joshua, the son
of Nun, a heritage among them; 50 By the orders of the Lord they gave him
the town for which he made request, Timnath-serah in the hill-country of
Ephraim: there, after building the town, he made his living-place. 51 These

are the heritages which Eleazar the priest and Joshua, the son of Nun, and the heads of families of the tribes of the children of Israel gave out at Shiloh, by the decision of the Lord, at the door of the Tent of meeting. So the distribution of the land was complete.

20

1 And the Lord said to Joshua, 2 Say to the children of Israel, Let certain towns be marked out as safe places, as I said to you by the mouth of Moses, 3 So that any man who in error and without design has taken the life of another, may go in flight to them: and they will be safe places for you from him who has the right of punishment for blood. 4 And if anyone goes in flight to one of those towns, and comes into the public place of the town, and puts his cause before the responsible men of the town, they will take him into the town and give him a place among them where he may be safe. 5 And if the one who has the right of punishment comes after him, they are not to give the taker of life up to him; because he was the cause of his neighbour's death without designing it and not in hate. 6 And he is to go on living in that town till he has to come before the meeting of the people to be judged; (till the death of him who is high priest at that time:) then the taker of life may come back to his town and to his house, to the town from which he had gone in flight. 7 So they made selection of Kedesh in Galilee in the hill-country of Naphtali, and Shechem in the hill-country of Ephraim, and Kiriath-arba (which is Hebron) in the hill-country of Judah. 8 And on the east side of Jordan at Jericho, they made selection of Bezer in the waste land, in the table-land, out of the tribe of Reuben, and Ramoth in Gilead out of the tribe of Gad, and Golan in Bashan out of the tribe of Manasseh. 9 These were the towns marked out for all the children of Israel and for the man from a strange country living among them, so that anyone causing the death of another in error, might go in flight there, and not be put to death by him who has the right of punishment for blood till he had come before the meeting of the people.

21

1 Then the heads of the families of the Levites came to Eleazar the priest and Joshua, the son of Nun, and to the heads of families of the tribes of the children of Israel; 2 And said to them in Shiloh in the land of Canaan, The Lord gave orders by Moses that we were to have towns for living in, with their grass-lands for our cattle. 3 And the children of Israel out of their heritage gave to the Levites these towns with their grass-lands, by the order

of the Lord. 4 And the heritage came out for the families of the Kohathites: the children of Aaron the priest, who were of the Levites, were given thirteen towns from the tribes of Judah, Simeon, and Benjamin. 5 The rest of the children of Kohath by their families were given ten towns from the tribes of Ephraim and Dan and the half-tribe of Manasseh. 6 The children of Gershon by their families were given thirteen towns from the tribes of Issachar and Asher and Naphtali and the half-tribe of Manasseh which was in Bashan. 7 The children of Merari by their families were given twelve towns from the tribes of Reuben and Gad and Zebulun. 8 All these towns with their grass-lands the children of Israel gave by the decision of the Lord to the Levites, as the Lord had given orders by Moses. 9 From the tribes of the children of Judah and the children of Simeon they gave these towns, listed here by name: 10These were for the children of Aaron among the families of the Kohathites, of the children of Levi: for they came first in the distribution. 11 They gave them Kiriath-arba, the town of Arba, the father of Anak, (which is Hebron) in the hill-country of Judah, with its grass-lands. 12 But the open country round the town, and its unwalled places, they gave to Caleb, the son of Jephunneh, as his property. 13 And to the children of Aaron the priest they gave Hebron with its grass-lands, the town where the taker of life might be safe, and Libnah with its grass-lands; 14 And Jattir with its grass-lands, and Eshtemoa with its grass-lands; 15And Holon with its grass-lands, and Debir with its grass-lands; 16 And Ain, and Juttah, and Beth-shemesh, with their grass-lands; nine towns from those two tribes. 17 And from the tribe of Benjamin they gave Gibeon and Geba with their grass-lands; 18 Anathoth and Almon with their grass-lands, four towns. 19 Thirteen towns with their grass-lands were given to the children of Aaron, the priests. 20 The rest of the families of the children of Kohath, the Levites, were given towns from the tribe of Ephraim. 21And they gave them Shechem with its grass-lands in the hill-country of Ephraim, the town where the taker of life might be safe, and Gezer with its grass-lands; 22 And Kibzaim and Beth-horon with their grass-lands, four towns. 23 And from the tribe of Dan, Elteke and Gibbethon with their grass-lands; 24 Aijalon and Gath-rimmon with their grass-lands, four towns. 25 And from the half-tribe of Manasseh, Taanach and Gath-rimmon with their grass-lands, two towns. 26 All the towns of the rest of the families of the children of Kohath were ten with their grass-lands. 27 And to the children of Gershon, of the families of the Levites, they gave from the half-tribe of Manasseh, Golan in Bashan with its grass-lands, the town where the taker of life might be safe, and Ashtaroth with its grass-lands, two towns. 28 And from the tribe of Issachar, Kishion and Daberath with their grass-lands; 29 Jarmuth and En-gannim with their grass-lands, four towns. 30 And from the tribe of Asher, Mishal and Abdon, with their grass-lands: 31 Helkath and Rehob with their grass-lands, four towns. 32 And from the tribe of Naphtali, Kedesh in

Galilee with its grass-lands, the town where the taker of life might be safe,
and Hammoth-dor and Kartan with their grass-lands, three towns. 33 All
the towns of the Gershonites with their families were thirteen with their
grass-lands. 34 And to the rest of the Levites, that is, the families of the
children of Merari, they gave from the tribe of Zebulun, Jokneam and
Kartah with their grass-lands; 35 Dimnah and Nahalal with their grass-
lands, four towns. 36 And from the tribe of Reuben, Bezer and Jahaz with
their grass-lands; 37Kedemoth and Mephaath with their grass-lands, four
towns. 38 And from the tribe of Gad, Ramoth in Gilead, the town where
the taker of life might be safe, and Mahanaim with their grass-lands; 39
Heshbon and Jazer with their grass-lands, four towns. 40 All these towns
were given to the children of Merari by their families, that is, the rest of the
families of the Levites; and their heritage was twelve towns. 41 All the
towns of the Levites, among the heritage of the children of Israel, were
forty-eight towns with their grass-lands. 42 Every one of these towns had
grass-lands round it. 43 So the Lord gave to Israel all the land which he
gave by oath to their fathers; so it became their heritage and their living-
place. 44 And the Lord gave them peace on every side, as he had said to
their fathers: all those who were against them gave way before them, for the
Lord gave them all up into their hands. 45 The Lord kept faith with the
house of Israel about all the good which he said he would do for them, and
all his words came true.

22

1 Then Joshua sent for the Reubenites and the Gadites and the half-tribe of
Manasseh, 2 And said to them, You have kept all the orders of Moses, the
Lord's servant, and have done everything I gave you orders to do: 3 You
have now been with your brothers for a long time; till this day you have
been doing the orders of the Lord your God. 4 And now the Lord your
God has given your brothers rest, as he said: so now you may go back to
your tents, to the land of your heritage, which Moses, the Lord's servant,
gave to you on the other side of Jordan. 5 Only take great care to do the
orders and the law which Moses, the Lord's servant, gave you; to have love
for the Lord your God and to go in all his ways; and to keep his laws and to
be true to him and to be his servants with all your heart and with all your
soul. 6 Then Joshua gave them his blessing and sent them away: and they
went back to their tents. 7 Now to the one half of the tribe of Manasseh,
Moses had given a heritage in Bashan; but to the other half, Joshua gave a
heritage among their brothers on the west side of Jordan. Now when
Joshua sent them away to their tents, he gave them his blessing, 8 And said
to them, Go back with much wealth to your tents, and with very much

cattle, with silver and gold and brass and iron, and with a very great store of
clothing; give your brothers a part of the goods taken in the war. 9 So
Reuben and Gad and the half-tribe of Manasseh went back, parting from
the children of Israel at Shiloh in the land of Canaan, to go to the land of
Gilead, to the land of their heritage which had been given to them by the
Lord's order to Moses. 10 Now when they came to the country by Jordan in
the land of Canaan, the children of Reuben and the children of Gad and the
half-tribe of Manasseh put up there, by Jordan, a great altar, seen from far.
11 And news came to the children of Israel, See, the children of Reuben
and the children of Gad and the half-tribe of Manasseh have put up an altar
opposite the land of Canaan, in the country by Jordan on the side which is
Israel's. 12 Then all the meeting of the children of Israel, hearing this, came
together at Shiloh to go up against them to war. 13And the children of
Israel sent Phinehas, the son of Eleazar the priest, to the children of
Reuben and the children of Gad and the half-tribe of Manasseh, to the land
of Gilead, 14 And with him they sent ten chiefs, one for every tribe of the
children of Israel, every one of them the head of his house among the
families of Israel. 15 And they came to the children of Reuben and the
children of Gad and the half-tribe of Manasseh, to the land of Gilead, and
said to them, 16 This is what all the meeting of the people of the Lord has
said, What is this wrong which you have done against the God of Israel,
turning back this day from the Lord and building an altar for yourselves,
and being false to the Lord? 17 Was not the sin of Baal-peor great enough,
from which we are not clear even to this day, though punishment came on
the people of the Lord, 18 That now you are turned back from the Lord?
and, because you are false to him today, tomorrow his wrath will be let
loose on all the people of Israel. 19 But if the land you now have is unclean,
come over into the Lord's land where his House is, and take up your
heritage among us: but do not be false to the Lord and to us by building
yourselves an altar in addition to the altar of the Lord our God. 20 Did not
Achan, the son of Zerah, do wrong about the cursed thing, causing wrath
to come on all the people of Israel? And not on him only came the
punishment of death. 21 Then the children of Reuben and the children of
Gad and the half-tribe of Manasseh said in answer to the heads of the
families of Israel, 22 God, even God the Lord, God, even God the Lord, he
sees, and Israel will see--if it is in pride or in sin against the Lord, 23 That
we have made ourselves an altar, being false to the Lord, keep us not safe
from death this day; and if for the purpose of offering burned offerings on
it and meal offerings, or peace-offerings, let the Lord himself send
punishment for it; 24 And if we have not, in fact, done this designedly and
with purpose, having in our minds the fear that in time to come your
children might say to our children, What have you to do with the Lord, the
God of Israel? 25 For the Lord has made Jordan a line of division between

us and you, the children of Reuben and the children of Gad; you have no
part in the Lord: so your children will make our children give up fearing the
Lord. 26 So we said, Let us now make an altar for ourselves, not for burned
offerings or for the offerings of beasts: 27 But to be a witness between us
and you, and between the future generations, that we have the right of
worshipping the Lord with our burned offerings and our offerings of beasts
and our peace-offerings; so that your children will not be able to say to our
children in time to come, You have no part in the Lord. 28 For we said to
ourselves, If they say this to us or to future generations, then we will say,
See this copy of the Lord's altar which our fathers made, not for burned
offerings or offerings of beasts, but for a witness between us and you. 29
Never let it be said that we were false to the Lord, turning back this day
from him and building an altar for burned offerings and meal offerings and
offerings of beasts, in addition to the altar of the Lord our God which is
before his House. 30 Then Phinehas the priest and the chiefs of the
meeting and the heads of the families of Israel who were with him, hearing
what the children of Reuben and the children of Gad and the children of
Manasseh said, were pleased. 31 And Phinehas, the son of Eleazar the
priest, said to the children of Reuben and the children of Gad and the
children of Manasseh, Now we are certain that the Lord is among us,
because you have not done this wrong against the Lord: and you have kept
us from falling into the hands of the Lord. 32 Then Phinehas, the son of
Eleazar the priest, and the chiefs went back from the land of Gilead, from
the children of Reuben and the children of Gad, and came to the children
of Israel in Canaan and gave them the news. 33 And the children of Israel
were pleased about this; and they gave praise to God, and had no more
thought of going to war against the children of Reuben and the children of
Gad for the destruction of their land. 34 And the children of Reuben and
the children of Gad gave to that altar the name of Ed. For, they said, It is a
witness between us that the Lord is God.

23

1 Now after a long time, when the Lord had given Israel rest from wars on
every side, and Joshua was old and full of years, 2 Joshua sent for all Israel,
for their responsible men and their chiefs and their judges and their
overseers, and said to them, I am old, and full of years: 3 You have seen
everything the Lord your God has done to all these nations because of you;
for it is the Lord your God who has been fighting for you. 4 Now I have
given to you, as the heritage of your tribes, all these nations which are still
in the land, together with those cut off by me, from Jordan as far as the
Great Sea on the west 5 The Lord your God will send them away by force,

driving them out before you; and you are to take their land for your
heritage, as the Lord your God said to you. 6 So be very strong to keep and
do whatever is recorded in the book of the law of Moses, not turning away
from it to the right or to the left; 7 Have nothing to do with these nations
who still are living among you; let not their gods be named by you or used
in your oaths; do not be their servants or give them worship: 8 But be true
to the Lord your God as you have been till this day. 9 For the Lord has sent
out from before you nations great and strong: and they have all given way
before you till this day. 10 One man of you is able to put to flight a
thousand; for it is the Lord your God who is fighting for you, as he has said
to you. 11 So keep watch on yourselves, and see that you have love for the
Lord your God. 12 For if you go back, joining yourselves to the rest of
these nations who are still among you, getting married to them and living
with them and they with you: 13 Then you may be certain that the Lord
your God will not go on driving these nations out from before you; but
they will become a danger and a cause of sin to you, a whip for your sides
and thorns in your eyes, till you are cut off from this good land which the
Lord your God has given you. 14 Now I am about to go the way of all the
earth: and you have seen and are certain, all of you, in your hearts and souls,
that in all the good things which the Lord said about you, he has kept faith
with you; everything has come true for you 15 And you will see that, as all
the good things which the Lord your God undertook to do for you, have
come to you, so the Lord will send down on you all the evil things till he
has made your destruction complete, and you are cut off from the good
land which the Lord your God has given you. 16 If the agreement of the
Lord your God, which was given to you by his orders, is broken, and you
become the servants of other gods and give them worship, then the wrath
of the Lord will be burning against you, and you will quickly be cut off
from the good land which he has given you.

24

1 Then Joshua got all the tribes of Israel together at Shechem; and he sent
for the responsible men of Israel and their chiefs and their judges and their
overseers; and they took their place before God. 2 And Joshua said to all
the people, These are the words of the Lord, the God of Israel: In the past
your fathers, Terah, the father of Abraham, and the father of Nahor, were
living on the other side of the River: and they were worshipping other gods.
3 And I took your father Abraham from the other side of the River, guiding
him through all the land of Canaan; I made his offspring great in number,
and gave him Isaac. 4 And to Isaac I gave Jacob and Esau: to Esau I gave
Mount Seir, as his heritage; but Jacob and his children went down to Egypt.

5 And I sent Moses and Aaron, troubling Egypt by all the signs I did among
them: and after that I took you out. 6 I took your fathers out of Egypt: and
you came to the Red Sea; and the Egyptians came after your fathers to the
Red Sea, with their war-carriages and their horsemen. 7 And at their cry, the
Lord made it dark between you and the Egyptians, and made the sea go
over them, covering them with its waters; your eyes have seen what I did in
Egypt: then for a long time you were living in the waste land. 8 And I took
you into the lands of the Amorites on the other side of Jordan; and they
made war on you, and I gave them into your hands and you took their land;
and I sent destruction on them before you. 9 Then Balak, the son of
Zippor, king of Moab, went up to war against Israel; and he sent for
Balaam, the son of Beor, to put a curse on you: 10 But I did not give ear to
Balaam; and so he went on blessing you; and I kept you safe from him. 11
Then you went over Jordan and came to Jericho: and the men of Jericho
made war on you, the Amorites and the Perizzites and the Canaanites and
the Hittites and the Girgashites and the Hivites and the Jebusites: and I
gave them up into your hands. 12 And I sent the hornet before you, driving
out the two kings of the Amorites before you, not with your sword and
your bow.13 And I gave you a land on which you had done no work, and
towns not of your building, and you are now living in them; and your food
comes from vine-gardens and olive-gardens not of your planting. 14 So
now, go in fear of the Lord, and be his servants with true hearts: put away
the gods worshipped by your fathers across the River and in Egypt, and be
servants of the Lord. 15 And if it seems evil to you to be the servants of the
Lord, make the decision this day whose servants you will be: of the gods
whose servants your fathers were across the River, or of the gods of the
Amorites in whose land you are living: but I and my house will be the
servants of the Lord. 16 Then the people in answer said, Never will we give
up the Lord to be the servants of other gods; 17 For it is the Lord our God
who has taken us and our fathers out of the land of Egypt, out of the
prison-house, and who did all those great signs before our eyes, and kept us
safe on all our journeys, and among all the peoples through whom we went:
18 And the Lord sent out from before us all the peoples, the Amorites
living in the land: so we will be the servants of the Lord, for he is our God.
19 And Joshua said to the people, You are not able to be the servants of the
Lord, for he is a holy God, a God who will not let his honour be given to
another: he will have no mercy on your wrongdoing or your sins. 20 If you
are turned away from the Lord and become the servants of strange gods,
then turning against you he will do you evil, cutting you off, after he has
done you good. 21 And the people said to Joshua, No! But we will be the
servants of the Lord. 22 And Joshua said to the people, You are witnesses
against yourselves that you have made the decision to be the servants of the
Lord. And they said, We are witnesses. 23 Then, he said, put away the

strange gods among you, turning your hearts to the Lord, the God of Israel.
24 And the people said to Joshua, We will be the servants of the Lord our
God, and we will give ear to his voice. 25 So Joshua made an agreement
with the people that day, and gave them a rule and a law in Shechem. 26
And Joshua put these words on record, writing them in the book of the law
of God; and he took a great stone, and put it up there under the oak-tree
which was in the holy place of the Lord. 27 And Joshua said to all the
people, See now, this stone is to be a witness against us; for all the words of
the Lord have been said to us in its hearing: so it will be a witness against
you if you are false to the Lord your God. 28 Then Joshua let the people go
away, every man to his heritage. 29 Now after these things, the death of
Joshua, the son of Nun, the servant of the Lord, took place, he being then a
hundred and ten years old. 30 And they put his body in the earth in the land
of his heritage in Timnath-serah, in the hill-country of Ephraim, to the
north of Mount Gaash. 31 And Israel was true to the Lord all the days of
Joshua, and all the days of the older men who were still living after Joshua's
death, and had seen what the Lord had done for Israel. 32 And the bones
of Joseph, which the children of Israel had taken up from Egypt, they put
in the earth in Shechem, in the property which Jacob had got from the sons
of Hamor, the father of Shechem, for a hundred shekels: and they became
the heritage of the children of Joseph. 33 Then the death of Eleazar, the
son of Aaron, took place; and his body was put in the earth in the hill of
Phinehas his son, which had been given to him in the hill-country of
Ephraim.

JOSHUA

WEBSTER BIBLE

1

1:1 Now after the death of Moses the servant of the LORD, it came to pass, that the LORD spoke to Joshua the son of Nun, Moses's minister, saying,
1:2 Moses my servant is dead; now therefore arise, go over this Jordan, thou, and all this people, to the land which I do give to them, even to the children of Israel.
1:3 Every place that the sole of your foot shall tread upon, that have I given to you, as I said to Moses.
1:4 From the wilderness and this Lebanon even to the great river, the river Euphrates, all the land of the Hittites, and to the great sea towards the setting of the sun, shall be your border.
1:5 There shall not any man be able to stand before thee all the days of thy life: as I was with Moses, so I will be with thee: I will not fail thee, nor forsake thee.
1:6 Be strong and of a good courage: for to this people shalt thou divide for an inheritance the land which I swore to their fathers to give them.
1:7 Only be thou strong and very courageous, that thou mayest observe to do according to all the law which Moses my servant commanded thee: turn not from it to the right hand or to the left, that thou mayest prosper whithersoever thou goest.
1:8 This book of the law shall not depart out of thy mouth; but thou shalt meditate in it day and night, that thou mayest observe to do according to all

that is written therein: for then thou shalt make thy way prosperous, and then thou shalt have good success.
1:9 Have not I commanded thee? Be strong and of a good courage; be not afraid, neither be thou dismayed: for the LORD thy God is with thee whithersoever thou goest.
1:10 Then Joshua commanded the officers of the people, saying,
1:11 Pass through the host, and command the people, saying, Prepare you provisions; for within three days ye shall pass over this Jordan, to go in to possess the land which the LORD your God giveth you to possess it.
1:12 And to the Reubenites, and to the Gadites, and to half the tribe of Manasseh, spoke Joshua, saying,
1:13 Remember the word which Moses the servant of the LORD commanded you, saying, The LORD your God hath given you rest, and hath given you this land.
1:14 Your wives, your little ones, and your cattle shall remain in the land which Moses gave you on this side of Jordan; but ye shall pass before your brethren armed, all the mighty men of valor, and help them;
1:15 Until the LORD shall have given your brethren rest, as he hath given you, and they also have possessed the land which the LORD your God giveth them: then ye shall return to the land of your possession, and enjoy it, which Moses the LORD'S servant gave you on this side of Jordan towards the sun-rising.
1:16 And they answered Joshua, saying, All that thou commandest us, we will do, and whithersoever thou sendest us, we will go.
1:17 According as we hearkened to Moses in all things, so will we hearken to thee: only the LORD thy God be with thee, as he was with Moses.
1:18 Every one that doth rebel against thy commandment, and will not hearken to thy words in all that thou commandest him, shall be put to death: only be strong and of a good courage.

2

2:1 And Joshua the son of Nun sent from Shittim two men to spy secretly, saying, Go, view the land, even Jericho. And they went, and came into the house of a harlot, named Rahab, and lodged there.
2:2 And it was told the king of Jericho, saying, Behold, there came men in hither to-night of the children of Israel, to search out the country.
2:3 And the king of Jericho sent to Rahab, saying, Bring forth the men that have come to thee, who have entered into thy house: for they have come to search out all the country.
2:4 And the woman took the two men, and hid them, and said thus, There

came men to me, but I knew not whence they were:
2:5 And it came to pass about the time of shutting the gate, when it was dark, that the men went out: whither the men went, I know not: pursue after them quickly; for ye will overtake them.
2:6 But she had brought them up to the roof of the house, and hid them with the stalks of flax, which she had laid in order upon the roof.
2:7 And the men pursued them the way to Jordan to the fords: and as soon as they who pursued them had gone out, they shut the gate.
2:8 And before they had lain down, she came up to them upon the roof;
2:9 And she said to the men, I know that the LORD hath given you the land, and that your terror hath fallen upon us, and that all the inhabitants of the land faint because of you.
2:10 For we have heard how the LORD dried up the water of the Red sea for you, when ye came out of Egypt; and what ye did to the two kings of the Amorites, that were on the other side of Jordan, Sihon and Og, whom ye utterly destroyed.
2:11 And as soon as we had heard these things, our hearts did melt, neither did there remain any more courage in any man, because of you: for the LORD your God, he is God in heaven above, and in earth beneath.
2:12 Now therefore, I pray you, swear to me by the LORD, since I have showed you kindness, that ye will also show kindness to my father's house, and give me a true token:
2:13 And that ye will save alive my father, and my mother, and my brethren, and my sisters, and all that they have, and deliver our lives from death.
2:14 And the men answered her, Our life for yours, if ye utter not this our business. And it shall be, when the LORD hath given us the land, that we will deal kindly and truly with thee.
2:15 Then she let them down by a cord through the window: for her house was upon the town-wall, and she dwelt upon the wall.
2:16 And she said to them, Depart to the mountain, lest the pursuers meet you; and hide yourselves there three days, until the pursuers have returned: and afterward ye may go your way.
2:17 And the men said to her, We will be blameless of this thy oath which thou hast made us swear.
2:18 Behold, when we come into the land, thou shalt bind this line of scarlet thread in the window by which thou didst let us down: and thou shalt bring thy father, and thy mother, and thy brethren, and all thy father's household home to thee.
2:19 And it shall be, that whoever shall go out of the doors of thy house into the street, his blood shall be upon his head, and we will be guiltless: and whoever shall be with thee in the house, his blood shall be on our head, if any hand be upon him.
2:20 And if thou shalt utter this our business, then we will be quit of thy

oath which thou hast made us to swear.
2:21 And she said, According to your words, so be it. And she sent them away, and they departed: and she bound the scarlet line in the window.
2:22 And they went, and came to the mountain, and abode there three days, until the pursuers had returned: and the pursuers sought them throughout all the way, but found them not.
2:23 So the two men returned, and descended from the mountain, and passed over, and came to Joshua the son of Nun, and told him all things that befell them:
2:24 And they said to Joshua, Truly the LORD hath delivered into our hands all the land; for even all the inhabitants of the country do faint because of us.

3

3:1 And Joshua rose early in the morning; and they removed from Shittim, and came to Jordan, he and all the children of Israel, and lodged there before they passed over.
3:2 And it came to pass after three days, that the officers went through the host;
3:3 And they commanded the people, saying, When ye see the ark of the covenant of the LORD your God, and the priests the Levites bearing it, then ye shall remove from your place, and go after it.
3:4 Yet there shall be a space between you and it, about two thousand cubits by measure: come not near to it, that ye may know the way by which ye must go: for ye have not passed this way heretofore.
3:5 And Joshua said to the people, Sanctify yourselves: for to-morrow the LORD will do wonders among you.
3:6 And Joshua spoke to the priests, saying, Take up the ark of the covenant, and pass over before the people. And they took up the ark of the covenant, and went before the people.
3:7 And the LORD said to Joshua, This day will I begin to magnify thee in the sight of all Israel, that they may know that as I was with Moses, so I will be with thee.
3:8 And thou shalt command the priests that bear the ark of the covenant, saying, When ye have come to the brink of the water of Jordan, ye shall stand still in Jordan.
3:9 And Joshua said to the children of Israel, Come hither, and hear the words of the LORD your God.
3:10 And Joshua said, By this ye shall know that the living God is among you, and that he will without fail drive out from before you the Canaanites,

and the Hittites, and the Hivites, and the Perizzites, and the Girgashites, and the Amorites, and the Jebusites.
3:11 Behold, the ark of the covenant of the Lord of all the earth passeth over before you into Jordan.
3:12 Now therefore take you twelve men out of the tribes of Israel, out of every tribe a man.
3:13 And it shall come to pass, as soon as the soles of the feet of the priests that bear the ark of the LORD, the Lord of all the earth, shall rest in the waters of Jordan, that the waters of Jordan shall be cut off from the waters that come down from above; and they shall stand in a heap.
3:14 And it came to pass, when the people removed from their tents to pass over Jordan, and the priests bearing the ark of the covenant before the people;
3:15 And as they that bore the ark had come to Jordan, and the feet of the priests that bore the ark were dipped in the brim of the water, (for Jordan overfloweth all its banks all the time of harvest,)
3:16 That the waters which came down from above stood and rose up in a heap very far from the city Adam, that is beside Zaretan; and those that came down towards the sea of the plain, even the salt sea, failed, and were cut off: and the people passed over right against Jericho.
3:17 And the priests that bore the ark of the covenant of the LORD stood firm on dry ground in the midst of Jordan, and all the Israelites passed over on dry ground, until all the people had passed quite over Jordan.

4

4:1 And it came to pass, when all the people had quite passed over Jordan, that the LORD spoke to Joshua, saying,
4:2 Take you twelve men from the people, from every tribe a man,
4:3 And command ye them, saying, Take you hence out of the midst of Jordan, from the place where the priests' feet stood firm, twelve stones, and ye shall carry them over with you, and leave them in the lodging-place where ye shall lodge this night.
4:4 Then Joshua called the twelve men, whom he had prepared of the children of Israel, of every tribe a man:
4:5 And Joshua said to them, Pass over before the ark of the LORD your God into the midst of Jordan, and take ye up every man of you a stone upon his shoulder, according to the number of the tribes of the children of Israel:
4:6 That this may be a sign among you, that when your children ask their fathers in time to come, saying, What mean ye by these stones?

4:7 Then ye shall answer them, That the waters of Jordan were cut off before the ark of the covenant of the LORD; when it passed over Jordan, the waters of Jordan were cut off: and these stones shall be for a memorial to the children of Israel for ever.
4:8 And the children of Israel did so as Joshua commanded, and took up twelve stones from the midst of Jordan, as the the LORD commanded Joshua, according to the number of the tribes of the children of Israel, and carried them over with them to the place where they lodged, and laid them down there.
4:9 And Joshua set up twelve stones in the midst of Jordan, in the place where the feet of the priests who bore the ark of the covenant stood: and they are there to this day.
4:10 For the priests who bore the ark stood in the midst of Jordan, until every thing was finished that the LORD commanded Joshua to speak to the people, according to all that Moses commanded Joshua: and the people hasted and passed over.
4:11 And it came to pass, when all the people had quite passed over, that the ark of the LORD passed over, and the priests in the presence of the people.
4:12 And the children of Reuben, and the children of Gad, and half the tribe of Manasseh, passed over armed before the children of Israel, as Moses directed them:
4:13 About forty thousand prepared for war passed over before the LORD to battle, to the plains of Jericho.
4:14 On that day the LORD magnified Joshua in the sight of all Israel, and they feared him, as they feared Moses, all the days of his life.
4:15 And the LORD spoke to Joshua, saying,
4:16 Command the priests that bear the ark of the testimony, that they come up out of Jordan.
4:17 Joshua therefore commanded the priests, saying, Come ye up out of Jordan.
4:18 And it came to pass, when the priests that bore the ark of the covenant of the LORD had come up out of the midst of Jordan, and the soles of the priests' feet were lifted up upon the dry land, that the waters of Jordan returned to their place, and flowed over all its banks, as they did before.
4:19 And the people came up out of Jordan on the tenth day of the first month, and encamped in Gilgal, in the east border of Jericho.
4:20 And those twelve stones which they took out of Jordan, did Joshua set up in Gilgal.
4:21 And he spoke to the children of Israel, saying, When your children shall ask their fathers in time to come, saying, What mean these stones?
4:22 Then ye shall let your children know, saying, Israel came over this Jordan on dry land.

4:23 For the LORD your God dried up the waters of Jordan from before you, until ye had passed over, as the LORD your God did to the Red sea, which he dried up from before us, until we had gone over:
4:24 That all the people of the earth might know the hand of the LORD that it is mighty: that ye might fear the LORD your God for ever.

5

5:1 And it came to pass, when all the kings of the Amorites who were on the side of Jordan westward, and all the kings of the Canaanites who were by the sea, heard that the LORD had dried up the waters of Jordan from before the children of Israel, until we had passed over, that their heart melted; neither was there spirit in them any more, because of the children of Israel.
5:2 At that time the LORD said to Joshua, Make thee sharp knives, and circumcise again the children of Israel the second time.
5:3 And Joshua made him sharp knives, and circumcised the children of Israel at the hill of the foreskins.
5:4 And this is the cause why Joshua did circumcise: All the people that came out of Egypt, that were males, even all the men of war died in the wilderness by the way, after they came out of Egypt.
5:5 Now all the people that came out were circumcised; but all the people that were born in the wilderness by the way as they came forth from Egypt, them they had not circumcised.
5:6 For the children of Israel walked forty years in the wilderness, till all the people that were men of war who came out of Egypt were consumed, because they obeyed not the voice of the LORD: to whom the LORD swore that he would not show them the land which the LORD swore to their fathers that he would give us, a land that floweth with milk and honey.
5:7 And their children, whom he raised up in their stead, them Joshua circumcised: for they were uncircumcised, because they had not circumcised them by the way.
5:8 And it came to pass when they had done circumcising all the people, that they abode in their places in the camp, till they were whole.
5:9 And the LORD said to Joshua, This day have I rolled away the reproach of Egypt from off you: Wherefore the name of the place is called Gilgal to this day.
5:10 And the children of Israel encamped in Gilgal, and kept the passover on the fourteenth day of the month at evening in the plains of Jericho.
5:11 And they ate of the old corn of the land on the morrow after the passover, unleavened cakes, and parched corn in the same day.

5:12 And the manna ceased on the morrow after they had eaten of the old corn of the land; neither had the children of Israel manna any more; but they ate of the fruit of the land of Canaan that year.
5:13 And it came to pass when Joshua was by Jericho, that he lifted up his eyes and looked, and behold, there stood a man over against him with his sword drawn in his hand: and Joshua went to him, and said to him, Art thou for us, or for our adversaries?
5:14 And he said, No; but as captain of the host of the LORD am I now come. And Joshua fell on his face to the earth, and worshiped, and said to him, What saith my lord to his servant?
5:15 And the captain of the LORD'S host said to Joshua, Loose thy shoe from off thy foot, for the place on which thou standest is holy: and Joshua did so.

6

6:1 Now Jericho was closely shut up because of the children of Israel: none went out, and none came in.
6:2 And the LORD said to Joshua, See, I have given into thy hand Jericho, and its king, and the mighty men of valor.
6:3 And ye shall compass the city, all ye men of war, and go round the city once: thus shalt thou do six days.
6:4 And seven priests shall bear before the ark seven trumpets of rams' horns: and the seventh day ye shall compass the city seven times, and the priests shall blow with the trumpets.
6:5 And it shall come to pass, that when they make a long blast with the ram's horn, and when ye hear the sound of the trumpet, all the people shall shout with a great shout: and the wall of the city shall fall down flat, and the people shall ascend every man straight before him.
6:6 And Joshua the son of Nun called the priests, and said to them, Take up the ark of the covenant, and let seven priests bear seven trumpets of rams' horns before the ark of the LORD.
6:7 And he said to the people, Pass on, and compass the city, and let him that is armed pass on before the ark of the LORD.
6:8 And it came to pass, when Joshua had spoken to the people, that the seven priests bearing the seven trumpets of rams' horns passed on before the LORD, and blew with the trumpets: and the ark of the covenant of the LORD followed them.
6:9 And the armed men went before the priests that blew with the trumpets, and the rear-guard came after the ark, the priests going on, and blowing with the trumpets.

6:10 And Joshua had commanded the people, saying, Ye shall not shout, nor make any noise with your voice, neither shall any word proceed from your mouth, until the day I bid you shout, then shall ye shout.
6:11 So the ark of the LORD compassed the city, going about it once: and they came into the camp, and lodged in the camp.
6:12 And Joshua rose early in the morning, and the priests took up the ark of the LORD.
6:13 And seven priests bearing seven trumpets of rams' horns before the ark of the LORD went on continually, and blew with the trumpets: and the armed men went before them; but the rear-guard came after the ark of the LORD, the priests going on, and blowing with the trumpets.
6:14 And the second day they compassed the city once, and returned into the camp. So they did six days.
6:15 And it came to pass on the seventh day, that they rose early about the dawning of the day, and compassed the city after the same manner seven times: only on that day they compassed the city seven times.
6:16 And it came to pass at the seventh time, when the priests blew with the trumpets, Joshua said to the people, Shout; for the LORD hath given you the city.
6:17 And the city shall be accursed, even it, and all that are in it, to the LORD: only Rahab the harlot shall live, she and all that are with her in the house, because she hid the messengers that we sent.
6:18 And ye, in any wise keep yourselves from the accursed thing, lest ye make yourselves accursed, when ye take of the accursed thing, and make the camp of Israel a curse, and trouble it.
6:19 But all the silver, and gold, and vessels of brass and iron, are consecrated to the LORD: they shall come into the treasury of the LORD.
6:20 So the people shouted when the priests blew with the trumpets: and it came to pass, when the people heard the sound of the trumpet, and the people shouted with a great shout, that the wall fell down flat, so that the people went up into the city, every man straight before him, and they took the city.
6:21 And they utterly destroyed all that was in the city, both man and woman, young and old, and ox, and sheep, and ass, with the edge of the sword.
6:22 But Joshua had said to the two men that spied out the country, Go into the harlot's house, and bring out thence the woman, and all that she hath, as ye swore to her.
6:23 And the young men that were spies went in, and brought out Rahab, and her father, and her mother, and her brethren, and all that she had; and they brought out all her kindred, and left them without the camp of Israel.
6:24 And they burnt the city with fire, and all that was in it: only the silver, and the gold, and the vessels of brass and of iron, they put into the treasury

of the house of the LORD.
6:25 And Joshua saved Rahab the harlot alive, and her father's household, and all that she had; and she dwelleth in Israel even to this day; because she hid the messengers which Joshua sent to spy out Jericho.
6:26 And Joshua adjured them at that time, saying, Cursed be the man before the LORD, that riseth up and buildeth this city Jericho: he shall lay its foundation in his first-born, and in his youngest son shall he set up the gates of it.
6:27 So the LORD was with Joshua; and his fame was noised throughout all the country.

7

7:1 But the children of Israel committed a trespass in the accursed thing: for Achan, the son of Carmi, the son of Zabdi, the son of Zerah, of the tribe of Judah, took of the accursed thing: and the anger of the LORD was kindled against the children of Israel.
7:2 And Joshua sent men from Jericho to Ai, which is beside Beth-aven, on the east side of Beth-el, and spoke to them, saying, Go up and view the country. And the men went up and viewed Ai.
7:3 And they returned to Joshua, and said to him, Let not all the people go up; but let about two or three thousand men go up and smite Ai; and make not all the people to labor thither; for they are but few.
7:4 So there went up thither of the people about three thousand men: and they fled before the men of Ai.
7:5 And the men of Ai smote of them about thirty and six men: for they chased them from before the gate even to Shebarim, and smote them in the going down: wherefore the hearts of the people melted, and became as water.
7:6 And Joshua rent his clothes, and fell to the earth upon his face before the ark of the LORD until the evening, he and the elders of Israel, and put dust upon their heads.
7:7 And Joshua said, Alas, O Lord GOD, why hast thou at all brought this people over Jordan, to deliver us into the hand of the Amorites, to destroy us? O that we had been content, and dwelt on the other side of Jordan.
7:8 O Lord, what shall I say, when Israel turn their backs before their enemies!
7:9 For the Canaanites, and all the inhabitants of the land will hear of it, and will environ us, and cut off our name from the earth: and what wilt thou do to thy great name?
7:10 And the LORD said to Joshua, Arise; Why liest thou thus upon thy

face?
7:11 Israel hath sinned, and they have also transgressed my covenant which
I commanded them: for they have even taken of the accursed thing, and
have also stolen, and dissembled also, and they have put it even among their
own goods.
7:12 Therefore the children of Israel could not stand before their enemies,
but turned their backs before their enemies, because they were accursed:
neither will I be with you any more, except ye destroy the accursed from
among you.
7:13 Rise, sanctify the people, and say, Sanctify yourselves against tomorrow: for thus saith the LORD God of Israel, There is an accursed thing
in the midst of thee, O Israel: thou canst not stand before thy enemies, until
ye take away the accursed thing from among you.
7:14 In the morning therefore ye shall be brought according to your tribes:
and it shall be, that the tribe which the LORD taketh shall come according
to their families: and the family which the LORD shall take shall come by
households; and the household which the LORD shall take shall come man
by man.
7:15 And it shall be, that he that is taken with the accursed thing shall be
burnt with fire, he and all that he hath: because he hath transgressed the
covenant of the LORD, and because he hath wrought folly in Israel.
7:16 So Joshua rose early in the morning, and brought Israel by their tribes;
and the tribe of Judah was taken:
7:17 And he brought the family of Judah; and he took the family of the
Zarhites: and he brought the family of the Zarhites man by man; and Zabdi
was taken:
7:18 And he brought his household man by man; and Achan the son of
Carmi, the son of Zabdi, the son of Zerah, of the tribe of Judah, was taken.
7:19 And Joshua said to Achan, My son, give, I pray thee, glory to the
LORD God of Israel, and make confession to him; and tell me now what
thou hast done, hide it not from me.
7:20 And Achan answered Joshua, and said, Indeed I have sinned against
the LORD God of Israel, and thus and thus have I done.
7:21 When I saw among the spoils a goodly Babylonish garment, and two
hundred shekels of silver, and a wedge of gold of fifty shekels weight, then
I coveted them, and took them, and behold, they are hid in the earth in the
midst of my tent, and the silver under it.
7:22 So Joshua sent messengers, and they ran to the tent, and behold, it was
hid in his tent, and the silver under it.
7:23 And they took them from the midst of the tent, and brought them to
Joshua, and to all the children of Israel, and laid them out before the
LORD.
7:24 And Joshua, and all Israel with him, took Achan the son of Zerah, and

the silver, and the garment, and the wedge of gold, and his sons, and his daughters, and his oxen, and his asses, and his sheep, and his tent, and all that he had: and they brought them to the valley of Achor.
7:25 And Joshua said, why hast thou troubled us? the LORD shall trouble thee this day. And all Israel stoned him with stones, and burned them with fire, after they had stoned them with stones.
7:26 And they raised over him a great heap of stones to this day. So the LORD turned from the fierceness of his anger: wherefore the name of that place was called the valley of Achor to this day.

8

8:1 And the LORD said to Joshua, Fear not, neither be thou dismayed: take all the people of war with thee, and arise, go up to Ai: see, I have given into thy hand the king of Ai, and his people, and his city, and his land:
8:2 And thou shalt do to Ai and her king, as thou didst to Jericho and her king: only its spoil, and its cattle, shall ye take for a prey to yourselves: lay thee an ambush for the city behind it.
8:3 So Joshua arose, and all the people of war, to go up against Ai: and Joshua chose out thirty thousand mighty men of valor, and sent them away by night.
8:4 And he commanded them, saying, Behold, ye shall lie in wait against the city, even behind the city: go not very far from the city, but be ye all ready:
8:5 And I, and all the people that are with me, will approach to the city: and it shall come to pass when they come out against us, as at the first, that we will flee before them,
8:6 (For they will come out after us) till we have drawn them from the city; for they will say, They flee before us, as at the first: therefore we will flee before them.
8:7 Then ye shall rise from the ambush and seize upon the city: for the LORD your God will deliver it into your hand,
8:8 And it shall be when ye have taken the city, that ye shall set the city on fire: according to the commandment of the LORD shall ye do. See, I have commanded you.
8:9 Joshua therefore sent them forth; and they went to lie in ambush, and abode between Beth-el and Ai, on the west side of Ai: but Joshua lodged that night among the people.
8:10 And Joshua rose early in the morning, and numbered the people, and went up, he and the elders of Israel, before the people to Ai.
8:11 And all the people, even the people of war that were with him, went up, and drew nigh, and came before the city, and pitched on the north side

of Ai: now there was a valley between them and Ai.
8:12 And he took about five thousand men; and set them to lie in ambush
between Beth-el and Ai, on the west side of the city.
8:13 And when they had set the people, even all the host that was on the
north of the city, and their liers in wait on the west of the city, Joshua went
that night into the midst of the valley.
8:14 And it came to pass when the king of Ai saw it, that they hasted and
rose early, and the men of the city went out against Israel to battle, he and
all his people, at a time appointed, before the plain: but he knew not that
there were liers in ambush against him behind the city.
8:15 And Joshua and all Israel made as if they were beaten before them, and
fled by the way of the wilderness.
8:16 And all the people that were in Ai were called together to pursue them:
and they pursued Joshua, and were drawn away from the city.
8:17 And there was not a man left in Ai, or Beth-el that went not out after
Israel: and they left the city open, and pursued Israel.
8:18 And the LORD said to Joshua, Stretch out the spear that is in thy hand
towards Ai; for I will give it into thy hand. And Joshua stretched out the
spear that he had in his hand towards the city.
8:19 And the ambush arose quickly out of their place, and they ran as soon
as he had stretched out his hand: and they entered into the city, and took it,
and hasted, and set the city on fire.
8:20 And when the men of Ai looked behind them, they saw, and behold,
the smoke of the city ascended to heaven, and they had no power to flee
this way or that way: and the people that fled to the wilderness turned back
upon the pursuers.
8:21 And when Joshua and all Israel saw that the ambush had taken the city,
and that the smoke of the city ascended, then they turned again and slew
the men of Ai.
8:22 And the other issued out of the city against them; so they were in the
midst of Israel, some on this side, and some on that side: and they smote
them, so that they let none of them remain or escape.
8:23 And the king of Ai they took alive, and brought him to Joshua.
8:24 And it came to pass when Israel had made an end of slaying all the
inhabitants of Ai in the field, in the wilderness in which they chased them,
and when they had all fallen on the edge of the sword, until they were
consumed, that all the Israelites returned to Ai, and smote it with the edge
of the sword.
8:25 And so it was, that all that fell that day, both of men and women, were
twelve thousand, even all the men of Ai.
8:26 For Joshua drew not his hand back with which he stretched out the
spear, until he had utterly destroyed all the inhabitants of Ai.
8:27 Only the cattle and the spoil of that city Israel took for a prey to

themselves, according to the word of the LORD which he commanded Joshua.
8:28 And Joshua burnt Ai, and made it a heap for ever, even a desolation to this day.
8:29 And the king of Ai he hanged on a tree until evening: and as soon as the sun was down, Joshua commanded that they should take his carcass down from the tree, and cast it at the entering of the gate of the city, and raise upon it a great heap of stones, that remaineth to this day.
8:30 Then Joshua built an altar to the LORD God of Israel in mount Ebal,
8:31 As Moses the servant of the LORD commanded the children of Israel, as it is written in the book of the law of Moses, an altar of whole stones, over which no man hath lifted up any iron: and they offered upon it burnt-offerings to the LORD, and sacrificed peace-offerings.
8:32 And he wrote there upon the stones a copy of the law of Moses, which he wrote in the presence of the children of Israel.
8:33 And all Israel, and their elders, and officers, and their judges, stood on this side of the ark, and on that side, before the priests the Levites, who bore the ark of the covenant of the LORD, as well the stranger, as he that was born among them; half of them over against mount Gerizim, and half of them over against mount Ebal; as Moses the servant of the LORD had commanded before, that they should bless the people of Israel.
8:34 And afterward he read all the words of the law, the blessings and cursings, according to all that is written in the book of the law.
8:35 There was not a word of all that Moses commanded, which Joshua read not before all the congregation of Israel, with the women, and the little ones, and the strangers that were conversant among them.

9

9:1 And it came to pass, when all the kings who were on this side Jordan, in the hills, and in the valleys, and in all the coasts of the great sea over against Lebanon, the Hittite, and the Amorite, the Canaanite, the Perizzite, the Hivite, and the Jebusite heard these things,
9:2 That they assembled themselves, to fight with Joshua and with Israel, with one accord.
9:3 And when the inhabitants of Gibeon heard what Joshua had done to Jericho and to Ai,
9:4 They did work craftily, and went and made as if they had been embassadors, and took old sacks upon their asses, and wine-bottles, old, and rent, and bound up;
9:5 And old shoes and patched upon their feet, and old garments upon

them; and all the bread of their provision was dry and moldy.
9:6 And they went to Joshua to the camp at Gilgal, and said to him, and to
the men of Israel, We have come from a far country: now therefore make
ye a league with us.
9:7 And the men of Israel said to the Hivites, It may be ye dwell among us;
and how shall we make a league with you?
9:8 And they said to Joshua, we are thy servants. And Joshua said to them,
Who are ye? and whence come ye?
9:9 And they said to him, From a very far country thy servants have come
because of the name of the LORD thy God: for we have heard the fame of
him, and all that he did in Egypt,
9:10 And all that he did to the two kings of the Amorites, that were beyond
Jordan, to Sihon king of Heshbon, and to Og king of Bashan, who was at
Ashtaroth.
9:11 Wherefore our elders, and all the inhabitants of our country spoke to
us, saying, Take provisions with you for the journey, and go to meet them,
and say to them, We are your servants: therefore now make ye a league with
us:
9:12 This our bread we took hot for our provision out of our houses on the
day we came forth to go to you; but now, behold, it is dry, and it is moldy:
9:13 And these bottles of wine which we filled, were new, and behold, they
are rent: and these our garments and our shoes are become old by reason of
the very long journey.
9:14 And the men took of their provisions, and asked not counsel at the
mouth of the LORD.
9:15 And Joshua made peace with them, and made a league with them, to
let them live: and the princes of the congregation swore to them.
9:16 And it came to pass at the end of three days after they had made a
league with them, that they heard that they were their neighbors, and that
they dwelt among them.
9:17 And the children of Israel journeyed, and came to their cities on the
third day. Now their cities were Gibeon, and Chephirah, and Beeroth, and
Kirjath-jearim.
9:18 And the children of Israel smote them not, because the princes of the
congregation had sworn to them by the LORD God of Israel. And all the
congregation murmured against the princes.
9:19 But all the princes said to all the congregation, We have sworn to them
by the LORD God of Israel: now therefore we may not touch them.
9:20 This we will do to them; we will even let them live, lest wrath be upon
us, because of the oath which we swore to them.
9:21 And the princes said to them, Let them live; but let them be hewers of
wood, and drawers of water to all the congregation; as the princes had
promised them.

9:22 And Joshua called for them, and he spoke to them, saying, Why have ye deceived us, saying, We are very far from you; when ye dwell among us?
9:23 Now therefore ye are cursed, and there shall none of you be freed from being bond-men, and hewers of wood and drawers of water for the house of my God.
9:24 And they answered Joshua, and said, Because it was certainly told thy servants, how the LORD thy God commanded his servant Moses to give you all the land, and to destroy all the inhabitants of the land from before you, therefore we were greatly afraid for our lives because of you, and have done this thing.
9:25 And now, behold, we are in thy hand: do as it seemeth good and right to thee to do to us,
9:26 And so did he to them, and delivered them out of the hand of the children of Israel, that they slew them not.
9:27 And Joshua made them that day hewers of wood and drawers of water for the congregation, and for the altar of the LORD, even to this day, in the place which he should choose.

10

10:1 Now it came to pass, when Adoni-zedec king of Jerusalem had heard how Joshua had taken Ai, and had utterly destroyed it; as he had done to Jericho and her king, so he had done to Ai and her king; and how the inhabitants of Gibeon had made peace with Israel, and were among them;
10:2 That they feared greatly, because Gibeon was a great city, as one of the royal cities, and because it was greater than Ai, and all the men of it were mighty.
10:3 Wherefore Adoni-zedec king of Jerusalem sent to Hoham king of Hebron, and to Piram king of Jarmuth, and to Japhia king of Lachish, and to Debir king of Eglon, saying,
10:4 Come up to me, and help me, that we may smite Gibeon: for it hath made peace with Joshua and with the children of Israel.
10:5 Therefore the five kings of the Amorites, the king of Jerusalem, the king of Hebron, the king of Jarmuth, the king of Lachish, the king of Eglon, assembled themselves, and went up, they and all their hosts, and encamped before Gibeon, and made war against it.
10:6 And the men of Gibeon sent to Joshua to the camp at Gilgal, saying, Slack not thy hand from thy servants; come up to us quickly, and save us, and help us: for all the kings of the Amorites that dwell in the mountains, are assembled against us.
10:7 So Joshua ascended from Gilgal, he, and all the people of war with him, and all the mighty men of valor.

10:8 And the LORD said to Joshua, Fear them not: for I have delivered them into thy hand; there shall not a man of them stand before thee.

10:9 Joshua therefore came to them suddenly, and went up from Gilgal all night.

10:10 And the LORD discomfited them before Israel, and slew them with a great slaughter at Gibeon, and chased them along the way that goeth up to Beth-horon, and smote them to Azekah, and to Makkedah.

10:11 And it came to pass as they fled from before Israel, and were in the descent to Beth-horon, that the LORD cast down great stones from heaven upon them to Azekah, and they died: they were more who died with hailstones than they whom the children of Israel slew with the sword.

10:12 Then spoke Joshua to the LORD in the day when the LORD delivered up the Amorites before the children of Israel, and he said in the sight of Israel, Sun, stand thou still upon Gibeon, and thou Moon, in the valley of Ajalon.

10:13 And the sun stood still, and the moon stayed, until the people had avenged themselves upon their enemies. Is not this written in the book of Jasher? So the sun stood still in the midst of heaven, and hasted not to go down about a whole day.

10:14 And there was no day like that before it or after it, that the LORD hearkened to the voice of a man: for the LORD fought for Israel.

10:15 And Joshua returned, and all Israel with him, to the camp at Gilgal.

10:16 But these five kings fled, and hid themselves in a cave at Makkedah.

10:17 And it was told Joshua, saying, The five kings are found hid in a cave at Makkedah.

10:18 And Joshua said, Roll great stones upon the mouth of the cave, and set men by it to keep them:

10:19 And stay you not, but pursue your enemies, and smite the hindmost of them; suffer them not to enter into their cities: for the LORD your God hath delivered them into your hand.

10:20 And it came to pass, when Joshua and the children of Israel had made an end of slaying them with a very great slaughter, till they were consumed, that the rest who remained of them entered into fortified cities.

10:21 And all the people returned to the camp to Joshua at Makkedah in peace: none moved his tongue against any of the children of Israel.

10:22 Then said Joshua, Open the mouth of the cave, and bring those five kings to me out of the cave.

10:23 And they did so, and brought those five kings to him out of the cave, the king of Jerusalem, the king of Hebron, the king of Jarmuth, the king of Lachish, and the king of Eglon.

10:24 And it came to pass, when they brought out those kings to Joshua, that Joshua called for all the men of Israel, and said to the captains of the men of war who went with him, Come near, put your feet upon the necks

of these kings. And they came near, and put their feet upon the necks of
them.
10:25 And Joshua said to them, Fear not, nor be dismayed, be strong and of
good courage: for thus shall the LORD do to all your enemies against
whom ye fight.
10:26 And afterward Joshua smote them, and slew them, and hanged them
on five trees: and they were hanging upon the trees until the evening.
10:27 And it came to pass at the time of the setting of the sun, that Joshua
commanded, and they took them down from the trees, and cast them into
the cave in which they had been hid, and laid great stones upon the cave's
mouth, which remain until this very day.
10:28 And that day Joshua took Makkedah, and smote it with the edge of
the sword, and the king of it he utterly destroyed, them, and all the souls
that were in it; he let none remain: and he did to the king of Makkedah as
he did to the king of Jericho.
10:29 Then Joshua passed from Makkedah, and all Israel with him, to
Libnah, and fought against Libnah:
10:30 And the LORD delivered it also, and its king, into the hand of Israel;
and he smote it with the edge of the sword, and all the souls that were in it;
he let none remain in it; but did to the king of it as he did to the king of
Jericho.
10:31 And Joshua passed from Libnah, and all Israel with him, to Lachish,
and encamped against it, and fought against it:
10:32 And the LORD delivered Lachish into the hand of Israel, who took it
on the second day, and smote it with the edge of the sword, and all the
souls that were in it, according to all that he had done to Libnah.
10:33 Then Horam king of Gezer came up to help Lachish; and Joshua
smote him and his people, until he had left him none remaining.
10:34 And from Lachish Joshua passed to Eglon, and all Israel with him;
and they encamped against it, and fought against it:
10:35 And they took it on that day, and smote it with the edge of the sword,
and all the souls that were in it he utterly destroyed that day, according to all
that he had done to Lachish.
10:36 And Joshua went up from Eglon, and all Israel with him, to Hebron;
and they fought against it:
10:37 And they took it, and smote it with the edge of the sword, and its
king, and all its cities, and all the souls that were in them; he left none
remaining (according to all that he had done to Eglon) but destroyed it
utterly, and all the souls that were in it.
10:38 And Joshua returned, and all Israel with him, to Debir; and fought
against it:
10:39 And he took it, and its king, and all its cities, and they smote them
with the edge of the sword, and utterly destroyed all the souls that were in

them; he left none remaining: as he had done to Hebron, so he did to
Debir, and to its king; as he had done also to Libnah, and to its king.
10:40 So Joshua smote all the country of the hills, and of the south, and of
the vale, and of the springs, and all their kings: he left none remaining, but
utterly destroyed all that breathed, as the LORD God of Israel commanded.
10:41 And Joshua smote them from Kadesh-barnea even to Gaza, and all
the country of Goshen, even to Gibeon.
10:42 And all these kings and their land did Joshua take at one time;
because the LORD God of Israel fought for Israel.
10:43 And Joshua returned, and all Israel with him, to the camp in Gilgal.

11

11:1 And it came to pass, when Jabin king of Hazor had heard those things,
that he sent to Jobab king of Madon, and to the king of Shimron, and to
the king Achshaph,
11:2 And to the kings that were on the north of the mountains, and of the
plains south of Cinneroth, and in the valley, and in the borders of Dor on
the west,
11:3 And to the Canaanite on the east and on the west, and to the Amorite,
and the Hittite, and the Perizzite, and the Jebusite in the mountains, and to
the Hivite under Hermon in the land of Mizpeh.
11:4 And they went out, they and all their hosts with them, many people,
even as the sand that is upon the sea-shore in multitude, with horses and
chariots very numerous.
11:5 And when all these kings were met together, they came and encamped
together at the waters of Merom, to fight against Israel.
11:6 And the LORD said to Joshua, Be not afraid because of them: for tomorrow about this time will I deliver them up all slain before Israel: thou
shalt hough their horses, and burn their chariots with fire.
11:7 So Joshua came, and all the people of war with him, against them by
the waters of Merom suddenly, and they fell upon them.
11:8 And the LORD delivered them into the hand of Israel, who smote
them, and chased them to great Zidon, and to Misrephoth-maim, and to the
valley of Mizpeh eastward; and they smote them, until they left to them
none remaining.
11:9 And Joshua did to them as the LORD bade him: he houghed their
horses, and burnt their chariots with fire.
11:10 And Joshua at that time turned back, and took Hazor, and smote its
king with the sword: for Hazor before-time was the head of all those
kingdoms.
11:11 And they smote all the souls that were in it with the edge of the

sword, utterly destroying them: there was not any left to breathe: and he burnt Hazor with fire.
11:12 And all the cities of those kings, and all the kings of them, Joshua took, and smote them with the edge of the sword, and he utterly destroyed them, as Moses the servant of the LORD commanded.
11:13 But as for the cities that stood still in their strength, Israel burned none of them, save Hazor only; that did Joshua burn.
11:14 And all the spoil of these cities, and the cattle, the children of Israel took for a prey to themselves: but every man they smote with the edge of the sword, until they had destroyed them, neither left they any to breathe.
11:15 As the LORD commanded Moses his servant, so did Moses command Joshua, and so did Joshua: he left nothing undone of all that the LORD commanded Moses.
11:16 So Joshua took all that land, the hills, and all the south country, and all the land of Goshen, and the valley, and the plain, and the mountain of Israel, and the valley of the same;
11:17 Even from the mount Halak, that goeth up to Seir, even to Baal-gad, in the valley of Lebanon under mount Hermon: and all their kings he took, and smote them, and slew them.
11:18 Joshua made war a long time with all those kings.
11:19 There was not a city that made peace with the children of Israel, save the Hivites the inhabitants of Gibeon: all other they took in battle.
11:20 For it was of the LORD to harden their hearts, that they should come against Israel in battle, that he might destroy them utterly, and that they might have no favor, but that he might destroy them, as the LORD commanded Moses.
11:21 And at that time came Joshua and cut off the Anakims from the mountains, from Hebron, from Debir, from Anab, and from all the mountains of Judah, and from all the mountains of Israel: Joshua destroyed them utterly with their cities.
11:22 There was none of the Anakims left in the land of the children of Israel: only in Gaza, in Gath, and in Ashdod, there remained.
11:23 So Joshua took the whole land, according to all that the LORD said to Moses, and Joshua gave it for an inheritance to Israel according to their divisions by their tribes. And the land rested from war.

12

12:1 Now these are the kings of the land, whom the children of Israel smote, and possessed their land on the other side of Jordan towards the rising of the sun, from the river Arnon, to mount Hermon, and all the plain

on the east:
12:2 Sihon king of the Amorites, who dwelt in Heshbon, and ruled from
Aroer, which is upon the bank of the river Arnon, and from the middle of
the river, and from half Gilead, even to the river Jabbok, which is the
border of the children of Ammon;
12:3 And from the plain to the sea of Cinneroth on the east, and to the sea
of the plain, even the salt sea on the east, the way to Beth-jeshimoth; and
from the south, under Ashdoth-pisgah:
12:4 And the coast of Og king of Bashan, who was of the remnant of the
giants, that dwelt at Ashtaroth and at Edrei,
12:5 And reigned in mount Hermon, and in Salcah, and in all Bashan, to the
border of the Geshurites, and the Maachathites, and half Gilead, the border
of Sihon king of Heshbon.
12:6 Them did Moses the servant of the LORD, and the children of Israel
smite: and Moses the servant of the LORD gave it for a possession to the
Reubenites, and the Gadites, and the half-tribe of Manasseh.
12:7 And these are the kings of the country whom Joshua and the children
of Israel smote on this side of Jordan on the west, from Baal-gad in the
valley of Lebanon, even to the mount Halak that goeth up to Seir; which
Joshua gave to the tribes of Israel for a possession according to their
divisions;
12:8 In the mountains, and in the valleys, and in the plains, and in the
springs, and in the wilderness, and in the south country; the Hittites, the
Amorites, and the Canaanites, the Perizzites, the Hivites, and the Jebusites:
12:9 The king of Jericho one; the king of Ai, which is beside Beth-el, one;
12:10 The king of Jerusalem, one; the king of Hebron, one;
12:11 The king of Jarmuth, one; the king of Lachish, one;
12:12 The king of Eglon, one; the king of Gezer, one;
12:13 The king of Debir, one; the king of Geder, one;
12:14 The king of Hormah, one; the king of Arad, one;
12:15 The king of Libnah, one; the king of Adullam, one;
12:16 The king of Makkedah, one; the king of Beth-el, one;
12:17 The king of Tappuah, one; the king of Hepher, one;
12:18 The king of Aphek, one; the king of Lasharon, one;
12:19 The king of Madon, one; the king of Hazor, one;
12:20 The king of Shimron-meron, one; the king of Achshaph, one;
12:21 The king of Taanach, one; the king of Megiddo, one;
12:22 The king of Kedesh, one; the king of Jokneam of Carmel, one;
12:23 The king of Dor in the border of Dor, one; the king of the nations of
Gilgal, one;
12:24 The king of Tirzah, one: all the kings thirty and one.

13

13:1 Now Joshua was old and advanced in years; and the LORD said to him Thou art old and advanced in years, and there remaineth yet very much land to be possessed.
13:2 This is the land that yet remaineth: all the borders of the Philistines, and all Geshuri,
13:3 From Sihor, which is before Egypt, even to the borders of Ekron northward, which is counted to the Canaanite: five lords of the Philistines; the Gazathites, and the Ashdothites, the Eshkalonites, the Gittites, and the Ekronites; also the Avites:
13:4 From the south all the land of the Canaanites, and Mearah that is beside the Sidonians, to Aphek to the borders of the Amorites:
13:5 And the land of the Giblites, and all Lebanon towards the sun-rising, from Baal-gad under mount Hermon to the entering into Hamath.
13:6 And the inhabitants of the hill-country from Lebanon to Misrephoth-maim, and all the Sidonians, them will I drive out from before the children of Israel: only divide thou it by lot to the Israelites for an inheritance, as I have commanded thee.
13:7 Now therefore divide this land for an inheritance to the nine tribes, and the half tribe of Manasseh,
13:8 With whom the Reubenites and the Gadites have received their inheritance, which Moses gave them, beyond Jordan eastward, even as Moses the servant of the LORD gave them.
13:9 From Aroer that is upon the bank of the river Arnon, and the city that is in the midst of the river, and all the plain of Medeba to Dibon;
13:10 And all the cities of Sihon king of the Amorites, who reigned in Heshbon, to the border of the children of Ammon;
13:11 And Gilead, and the border of the Geshurites and Maachathites, and all mount Hermon, and all Bashan to Salcah;
13:12 All the kingdom of Og in Bashan, who reigned in Ashtaroth and in Edrei, who remained of the remnant of the giants. For these did Moses smite, and cast them out.
13:13 Nevertheless, the children of Israel expelled not the Geshurites, nor the Maachathites: but the Geshurites and the Maachathites dwell among the Israelites until this day.
13:14 Only to the tribe of Levi he gave no inheritance; the sacrifices of the LORD God of Israel made by fire are their inheritance, as he said to them.
13:15 And Moses gave to the tribe of the children of Reuben inheritance according to their families.
13:16 And their border was from Aroer that is on the bank of the river Arnon, and the city that is in the midst of the river, and all the plain by

Medeba;
13:17 Heshbon, and all her cities that are in the plain; Dibon, and Bamoth-baal, and Beth-baal-meon,
13:18 And Jahaza, and Kedemoth, and Mephaath,
13:19 And Kirjathaim, and Sibmah, and Zareth-shahar in the mount of the valley,
13:20 And Beth-peor, and Ashdoth-pisgah, and Beth-jeshimoth,
13:21 And all the cities of the plain, and all the kingdom of Sihon king of the Amorites, who reigned in Heshbon, whom Moses smote with the princes of Midian, Evi, and Rekem, and Zur, and Hur, and Reba, dukes of Sihon, dwelling in the country.
13:22 Balaam also the son of Beor, the sooth-sayer, did the children of Israel slay with the sword, among them that were slain by them.
13:23 And the border of the children of Reuben was Jordan, and its border. This was the inheritance of the children of Reuben after their families, the cities and their villages.
13:24 And Moses gave inheritance to the tribe of Gad, even to the children of Gad according to their families.
13:25 And their border was Jazer, and all the cities of Gilead, and half the land of the children of Ammon, to Aroer that is before Rabbah;
13:26 And from Heshbon to Ramath-mizpeh, and Betonim; and from Mahanaim to the border of Debir;
13:27 And in the valley, Beth-aram, and Beth-nimrah, and Succoth, and Zaphon, the rest of the kingdom of Sihon king of Heshbon, Jordan and its border, even to the edge of the sea of Cinneroth, on the other side of Jordan eastward.
13:28 This is the inheritance of the children of Gad after their families, the cities, and their villages.
13:29 And Moses gave inheritance to the half-tribe of Manasseh: and this was the possession of the half-tribe of the children of Manasseh by their families.
13:30 And their border was from Mahanaim, all Bashan, all the kingdom of Og king of Bashan, and all the towns of Jair, which are in Bashan, sixty cities:
13:31 And half Gilead, and Ashtaroth, and Edrei, cities of the kingdom of Og in Bashan, were pertaining to the children of Machir the son of Manasseh, even to the one half of the children of Machir by their families.
13:32 These are the countries which Moses distributed for inheritance in the plains of Moab, on the other side of Jordan by Jericho eastward.
13:33 But to the tribe of Levi Moses gave not any inheritance: the LORD God of Israel was their inheritance, as he said to them.

14

14:1 And these are the countries which the children of Israel inherited in the land of Canaan, which Eleazar the priest, and Joshua the son of Nun, and the heads of the fathers of the tribes of the children of Israel distributed for inheritance to them.
14:2 By lot was their inheritance, as the LORD commanded by the hand of Moses, for the nine tribes, and for the half-tribe.
14:3 For Moses had given the inheritance of two tribes and a half-tribe on the other side of Jordan: but to the Levites he gave no inheritance among them.
14:4 For the children of Joseph were two tribes, Manasseh and Ephraim: therefore they gave no part to the Levites in the land, save cities to dwell in, with their suburbs for their cattle, and for their substance.
14:5 As the LORD commanded Moses, so the children of Israel did, and they divided the land.
14:6 Then the children of Judah came to Joshua in Gilgal: and Caleb the son of Jephunneh the Kenezite said to him, Thou knowest the thing that the LORD said to Moses the man of God concerning me and thee in Kadesh-barnea.
14:7 Forty years old was I when Moses the servant of the LORD sent me from Kadesh-barnea to explore the land; and I brought him word again as it was in my heart.
14:8 Nevertheless, my brethren that went up with me made the heart of the people melt: but I wholly followed the LORD my God.
14:9 And Moses swore on that day, saying, Surely the land on which thy feet have trodden shall be thy inheritance, and thy children's for ever; because thou hast wholly followed the LORD my God.
14:10 And now, behold, the LORD hath kept me alive, as he said, these forty and five years, even since the LORD spoke this word to Moses, while the children of Israel wandered in the wilderness: and now, lo, I am this day eighty five years old.
14:11 As yet I am as strong this day, as I was in the day that Moses sent me: as my strength was then, even so is my strength now, for war, both to go out, and to come in.
14:12 Now therefore give me this mountain, of which the LORD spoke in that day; for thou heardest in that day how the Anakims were there, and that the cities were great and fortified: if the LORD will be with me, then I shall be able to drive them out, as the LORD said.
14:13 And Joshua blessed him, and gave to Caleb the son of Jephunneh Hebron for an inheritance.
14:14 Hebron therefore became the inheritance of Caleb the son of

Jephunneh the Kenezite to this day; because that he wholly followed the LORD God of Israel.
14:15 And the name of Hebron before was Kirjath-arba; which Arba was a great man among the Anakims. And the land had rest from war.

15

15:1 This then was the lot of the tribe of the children of Judah by their families; even to the border of Edom, the wilderness of Zin southward was the uttermost part of the south border.
15:2 And their south border was from the shore of the salt-sea, from the bay that looketh southward:
15:3 And it went out to the south side to Maaleh-acrabbim, and passed along to Zin, and ascended on the south side to Kadesh-barnea, and passed along to Hezron, and went up to Adar, and fetched a compass to Karkaa:
15:4 From thence it passed towards Azmon, and went out to the river of Egypt; and the limits of that border were at the sea: this shall be your south limit.
15:5 And the east border was the salt-sea, even to the end of Jordan: and their border in the north quarter was from the bay of the sea, at the uttermost part of Jordan:
15:6 And the border went up to Beth-hogla, and passed along by the north of Beth-arabah; and the border went up to the stone of Bohan the son of Reuben:
15:7 And the border went up towards Debir from the valley of Achor, and so northward looking towards Gilgal, that is before the going up to Adummim, which is on the south side of the river: and the border passed towards the waters of En-shemesh, and the borders of it were at En-rogel:
15:8 And the border went up by the valley of the son of Hinnom, to the south side of the Jebusite; the same is Jerusalem: and the border went up to the top of the mountain that lieth before the valley of Hinnom westward, which is at the end of the valley of the giants northward:
15:9 And the border was drawn from the top of the hill to the fountain of the water of Nephtoah, and went out to the cities of mount Ephron; and the border was drawn to Baalah, which is Kirjath-jearim:
15:10 And the border compassed from Baalah westward to mount Seir, and passed along to the side of mount Jearim (which is Chesalon) on the north side, and went down to Beth-shemesh, and passed on to Timnah:
15:11 And the border went out to the side of Ekron northward: and the border was drawn to Shicron, and passed along to mount Baalah, and went out to Jabneel; and the terminations of the border were at the sea.

15:12 And the west border was to the great sea, and its coast: this is the border of the children of Judah round about, according to their families.
15:13 And to Caleb the son of Jephunneh he gave a part among the children of Judah, according to the commandment of the LORD to Joshua, even the city of Arba the father of Anak, which city is Hebron.
15:14 And Caleb drove thence the three sons of Anak, Sheshai, and Ahiman, and Talmai, the children of Anak.
15:15 And he went up thence to the inhabitants of Debir: and the name of Debir before was Kirjath-sepher.
15:16 And Caleb said, He that smiteth Kirjath-sepher, and taketh it, to him will I give Achsah my daughter for a wife.
15:17 And Othniel the son of Kenaz, the brother of Caleb, took it: and he gave him Achsah his daughter for a wife.
15:18 And it came to pass, as she came to him, that she moved him to ask of her father a field. And she lighted off her ass; and Caleb said to her, What wouldst thou?
15:19 Who answered, Give me a blessing; for thou hast given me a south land, give me also springs of water. And he gave her the upper springs, and the nether springs.
15:20 This is the inheritance of the tribe of the children of Judah according to their families.
15:21 And the uttermost cities of the tribe of the children of Judah towards the border of Edom southward were Kabzeel, and Eder, and Jagur,
15:22 And Kinah, and Dimonah, and Adadah,
15:23 And Kedesh, and Hazor, and Ithnan,
15:24 Ziph, and Telem, and Bealoth,
15:25 And Hazor, Hadattah, and Kerioth, and Hezron, which is Hazor,
15:26 Aman, and Shema, and Moladah,
15:27 And Hazar-gaddah, and Heshmon, and Beth-palet,
15:28 And Hazar-shual, and Beer-sheba, and Bizjothjah,
15:29 Baalah, and Iim, and Azem,
15:30 And Eltolad, and Chesil, and Hormah,
15:31 And Ziglag, and Madmannah, and Sansannah,
15:32 And Lebaoth, and Shilhim, and Ain, and Rimmon: all the cities are twenty and nine, with their villages:
15:33 And in the valley, Eshtaol, and Zoreah, and Ashnah,
15:34 And Zanoah, and En-gannim, Tappuah, and Enam,
15:35 Jarmuth, and Adullam, Socoh, and Azekah,
15:36 And Sharaim, and Adithaim, and Gederah, and Gederothaim; fourteen cities with their villages:
15:37 Zenan, and Hadashah, and Migdalgad,
15:38 And Dilean, and Mizpeh, and Joktheel,
15:39 Lachish, and Bozkath, and Eglon,

15:40 And Cabbon, and Lahman, and Kithlish,
15:41 And Gederoth, Beth-dagon, and Naamah, and Makkedah; sixteen cities with their villages:
15:42 Libnah, and Ether, and Ashan,
15:43 And Jiphtah, and Ashnah, and Nezib,
15:44 And Keilah, and Achzib, and Mareshah; nine cities with their villages:
15:45 Ekron, with her towns and her villages:
15:46 From Ekron even to the sea, all that lay near Ashdod, with their villages:
15:47 Ashdod, with her towns and her villages; Gaza, with her towns and her villages, to the river of Egypt, and the great sea, and its border:
15:48 And in the mountains, Shamir, and Jattir, and Socoh,
15:49 And Dannah, and Kirjath-sannah, which is Debir,
15:50 And Anab, and Eshtemoh, and Anim,
15:51 And Goshen, and Holon, and Giloh: eleven cities with their villages:
15:52 Arab, and Dumah, and Eshean,
15:53 And Janum, and Beth-tappuah, and Aphekah,
15:54 And Humtah, and Kirjath-arba (which is Hebron) and Zior; nine cities with their villages:
15:55 Maon, Carmel, and Ziph, and Juttah,
15:56 And Jezreel, and Jokdeam, and Zanoah,
15:57 Cain, Gibeah, and Timnah; ten cities with their villages:
15:58 Halhul, Beth-zur, and Gedor,
15:59 And Maarath, and Beth-anoth, and Eltekon; six cities with their villages:
15:60 Kirjath-baal (which is Kirjath-jearim) and Rabbah; two cities with their villages:
15:61 In the wilderness, Beth-arabah, Middin, and Secacah,
15:62 And Nibshan, and the city of Salt, and En-gedi; six cities with their villages.
15:63 As for the Jebusites, the inhabitants of Jerusalem, the children of Judah could not expel them: but the Jebusites dwell with the children of Judah at Jerusalem to this day.

16

16:1 And the lot of the children of Joseph fell from Jordan by Jericho, to the water of Jericho on the east, to the wilderness that goeth up from Jericho throughout mount Beth-el,
16:2 And goeth out from Beth-el to Luz, and passeth along to the borders of Archi to Ataroth,

16:3 And goeth down westward to the border of Japhleti, to the border of Beth-horon the nether, and to Gezer: and the limits of it are at the sea.
16:4 So the children of Joseph, Manasseh and Ephraim, took their inheritance.
16:5 And the border of the children of Ephraim according to their families was thus: even the border of their inheritance on the east side was Ataroth-adar, to Beth-horon the upper:
16:6 And the border went out towards the sea to Michmethah on the north side; and the border went about eastward to Taanath-shiloh, and passed by it on the east to Janohah;
16:7 And it went down from Janohah to Ataroth, and to Naarath, and came to Jericho, and terminated at Jordan.
16:8 The border went out from Tappuah westward to the river Kanah; and the limits of it were at the sea. This is the inheritance of the tribe of the children of Ephraim by their families.
16:9 And the separate cities for the children of Ephraim were among the inheritance of the children of Manasseh, all the cities with their villages.
16:10 And they did not expel the Canaanites that dwelt in Gezer: but the Canaanites dwell among the Ephraimites to this day, and serve under tribute.

17

17:1 There was also a lot for the tribe of Manasseh; for he was the first-born of Joseph; to wit, for Machir the first-born of Manasseh, the father of Gilead: because he was a man of war, therefore he had Gilead and Bashan.
17:2 There was also a lot for the rest of the children of Manasseh by their families; for the children of Abiezer, and for the children of Helek, and for the children of Asriel, and for the children of Shechem, and for the children of Hepher, and for the children of Shemida: these were the male children of Manasseh the son of Joseph by their families.
17:3 But Zelophehad, the son of Hepher, the son of Gilead, the son of Machir, the son of Manasseh, had no sons, but daughters: and these are the names of his daughters, Mahlah, and Noah, Hoglah, Milcah, and Tirzah.
17:4 And they came near before Eleazar the priest, and before Joshua the son of Nun, and before the princes, saying, The LORD commanded Moses to give us an inheritance among our brethren: therefore according to the commandment of the LORD he gave them an inheritance among the brethren of their father.
17:5 And there fell ten portions to Manasseh, besides the land of Gilead and Bashan, which were on the other side of Jordan;

17:6 Because the daughters of Manasseh had an inheritance among his sons: and the rest of Manasseh's sons had the land of Gilead.
17:7 And the border of Manasseh was from Asher to Michmethah, that lieth before Shechem; and the border went along on the right hand to the inhabitants of En-tappuah.
17:8 Now Manasseh had the land of Tappuah: but Tappuah on the border of Manasseh belonged to the children of Ephraim;
17:9 And the border descended to the river Kanah, southward of the river. These cities of Ephraim are among the cities of Manasseh: the border of Manasseh also was on the north side of the river, and the limits of it were at the sea:
17:10 Southward it was Ephraim's, and northward it was Manasseh's, and the sea is his border; and they met together in Asher on the north, and in Issachar on the east.
17:11 And Manasseh had in Issachar and in Asher Beth-shean and its towns, and Ibleam and its towns, and the inhabitants of Dor and its towns, and the inhabitants of En-dor and its towns, and the inhabitants of Tanach and its towns, and the inhabitants of Megiddo and its towns, even three countries.
17:12 Yet the children of Manasseh could not expel the inhabitants of those cities; but the Canaanites would dwell in that land.
17:13 Yet it came to pass, when the children of Israel had become strong, that they subjected the Canaanites to tribute; but did not utterly expel them.
17:14 And the children of Joseph spoke to Joshua, saying, Why hast thou given me but one lot and one portion to inherit, seeing I am a great people, forasmuch as the LORD hath hitherto blessed me?
17:15 And Joshua answered them, If thou art a great people, then go up to the wood, and cut down for thyself there in the land of the Perizzites and of the giants, if mount Ephraim is too narrow for thee.
17:16 And the children of Joseph said, The hill is not enough for us: and all the Canaanites that dwell in the land of the valley have chariots of iron, both they who are of Beth-shean and its towns, and they who are of the valley of Jezreel.
17:17 And Joshua spoke to the house of Joseph, even to Ephraim and to Manasseh, saying, Thou art a great people, and hast great power: thou shalt not have one lot only:
17:18 But the mountain shall be thine; for it is a wood, and thou shalt cut it down: and the limits of it shall be thine: for thou shalt drive out the Canaanites, though they have iron chariots, and though they are strong.

18

18:1 And the whole congregation of the children of Israel assembled at
Shiloh, and set up the tabernacle of the congregation there: and the land
was subdued before them.
18:2 And there remained among the children of Israel seven tribes, which
had not yet received their inheritance.
18:3 And Joshua said to the children of Israel, How long are ye slack to go
to possess the land which the LORD God of your fathers hath given you?
18:4 Select from among you three men for each tribe: and I will send them,
and they shall rise, and go through the land, and describe it according to the
inheritance of them, and they shall come again to me.
18:5 And they shall divide it into seven parts: Judah shall abide in their
border on the south, and the house of Joseph shall abide in their borders on
the north.
18:6 Ye shall therefore describe the land in seven parts, and bring the
description hither to me, that I may cast lots for you here before the LORD
our God.
18:7 But the Levites have no part among you; for the priesthood of the
LORD is their inheritance. And Gad, and Reuben, and half the tribe of
Manasseh, have received their inheritance beyond Jordan on the east, which
Moses the servant of the LORD gave them.
18:8 And the men arose, and departed: and Joshua charged them that went
to describe the land, saying, Go, and walk through the land, and describe it,
and come again to me, that I may here cast lots for you before the LORD
in Shiloh.
18:9 And the men went and passed through the land, and described it by
cities in seven parts in a book, and came again, to Joshua to the host at
Shiloh.
18:10 And Joshua cast lots for them in Shiloh before the LORD: and there
Joshua divided the land to the children of Israel according to their divisions.
18:11 And the lot of the tribe of the children of Benjamin came up
according to their families: and the border of their lot came forth between
the children of Judah and the children of Joseph.
18:12 And their border on the north side was from Jordan; and the border
went up to the side of Jericho on the north side, and went up through the
mountains westward; and the limits of it were at the wilderness of Beth-
aven.
18:13 And the border went over from thence towards Luz, to the side of
Luz (which is Beth-el) southward; and the border descended to Ataroth-
adar, near the hill that lieth on the south side of the nether Beth-horon.
18:14 And the border was drawn thence, and compassed the corner of the
sea southward, from the hill that lieth before Beth-horon southward; and
the limits of it were at Kirjath-baal (which is Kirjath-jearim) a city of the

children of Judah. This was the west quarter.
18:15 And the south quarter was from the end of Kirjah-jearim, and the
border went out on the west, and went out to the well of waters of
Nephtoah:
18:16 And the border came down to the end of the mountain that lieth
before the valley of the son of Hinnom, and which is in the valley of the
giants on the north, and descended to the valley of Hinnom, to the side of
Jebusi on the south, and descended to En-rogel,
18:17 And was drawn from the north, and went forth to En-shemesh, and
went forth towards Geliloth, which is over against the going up of
Adummim, and descended to the stone of Bohan the son of Reuben,
18:18 And passed along towards the side over against Arabah northward,
and went down to Arabah:
18:19 And the border passed along to the side of Beth-hoglah northward:
and the limits of the border were at the north bay of the salt sea at the
south end of Jordan. This was the south border.
18:20 And Jordan was the border of it on the east side. This was the
inheritance of the children of Benjamin, by the limits of it round about,
according to their families.
18:21 Now the cities of the tribe of the children of Benjamin, according to
their families, were Jericho, and Beth-hoglah, and the valley of Keziz,
18:22 And Beth-arabah, and Zemaraim, and Beth-el,
18:23 And Avim, and Parah, and Ophrah,
18:24 And Chephar-haamonai, and Ophni, and Gaba; twelve cities with
their villages:
18:25 Gibeon, and Ramah, and Beeroth,
18:26 And Mizpeh, and Chephirah, and Mozah,
18:27 And Rekem, and Irpeel, and Taralah,
18:28 And Zelah, Eleph, and Jebusi, (which is Jerusalem) Gibeath, and
Kirjath; fourteen cities with their villages. This is the inheritance of the
children of Benjamin according to their families.

19

19:1 And the second lot came forth to Simeon, even for the tribe of the
children of Simeon according to their families: and their inheritance was
within the inheritance of the children of Judah.
19:2 And they had in their inheritance, Beer-sheba, and Sheba, and
Moladah.
19:3 And Hazar-shual, and Balah, and Azem,
19:4 And Eltolad, and Bethul, and Hormah,

19:5 And Ziklag, and Beth-marcaboth, and Hazar-susah,
19:6 And Beth-lebaoth, and Sheruhen; thirteen cities and their villages:
19:7 Ain, Remmon, and Ether, and Ashan; four cities and their villages:
19:8 And all the villages that were around these cities to Baalath-beer, Ramath of the south. This is the inheritance of the tribe of the children of Simeon according to their families.
19:9 Out of the portion of the children of Judah was the inheritance of the children of Simeon: for the part of the children of Judah was too much for them: therefore the children of Simeon had their inheritance within the inheritance of them.
19:10 And the third lot came up for the children of Zebulun according to their families: and the border of their inheritance was to Sarid:
19:11 And their border went up towards the sea, and Maralah, and reached to Dabbasheth, and reached to the river that is before Jokneam,
19:12 And turned from Sarid eastward, towards the sun-rising, to the border of Chisloth-tabor, and then goeth out to Daberath, and goeth up to Japhia,
19:13 And from thence passeth along on the east to Gittah-hepher, to Ittah-kazin, and goeth out to Remmon-methoar to Neah;
19:14 And the border compasseth it on the north side to Hannathon: and the limits of it are in the valley of Jiphthah-el:
19:15 And Kattath, and Nahallal, and Shimron, and Idalah, and Beth-lehem; twelve cities with their villages.
19:16 This is the inheritance of the children of Zebulun according to their families, these cities with their villages.
19:17 And the fourth lot came out to Issachar, for the children of Issachar according to their families.
19:18 And their border was towards Jezreel, and Chesulloth, and Shunem,
19:19 And Hapharaim, and Shihon, and Anaharath,
19:20 And Rabbith, and Kishion, and Abez,
19:21 And Remeth, and En-gannim, and En-haddah, and Beth-pazzez;
19:22 And the border reacheth to Tabor, and Shahazimah, and Beth-shemesh, and the limits of their border were at Jordan: sixteen cities with their villages.
19:23 This is the inheritance of the tribe of the children of Issachar according to their families, the cities and their villages.
19:24 And the fifth lot came out for the tribe of the children of Asher according to their families.
19:25 And their border was Helkath, and Hali, and Beten, and Achshaph,
19:26 And Alammelech, and Amad, and Misheal; and reacheth to Carmel westward, and to Shihor-libnath;
19:27 And turneth towards the sun-rising to Beth-dagon, and reacheth to Zebulun, and to the valley of Jiphthah-el towards the north side of Beth-

emek, and Neiel, and goeth out to Cabul on the left hand,
19:28 And Hebron, and Rehob, and Hammon, and Kanah, even to great
Zidon;
19:29 And then the border turneth to Ramah, and to the strong city Tyre;
and the border turneth to Hosah: and the limits of it are at the sea from the
coast to Achzib:
19:30 Ummah also, and Aphek, and Rehob: twenty and two cities with their
villages.
19:31 This is the inheritance of the tribe of the children of Asher according
to their families, these cities with their villages.
19:32 The sixth lot came out to the children of Naphtali, even for the
children of Naphtali according to their families.
19:33 And their border was from Heleph, from Allon to Zaanannim, and
Adami, Nekeb, and Jabneel, to Lakum; and the limits thereof were at
Jordan:
19:34 And then the border turneth westward to Aznoth-tabor, and goeth
out from thence to Hukkok, and reacheth to Zebulun on the south side,
and reacheth to Asher on the west side, and to Judah upon Jordan towards
the sun-rising.
19:35 And the fortified cities are Ziddim, Zer, and Hammath, Rakkath, and
Chinnereth,
19:36 And Adamah, and Ramah, and Hazor,
19:37 And Kedesh, and Edrei, and En-hazor,
19:38 And Iron, and Migdal-el, Horem, and Beth-anath, and Beth-shemesh;
nineteen cities with their villages.
19:39 This is the inheritance of the tribe of the children of Naphtali
according to their families, the cities and their villages.
19:40 And the seventh lot came out for the tribe of the children of Dan
according to their families.
19:41 And the border of their inheritance was Zorah, and Eshtaol, and Ir-
shemesh,
19:42 And Shaalabbim, and Ajalon, and Jethlah,
19:43 And Elon, and Thimnathah, and Ekron,
19:44 And Eltekeh, and Gibbethon, and Baalath,
19:45 And Jehud, and Bene-berak, and Gath-rimmon,
19:46 And Me-jarkon, and Rakkon, with the border before Japho.
19:47 And the border of the children of Dan, went out too little for them:
therefore the children of Dan went up to fight against Leshem, and took it,
and smote it with the edge of the sword, and possessed it, and dwelt in it,
and called Leshem, Dan, after the name of Dan their father.
19:48 This is the inheritance of the tribe of the children of Dan according
to their families, these cities with their villages.
19:49 When they had made an end of dividing the land for inheritance by

their borders, the children of Israel gave an inheritance to Joshua the son of Nun among them:
19:50 According to the word of the LORD they gave him the city which he asked, even Timnath-serah in mount Ephraim: and he built the city, and dwelt in it.
19:51 These are the inheritances which Eleazar the priest, and Joshua the son of Nun, and the heads of the fathers of the tribes of the children of Israel, divided for an inheritance by lot in Shiloh before the LORD, at the door of the tabernacle of the congregation. So they made an end of dividing the country.

20

20:1 The LORD also spoke to Joshua, saying,
20:2 Speak to the children of Israel, saying, Appoint for you cities of refuge, of which I spoke to you by the hand of Moses:
20:3 That the slayer that killeth any person unawares and ignorantly, may flee thither: and they shall be your refuge from the avenger of blood.
20:4 And when he that doth flee to one of those cities shall stand at the entering of the gate of the city, and shall declare his cause in the ears of the elders of that city, they shall take him into the city to them, and give him a place, that he may dwell among them.
20:5 And if the avenger of blood shall pursue him, then they shall not deliver the slayer into his hand; because he smote his neighbor ignorantly, and had not hated him before.
20:6 And he shall dwell in that city, until he shall stand before the congregation for judgment, and until the death of the high-priest that shall be in those days: then shall the slayer return, and come to his own city, and to his own house, to the city from whence he fled.
20:7 And they appointed Kedesh in Galilee in mount Naphtali, and Shechem in mount Ephraim, and Kirjath-arba, (which is Hebron) in the mountain of Judah.
20:8 And on the other side of Jordan by Jericho eastward, they assigned Bezer in the wilderness upon the plain out of the tribe of Reuben, and Ramoth in Gilead out of the tribe of Gad, and Golan in Bashan out of the tribe of Manasseh.
20:9 These were the cities appointed for all the children of Israel, and for the stranger sojourning among them, that whoever should kill any person unawares might flee thither, and not die by the hand of the avenger of blood, until he stood before the congregation.

21

21:1 Then came near the heads of the fathers of the Levites to Eleazar the priest, and to Joshua the son of Nun, and to the heads of the fathers of the tribes of the children of Israel;
21:2 And they spoke to them at Shiloh in the land of Canaan, saying, the LORD commanded by the hand of Moses to give us cities to dwell in, with their suburbs for our cattle.
21:3 And the children of Israel gave to the Levites out of their inheritance, at the commandment of the LORD, these cities and their suburbs.
21:4 And the lot came out for the families of the Kohathites: and the children of Aaron the priest, who were of the Levites, had by lot out of the tribe of Judah, and out of the tribe of Simeon, and out of the tribe of Benjamin, thirteen cities.
21:5 And the rest of the children of Kohath had by lot out of the families of the tribe of Ephraim, and out of the tribe of Dan, and out of the half-tribe of Manasseh, ten cities.
21:6 And the children of Gershon had by lot out of the families of the tribe of Issachar, and out of the tribe of Asher, and out of the tribe of Naphtali, and out of the half-tribe of Manasseh in Bashan, thirteen cities.
21:7 The children of Merari by their families had out of the tribe of Reuben, and out of the tribe of Gad, and out of the tribe of Zebulun, twelve cities.
21:8 And the children of Israel gave by lot to the Levites these cities with their suburbs, as the LORD commanded by the hand of Moses.
21:9 And they gave out of the tribe of the children of Judah, and out of the tribe of the children of Simeon, these cities which are here mentioned by name,
21:10 Which the children of Aaron, being of the families of the Kohathites, who were of the children of Levi, had: for theirs was the first lot.
21:11 And they gave them the city of Arba the father of Anak (which city is Hebron) in the hill-country of Judah, with its suburbs round it.
21:12 But the fields of the city, and its villages, they gave to Caleb the son of Jephunneh for his possession.
21:13 Thus they gave to the children of Aaron the priest, Hebron with its suburbs, to be a city of refuge for the slayer; and Libnah with its suburbs,
21:14 And Jattir with its suburbs, and Eshtemoa with its suburbs,
21:15 And Holon with its suburbs, and Debir with its suburbs,
21:16 And Ain with its suburbs, and Juttah with its suburbs, and Beth-shemesh with its suburbs; nine cities out of those two tribes.
21:17 And out of the tribe of Benjamin, Gibeon with its suburbs, Geba with its suburbs,

21:18 Anathoth with its suburbs, and Almon with its suburbs; four cities.
21:19 All the cities of the children of Aaron, the priests, were thirteen cities with their suburbs.
21:20 And the families of the children of Kohath, the Levites who remained of the children of Kohath, even they had the cities of their lot out of the tribe of Ephraim.
21:21 For they gave them Shechem with its suburbs in mount Ephraim, to be a city of refuge for the slayer; and Gezer with its suburbs,
21:22 And Kibzaim with its suburbs, and Beth-horon with its suburbs; four cities.
21:23 And out of the tribe of Dan, Eltekeh with its suburbs, Gibbethon with its suburbs,
21:24 Ajalon with its suburbs, Gath-rimmon with its suburbs; four cities.
21:25 And out of the half-tribe of Manasseh, Taanach with its suburbs, and Gath-rimmon with its suburbs; two cities.
21:26 All the cities were ten with their suburbs, for the families of the children of Kohath that remained.
21:27 And to the children of Gershon, of the families of the Levites, out of the other half-tribe of Manasseh they gave Golan in Bashan with its suburbs, to be a city of refuge for the slayer, and Beesh-terah with its suburbs; two cities.
21:28 And out of the tribe of Issachar, Kishon with its suburbs, Dabareh with its suburbs,
21:29 Jarmuth with its suburbs, En-gannim with its suburbs; four cities.
21:30 And out of the tribe of Asher, Mishal with its suburbs, Abdon with its suburbs,
21:31 Helkath with its suburbs, and Rehob with its suburbs; four cities.
21:32 And out of the tribe of Naphtali, Kedesh in Galilee with its suburbs, to be a city of refuge for the slayer; and Hammoth-dor with its suburbs, and Kartan with its suburbs; three cities.
21:33 All the cities of the Gershonites, according to their families, were thirteen cities with their suburbs.
21:34 And to the families of the children of Merari, the rest of the Levites, out of the tribe of Zebulun, Jokneam with its suburbs, and Kartah with its suburbs,
21:35 Dimnah with its suburbs, Nahalal with its suburbs; four cities.
21:36 And out of the tribe of Reuben, Bezer with its suburbs, and Jahazah with its suburbs,
21:37 Kedemoth with its suburbs, and Mephaath with its suburbs; four cities.
21:38 And out of the tribe of Gad, Ramoth in Gilead with its suburbs to be a city of refuge for the slayer; and Mahanaim with its suburbs,
21:39 Heshbon with its suburbs, Jazer with its suburbs; four cities in all.

21:40 So all the cities for the children of Merari by their families, which were remaining of the families of the Levites, were by their lot twelve cities.
21:41 All the cities of the Levites within the possession of the children of Israel were forty and eight cities with their suburbs.
21:42 These cities were every one with their suburbs around them. Thus were all these cities.
21:43 And the LORD gave to Israel all the land which he swore to give to their fathers: and they possessed it, and dwelt in it.
21:44 And the LORD gave them rest on all sides, according to all that he swore to their fathers: and there stood not a man of all their enemies before them; the LORD delivered all their enemies into their hand.
21:45 There failed not aught of any good thing which the LORD had spoken to the house of Israel; all came to pass.

22

22:1 Then Joshua called the Reubenites, and the Gadites, and the half-tribe of Manasseh,
22:2 And said to them, Ye have kept all that Moses the servant of the LORD commanded you, and have obeyed my voice in all that I commanded you:
22:3 Ye have not left your brethren these many days to this day, but have kept the charge of the commandment of the LORD your God.
22:4 And now the LORD your God hath given rest to your brethren, as he promised them: therefore now return ye, and go to your tents, and to the land of your possession, which Moses the servant of the LORD gave you on the other side of Jordan.
22:5 But take diligent heed to perform the commandment and the law, which Moses the servant of the LORD charged you, to love the LORD your God, and to walk in all his ways, and to keep his commandments, and to cleave to him, and to serve him with all your heart, and with all your soul.
22:6 So Joshua blessed them and sent them away; and they went to their tents.
22:7 Now to the one half of the tribe of Manasseh Moses had given possession in Bashan: but to the other half of it gave Joshua among their brethren on this side of Jordan westward. And when Joshua sent them away also to their tents, then he blessed them,
22:8 And he spoke to them, saying, Return with much riches to your tents, and with very many cattle, with silver, and with gold, and with brass, and with iron, and with very much raiment: divide the spoil of your enemies with your brethren.

22:9 And the children of Reuben, and the children of Gad, and the half-tribe of Manasseh returned, and departed from the children of Israel out of Shiloh, which is in the land of Canaan, to go to the country of Gilead, to the land of their possession, of which they were possessed, according to the word of the LORD by the hand of Moses.
22:10 And when they came to the borders of Jordan, that are in the land of Canaan, the children of Reuben, and the children of Gad, and the half-tribe of Manasseh built there an altar by Jordan, a great altar to the sight.
22:11 And the children of Israel heard it said, Behold, the children of Reuben, and the children of Gad, and the half-tribe of Manasseh, have built an altar over against the land of Canaan, in the borders of Jordan, at the passage of the children of Israel.
22:12 And when the children of Israel heard of it, the whole congregation of the children of Israel assembled at Shiloh, to go up to war against them.
22:13 And the children of Israel sent to the children of Reuben, and to the children of Gad, and to the half-tribe of Manasseh into the land of Gilead, Phinehas the son of Eleazar the priest,
22:14 And with him ten princes, of each chief house a prince throughout all the tribes of Israel; and each one was a head of the house of their fathers among the thousands of Israel.
22:15 And they came to the children of Reuben, and to the children of Gad, and to the half-tribe of Manasseh, to the land of Gilead, and they spoke with them, saying,
22:16 Thus saith the whole congregation of the LORD, What trespass is this that ye have committed against the God of Israel, to turn away this day from following the LORD, in that ye have built you an altar, that ye might rebel this day against the LORD?
22:17 Is the iniquity of Peor too little for us, from which we are not cleansed until this day, although there was a plague in the congregation of the LORD,
22:18 But that ye must turn away this day from following the LORD? and it will be, seeing ye rebel to-day against the LORD, that to-morrow he will be wroth with the whole congregation of Israel.
22:19 Not withstanding, if the land of your possession is unclean, then pass ye over to the land of the possession of the LORD, in which the LORD'S tabernacle dwelleth, and take possession among us: but rebel not against the LORD, nor rebel against us, in building you an altar besides the altar of the LORD our God.
22:20 Did not Achan the son of Zerah commit a trespass in the accursed thing, and wrath fall on all the congregation of Israel? and that man perished not alone in his iniquity.
22:21 Then the children of Reuben, and the children of Gad, and the half-tribe of Manasseh answered, and said to the heads of the thousands of

Israel, 22:22 The LORD God of gods, the LORD God of gods, he knoweth, and Israel he shall know; if it is in rebellion, or if in transgression against the LORD, (save us not this day,)
22:23 That we have built us an altar to turn from following the LORD, or if to offer on it burnt-offering, or meat-offering, or if to offer peace-offerings on it, let the LORD himself require it;
22:24 And if we have not rather done it for fear of this thing, saying, In time to come your children may speak to our children, saying, What have ye to do with the LORD God of Israel?
22:25 For the LORD hath made Jordan a boundary between us and you, ye children of Reuben and children of Gad; ye have no part in the LORD. So shall your children make our children cease from fearing the LORD.
22:26 Therefore we said, Let us now prepare to build us an altar, not for burnt-offering, nor for sacrifice:
22:27 But that it may be a witness between us, and you, and our generations after us, that we may do the service of the LORD before him with our burnt-offerings, and with our sacrifices, and with our peace-offerings; that your children may not say to our children in time to come, Ye have no part in the LORD.
22:28 Therefore said we, that it shall be, when they shall so say to us or to our generations in time to come, that we may say, Behold the pattern of the altar of the LORD, which our fathers made, not for burnt-offerings, nor for sacrifices; but it is a witness between us and you.
22:29 Far be it from us that we should rebel against the LORD, and turn this day from following the LORD, to build an altar for burnt-offerings, for meat-offerings, or for sacrifices, besides the altar of the LORD our God that is before his tabernacle.
22:30 And when Phinehas the priest, and the princes of the congregation, and heads of the thousands of Israel who were with him, heard the words that the children of Reuben, and the children of Gad, and the children of Manasseh spoke, it pleased them.
22:31 And Phinehas the son of Eleazar the priest said to the children of Reuben, and to the children of Gad, and to the children of Manasseh, This day we perceive that the LORD is among us, because ye have not committed this trespass against the LORD: now ye have delivered the children of Israel out of the hand of the LORD.
22:32 And Phinehas the son of Eleazar the priest, and the princes, returned from the children of Reuben, and from the children of Gad, from the land of Gilead, to the land of Canaan, to the children of Israel, and brought them word again.
22:33 And the thing pleased the children of Israel; and the children of Israel blessed God, and did not intend to go up against them in battle, to destroy the land in which the children of Reuben and Gad dwelt.

22:34 And the children of Reuben and the children of Gad called the altar Ed: for it shall be a witness between us that the LORD is God.

23

23:1 And it came to pass, a long time after that the LORD had given rest to Israel from all their enemies on all sides, that Joshua became old and advanced in age.
23:2 And Joshua called for all Israel, and for their elders, and for their heads, and for their judges, and for their officers, and said to them, I am old and advanced in age:
23:3 And ye have seen all that the LORD your God hath done to all these nations because of you; for the LORD your God is he that hath fought for you.
23:4 Behold, I have divided to you by lot these nations that remain, to be an inheritance for your tribes, from Jordan, with all the nations that I have cut off, even to the great sea westward.
23:5 And the LORD your God, he shall expel them from before you, and drive them from your sight; and ye shall possess their land, as the LORD your God hath promised to you.
23:6 Be ye therefore very courageous to keep and to do all that is written in the book of the law of Moses, that ye turn not aside from it to the right hand or to the left;
23:7 That ye come not among these nations, these that remain among you; neither make mention of the name of their gods, nor cause to swear by them, neither serve them, nor bow yourselves to them:
23:8 But cleave to the LORD your God, as ye have done to this day.
23:9 For the LORD hath driven out from before you great nations and strong: but as for you, no man hath been able to stand before you to this day.
23:10 One man of you shall chase a thousand: for the LORD your God, he it is that fighteth for you, as he hath promised you.
23:11 Take good heed therefore to yourselves, that ye love the LORD your God.
23:12 Else if ye do in any wise go back, and cleave to the remnant of these nations, even these that remain among you, and shall make marriages with them, and associate with them, and they with you:
23:13 Know for a certainty that the LORD your God will no more drive out any of these nations from before you; but they shall be snares and traps to you, and scourges in your sides, and thorns in your eyes, until ye perish from off this good land which the LORD your God hath given you.

23:14 And behold, this day I am going the way of all the earth; and ye know in all your hearts and in all your souls, that not one thing hath failed of all the good things which the LORD your God spoke concerning you: all are come to pass to you, and not one thing hath failed of it.
23:15 Therefore it shall come to pass, that as all good things are come upon you, which the LORD your God promised you; so shall the LORD bring upon you all evil things, until he hath destroyed you from off this good land which the LORD your God hath given you.
23:16 When ye have transgressed the covenant of the LORD your God, which he commanded you, and have gone and served other gods, and bowed yourselves to them; then shall the anger of the LORD be kindled against you, and ye shall perish quickly from off the good land which he hath given to you.

24

24:1 And Joshua convened all the tribes of Israel to Shechem, and called for the elders of Israel, and for their heads, and for their judges, and for their officers; and they presented themselves before God.
24:2 And Joshua said to all the people, Thus saith the LORD God of Israel, Your fathers dwelt on the other side of the flood in old time, even Terah, the father of Abraham, and the father of Nahor: and they served other gods.
24:3 And I took your father Abraham from the other side of the flood, and led him throughout all the land of Canaan, and multiplied his seed, and gave him Isaac.
24:4 And I gave to Isaac Jacob and Esau: and I gave to Esau mount Seir, to possess it; but Jacob and his children went down into Egypt.
24:5 I sent Moses also and Aaron, and I plagued Egypt, according to that which I did among them: and afterward I brought you out.
24:6 And I brought your fathers out of Egypt: and ye came to the sea; and the Egyptians pursued after your fathers with chariots and horsemen to the Red sea.
24:7 And when they cried to the LORD, he put darkness between you and the Egyptians, and brought the sea upon them, and covered them; and your eyes have seen what I have done in Egypt: and ye dwelt in the wilderness a long season.
24:8 And I brought you into the land of the Amorites, who dwelt on the other side of Jordan, and they fought with you: and I gave them into your hand, that ye might possess their land; and I destroyed them from before you.

24:9 Then Balak the son of Zippor, king of Moab, arose and warred against
Israel, and sent and called Balaam the son of Beor to curse you:
24:10 But I would not hearken to Balaam; therefore he blessed you still: so
I delivered you out of his hand.
24:11 And ye went over Jordan, and came to Jericho: and the men of
Jericho fought against you, the Amorites, and the Perizzites, and the
Canaanites, and the Hittites, and the Girgashites, the Hivites, and the
Jebusites, and I delivered them into your hand.
24:12 And I sent the hornet before you, which drove them out from before
you, even the two kings of the Amorites; but not with thy sword, nor with
thy bow.
24:13 And I have given you a land for which ye did not labor, and cities
which ye built not, and ye dwell in them; of the vineyards and olive-yards
which ye planted not do ye eat.
24:14 Now therefore fear the LORD, and serve him in sincerity and in
truth; and put away the gods which your fathers served on the other side of
the flood, and in Egypt; and serve ye the LORD.
24:15 And if it seemeth evil to you to serve the LORD, choose you this day
whom ye will serve, whether the gods which your fathers served that were
on the other side of the flood, or the gods of the Amorites in whose land ye
dwell: but as for me and my house, we will serve the LORD.
24:16 And the people answered, and said, Be it far from us that we should
forsake the LORD, to serve other gods;
24:17 For the LORD our God, he it is that brought us, and our fathers, out
of the land of Egypt, from the house of bondage, and who did those great
signs in our sight, and preserved us in all the way in which we went, and
among all the people through whom we passed:
24:18 And the LORD drove out from before us all the people, even the
Amorites who dwelt in the land: therefore will we also serve the LORD; for
he is our God.
24:19 And Joshua said to the people, Ye cannot serve the LORD: for he is
a holy God; he is a jealous God; he will not forgive your transgressions, nor
your sins.
24:20 If ye forsake the LORD, and serve strange gods, then he will turn and
do you hurt, and consume you, after that he hath done you good.
24:21 And the people said to Joshua, No; but we will serve the LORD.
24:22 And Joshua said to the people, Ye are witnesses against yourselves
that ye have chosen you the LORD, to serve him. And they said, We are
witnesses.
24:23 Now therefore put away (said he) the strange gods which are among
you, and incline your heart to the LORD God of Israel.
24:24 And the people said to Joshua, The LORD our God will we serve,
and his voice will we obey.

24:25 So Joshua made a covenant with the people that day, and set them a
statute and an ordinance in Shechem.
24:26 And Joshua wrote these words in the book of the law of God, and
took a great stone, and set it up there under an oak that was by the
sanctuary of the LORD.
24:27 And Joshua said to all the people, Behold, this stone shall be a
witness to us; for it hath heard all the words of the LORD which he spoke
to us, it shall be therefore a witness to you, lest ye deny your God.
24:28 So Joshua let the people depart, every man to his inheritance.
24:29 And it came to pass after these things, that Joshua the son of Nun the
servant of the LORD died, being a hundred and ten years old.
24:30 And they buried him in the border of his inheritance in Timnath-
serah, which is in mount Ephraim, on the north side of the hill of Gaash.
24:31 And Israel served the LORD all the days of Joshua, and all the days
of the elders that outlived Joshua, and who had known all the works of the
LORD that he had done for Israel.
24:32 And the bones of Joseph which the children of Israel brought out of
Egypt, they buried in Shechem, in a parcel of ground which Jacob bought
of the sons of Hamor the father of Shechem for a hundred pieces of silver;
and it became the inheritance of the children of Joseph.
24:33 And Eleazar the son of Aaron died; and they buried him in a hill that
pertained to Phinehas his son, which was given him in mount Ephraim.

COMMENTARY

BY
MATTHEW HENRY

Introduction to Joshua

Here is the history of Israel's passing into the land of Canaan, conquering and dividing it, under the command of Joshua, and their history until his death. The power and truth of God in fulfilling his promises to Israel, and in executing his justly threatened vengeance on the Canaanites, are wonderfully displayed. This should teach us to regard the tremendous curses denounced in the word of God against impenitent sinners, and to seek refuge in Christ Jesus.

Joshua 1

Chapter Contents
The Lord appoints Joshua to succeed Moses. (1-4) God promises to assist Joshua. (5-9) Preparation to pass over Jordan. (10-15) The people promise to obey Joshua. (16-18)
Commentary on Joshua 1:1-4
Joshua had attended upon Moses. He who was called to honour, had been long used to business. Our Lord Jesus took upon him the form of a servant. Joshua was trained up under command. Those are fittest to rule, who have learned to obey. The removal of useful men should quicken survivors to be the more diligent in doing good. Arise, go over Jordan. At this place and at this time the banks were overflowed. Joshua had no bridge or boats, and yet

he must believe that God, having ordered the people over, would open a way.

Commentary on Joshua 1:5-9

Joshua is to make the law of God his rule. He is charged to meditate therein day and night, that he might understand it. Whatever affairs of this world we have to mind, we must not neglect the one thing needful. All his orders to the people, and his judgments, must be according to the law of God. Joshua must himself be under command; no man's dignity or dominion sets him above the law of God. He is to encourage himself with the promise and presence of God. Let not the sense of thine own infirmities dishearten thee; God is all-sufficient. I have commanded, called, and commissioned thee to do it, and will be sure to bear thee out in it. When we are in the way of duty, we have reason to be strong and very bold. Our Lord Jesus, as Joshua here, was borne up under his sufferings by a regard to the will of God, and the commandment from his Father.

Commentary on Joshua 1:10-15

Joshua says to the people, Ye shall pass over Jordan, and shall possess the land; because God had said so to him. We honour the truth of God, when we stagger not at the promise of God. The two tribes and a half were to go over Jordan with their brethren. When God, by his providence, has given us rest, we ought to consider what service we may do to our brethren.

Commentary on Joshua 1:16-18

The people of Israel engage to obey Joshua; All that thou commandest us to do we will readily do, without murmuring or disputing, and whithersoever thou sendest us we will go. The best we can ask of God for our magistrates, is, that they may have the presence of God; that will make them blessings to us, so that in seeking this for them, we consult our own interest. May we be enabled to enlist under the banner of the Captain of our salvation, to be obedient to his commands, and to fight the good fight of faith, with all that trust in and love his name, against all who oppose his authority; for whoever refuses to obey him must be destroyed.

Joshua 2

Chapter Contents

Rahab receives and hides two Israelites. (1-7) Rahab and the spies. (8-21) The return of the spies. (22-24)

Commentary on Joshua 2:1-7

Faith in God's promises ought not to do away, but to encourage our diligence in the use of proper means. The providence of God directed the spies to the house of Rahab. God knew where there was one that would be true to them, though they did not. Rahab appears to have been an innkeeper; and if she had formerly been one of bad life, which is doubtful, she had left her evil courses. That which seems to us most accidental, is often overruled by the Divine providence to serve great ends. It was by faith that Rahab received those with peace, against whom her king and country had war. We are sure this was a good work; it is so spoken of by the apostle, James 2:25; and she did it by faith, such a faith as set her above the fear of man. Those only are true believers, who find in their hearts to venture for God; they take his people for their people, and cast in their lot among them. The spies were led by the special providence of God, and Rahab entertained them out of regard to Israel and Israel's God, and not for lucre or for any evil purpose. Though excuses may be offered for the guilt of Rahab's falsehood, it seems best to admit nothing which tends to explain it away. Her views of the Divine law must have been very dim: a falsehood like this, told by those who enjoy the light of revelation, whatever the motive, would deserve heavy censure.

Commentary on Joshua 2:8-21

Rahab had heard of the miracles the Lord wrought for Israel. She believed that his promises would certainly be fulfilled, and his threatenings take effect; and that there was no way of escape but by submitting to him, and joining with his people. The conduct of Rahab proved that she had the real principle of Divine faith. Observe the promises the spies made to her. The goodness of God is often expressed by his kindness and truth, Psalm 117:2; in both these we must be followers of him. Those who will be conscientious in keeping promises, are cautious in making them. The spies make needful conditions. The scarlet cord, like the blood upon the doorpost at the passover, recalls to remembrance the sinner's security under the atoning blood of Christ; and that we are to flee thereto for refuge from the wrath of a justly offended God. The same cord Rahab used for the saving of these Israelites, was to be used for her own safety. What we serve and honour God with, we may expect he will bless, and make useful to us.

Commentary on Joshua 2:22-24

The report the spies brought was encouraging. All the people of the country faint because of Israel; they have neither wisdom to yield, nor courage to fight. Those terrors of conscience, and that sense of Divine wrath, which dismay the ungodly, but bring not to repentance, are fearful forebodings of approaching destruction. But grace yet abounds to the chief of sinners. Let them, without delay, flee to Christ, and all shall be well.

Joshua 3

Chapter Contents

The Israelites come to Jordan. (1-6) The Lord encourages joshua-Joshua encourages the people. (7-13) The Israelites pass through Jordan on dry land. (14-17)

Commentary on Joshua 3:1-6

The Israelites came to Jordan in faith, having been told that they should pass it. In the way of duty, let us proceed as far as we can, and depend on the Lord. Joshua led them. Particular notice is taken of his early rising, as afterwards upon other occasions, which shows how little he sought his own ease. Those who would bring great things to pass, must rise early. Love not sleep, lest thou come to poverty. All in public stations should always attend to the duty of their place. The people were to follow the ark. Thus must we walk after the rule of the word, and the direction of the Spirit, in everything; so shall peace be upon us as upon the Israel of God; but we must follow our ministers only as they follow Christ. All their way through the wilderness was an untrodden path, but most so this through Jordan. While we are here, we must expect and prepare to pass ways that we have not passed before; but in the path of duty we may proceed with boldness and cheerfulness. Whether we are called to suffer poverty, pain, labour, persecution, reproach, or death, we are following the Author and Finisher of our faith; nor can we set our feet in any dangerous or difficult spot, through our whole journey, but faith will there see the prints of the Redeemer's feet, who trod that very path to glory above, and bids us follow him, that where he is, we may be also. They were to sanctify themselves. Would we experience the effects of God's love and power, we must put away sin, and be careful not to grieve the Holy Spirit of God.

Commentary on Joshua 3:7-13

The waters of Jordan shall be cut off. This must be done in such a way as never was done, but in the dividing of the Red sea. That miracle is here repeated; God has the same power to finish the salvation of his people, as to begin it; the WORD of the Lord was as truly with Joshua as with Moses. God's appearances for his people ought to encourage faith and hope. God's work is perfect, he will keep his people. Jordan's flood cannot keep out Israel, Canaan's force cannot turn them out again.

Commentary on Joshua 3:14-17

Jordan overflowed all its banks. This magnified the power of God, and his kindness to Israel. Although those who oppose the salvation of God's people have all advantages, yet God can and will conquer. This passage over Jordan, as an entrance to Canaan, after their long, weary wanderings in the wilderness, shadowed out the believer's passage through death to heaven, after he has finished his wanderings in this sinful world. Jesus, typified by the ark, hath gone before, and he crossed the river when it most flooded the country around. Let us treasure up experiences of His faithful and tender care, that they may help our faith and hope in the last conflict.

Joshua 4

Chapter Contents
Stones taken out of Jordan. (1-9) The people pass through Jordan. (10-19) The twelve stones placed in Gilgal. (20-24)
Commentary on Joshua 4:1-9
The works of the Lord are so worthy of rememberance, and the heart of man is so prone to forget them, that various methods are needful to refresh our memories, for the glory of God, our advantage, and that of our children. God gave orders for preparing this memorial.
Commentary on Joshua 4:10-19
The priests with the ark did not stir till ordered to move. Let none be weary of waiting, while they have the tokens of God's presence with them, even the ark of the covenant, though it be in the depths of adversity. Notice is taken of the honour put upon Joshua. Those are feared in the best manner, and to the best purpose, who make it appear that God is with them, and that they set him before them.
Commentary on Joshua 4:20-24
It is the duty of parents to tell their children betimes of the words and works of God, that they may be trained up in the way they should go. In all the instruction parents give their children, they should teach them to fear God. Serious godliness is the best learning. Are we not called, as much as the Israelites, to praise the loving-kindness of our God? Shall we not raise a pillar to our God, who has brought us through dangers and distresses in so wonderful a way? For hitherto the Lord hath helped us, as much as he did his saints of old. How great the stupidity and ingratitude of men, who perceive not His hand, and will not acknowledge his goodness, in their frequent deliverances!

Joshua 5

Chapter Contents
The Canaanites are afraid, Circumcision renewed. (1-9) The passover at Gilgal The manna ceases. (10-12) The Captain of the Lord's host appears to Joshua. (13-15)
Commentary on Joshua 5:1-9
How dreadful is their case, who see the wrath of God advancing towards them, without being able to turn it aside, or escape it! Such will be the horrible situation of the wicked; nor can words express the anguish of their feelings, or the greatness of their terror. Oh that they would now take warning, and before it be too late, flee for refuge to lay hold upon that hope

set before them in the gospel! God impressed these fears on the Canaanites, and dispirited them. This gave a short rest to the Israelites, and circumcision rolled away the reproach of Egypt. They were hereby owned to be the free-born children of God, having the seal of the covenant. When God glorifies himself in perfecting the salvation of his people, he not only silences all enemies, but rolls back their reproaches upon themselves.

Commentary on Joshua 5:10-12

A solemn passover was kept, at the time appointed by the law, in the plains of Jericho, in defiance of the Canaanites round about them. It was a performance of the promise, that when they went up to keep the feasts, their land should be under the special protection of the Divine providence, Exodus 34:24. Notice is taken of the ceasing of the manna as soon as they had eaten the old corn of the land. For as it came just when they needed, so it continued as long as they needed it. This teaches us not to expect supplies by miracles, when they may be had in a common way. The word and ordinances of God are spiritual manna, with which God nourishes his people in this wilderness. Though often forfeited, yet they are continued while we are here; but when we come to the heavenly Canaan, this manna will cease, for we shall no longer need it.

Commentary on Joshua 5:13-15

We read not of any appearance of God's glory to Joshua till now. There appeared to him one as a man to be noticed. This Man was the Son of God, the eternal Word. Joshua gave him Divine honours: he received them, which a created angel would not have done, and he is called Jehovah, Joshua 6:2. To Abraham he appeared as a traveller; to Joshua as a man of war. Christ will be to his people what their faith needs. Christ had his sword drawn, which encouraged Joshua to carry on the war with vigour. Christ's sword drawn in his hand, denotes how ready he is for the defence and salvation of his people. His sword turns every way. Joshua will know whether he is a friend or a foe. The cause between the Israelites and Canaanites, between Christ and Beelzebub, will not admit of any man's refusing to take one part or the other, as he may do in worldly contests. Joshua's inquiry shows an earnest desire to know the will of Christ, and a cheerful readiness and resolution to do it. All true Christians must fight under Christ's banner, and they will conquer by his presence and assistance.

Joshua 6

Chapter Contents

The siege of Jericho. (1-5) The city is compassed. (6-16) Jericho is taken, Rahab and her family are saved. (17-27)

Commentary on Joshua 6:1-5

Jericho resolves Israel shall not be its master. It shut itself up, being strongly fortified both by art and nature. Thus were they foolish, and their hearts hardened to their destruction; the miserable case of all that strengthen themselves against the Almighty. God resolves Israel shall be its master, and that quickly. No warlike preparations were to be made. By the uncommon method of besieging the city, the Lord honoured the ark, as the symbol of his presence, and showed that all the victories were from him. The faith and patience of the people were proved and increased.

Commentary on Joshua 6:6-16

Wherever the ark went, the people attended it. God's ministers, by the trumpet of the everlasting gospel, which proclaims liberty and victory, must encourage the followers of Christ in their spiritual warfare. As promised deliverances must be expected in God's way, so they must be expected in his time. At last the people were to shout: they did so, and the walls fell. This was a shout of faith; they believed the walls of Jericho would fall. It was a shout of prayer; they cry to Heaven for help, and help came.

Commentary on Joshua 6:17-27

Jericho was to be a solemn and awful sacrifice to the justice of God, upon those who had filled up the measure of their sins. So He appoints, from whom, as creatures, they received their lives, and to whom, as sinners, they had forfeited them. Rahab perished not with them that believed not, Hebrews 11:31. All her kindred were saved with her; thus faith in Christ brings salvation to the house, Acts 14:31. She, and they with her, were plucked as brands from the burning. With Rahab, or with the men of Jericho; our portion must be assigned, as we posses or disregard the sign of salvation; even faith in Christ, which worketh by love. Let us remember what depends upon our choice, and let us choose accordingly. God shows the weight of a Divine curse; where it rests there is no getting from under it; for it brings ruin without remedy.

Joshua 7

Chapter Contents

The Israelites smitten at Ai. (1-5) Joshua's humiliation and prayer. (6-9) God instructs Joshua what to do. (10-5) Achan is detected, He is destroyed. (16-26)

Commentary on Joshua 7:1-5

Achan took some of the spoil of Jericho. The love of the world is that root of bitterness, which of all others is most hardly rooted up. We should take heed of sin ourselves, lest by it many be defiled or disquieted, Hebrews 12:15; and take heed of having fellowship with sinners, lest we share their guilt. It concerns us to watch over one another to prevent sin, because others' sins may be to our damage. The easy conquest of Jericho excited contempt of the enemy, and a disposition to expect the Lord to do all for them without their using proper means. Thus men abuse the doctrines of Divine grace, and the promises of God, into excuses for their own sloth and self-indulgence. We are to work out our own salvation, though it is God that works in us. It was a dear victory to the Canaanites, whereby Israel was awakened and reformed, and reconciled to their God, and the people of Canaan hardened to their own ruin.

Commentary on Joshua 7:6-9

Joshua's concern for the honour of God, more than even for the fate of Israel, was the language of the Spirit of adoption. He pleaded with God. He laments their defeat, as he feared it would reflect on God's wisdom and power, his goodness and faithfulness. We cannot at any time urge a better plea than this, Lord, what wilt thou do for thy great name? Let God be glorified in all, and then welcome his whole will.

Commentary on Joshua 7:10-15

God awakens Joshua to inquiry, by telling him that when this accursed thing was put away, all would be well. Times of danger and trouble should be times of reformation. We should look at home, into our own hearts, into our own houses, and make diligent search to find out if there be not some accursed thing there, which God sees and abhors; some secret lust, some unlawful gain, some undue withholding from God or from others. We cannot prosper, until the accursed thing be destroyed out of our hearts, and put out of our habitations and our families, and forsaken in our lives. When the sin of sinners finds them out, God is to be acknowledged. With a certain and unerring judgment, the righteous God does and will distinguish between the innocent and the guilty; so that though the righteous are of the same tribe, and family, and household with the wicked, yet they never shall be treated as the wicked.

Commentary on Joshua 7:16-26

See the folly of those that promise themselves secrecy in sin. The righteous God has many ways of bringing to light the hidden works of darkness. See also, how much it is our concern, when God is contending with us, to find out the cause that troubles us. We must pray with holy Job, Lord, show me wherefore thou contendest with me. Achan's sin began in the eye. He saw these fine things, as Eve saw the forbidden fruit. See what comes of suffering the heart to walk after the eyes, and what need we have to make this covenant with our eyes, that if they wander they shall be sure to weep for it. It proceeded out of the heart. They that would be kept from sinful actions, must mortify and check in themselves sinful desires, particularly the desire of worldly wealth. Had Achan looked upon these things with an eye of faith, he would have seen they were accursed things, and would have dreaded them; but looking on them with an eye of sense only, he saw them as goodly things, and coveted them. When he had committed the sin, he tried to hide it. As soon as he had got this plunder, it became his burden, and he dared not to use his ill-gotten treasure. So differently do objects of temptation appear at a distance, to what they do when they have been gotten. See the deceitfulness of sin; that which is pleasing in the commission, is bitter in the reflection. See how they will be deceived that rob God. Sin is a very troublesome thing, not only to a sinner himself, but to all about him. The righteous God will certainly recompense tribulation to them that trouble his people. Achan perished not alone in his sin. They lose their own, who grasp at more than their own. His sons and daughters were put to death with him. It is probable that they helped to hide the things; they must have known of them. What fatal consequences follow, even in this world, to the sinner himself, and to all belonging him! One sinner destroys much good. What, then, will be the wrath to come? Let us flee from it to Christ Jesus as the sinner's Friend. There are circumstances in the confession of Achan, marking the progress of sin, from its first entrance into the heart to its being done, which may serve as the history of almost every offence against the law of God, and the sacrifice of Jesus Christ.

Joshua 8

Chapter Contents

God encourages Joshua. (1,2) The taking of Ai. (3-22) The destruction of Ai and its king. (23-29) The law read on Ebal and Gerizim. (30-35)

Commentary on Joshua 8:1, 2

When we have faithfully put away sin, that accursed thing which separates between us and God, then, and not till then, we may look to hear from God to our comfort; and God's directing us how to go on in our Christian work and warfare, is a good evidence of his being reconciled to us. God encouraged Joshua to proceed. At Ai the spoil was not to be destroyed as at Jericho, therefore there was no danger of the people's committing such a trespass. Achan, who caught at forbidden spoil, lost that, and life, and all; but the rest of the people, who kept themselves from the accursed thing, were quickly rewarded for their obedience. The way to have the comfort of what God allows us, is, to keep from what he forbids us. No man shall lose by self-denial.

Commentary on Joshua 8:3-22

Observe Joshua's conduct and prudence. Those that would maintain their spiritual conflicts must not love their ease. Probably he went into the valley alone, to pray to God for a blessing, and he did not seek in vain. He never drew back till the work was done. Those that have stretched out their hands against their spiritual enemies, must never draw them back.

Commentary on Joshua 8:23-29
God, the righteous Judge, had sentenced the Canaanites for their wickedness; the Israelites only executed his doom. None of their conduct can be drawn into an example for others. Especial reason no doubt there was for this severity to the king of Ai; it is likely he had been notoriously wicked and vile, and a blasphemer of the God of Israel.
Commentary on Joshua 8:30-35
As soon as Joshua got to the mountains Ebal and Gerizim, without delay, and without caring for the unsettled state of Israel, or their enemies, he confirmed the covenant of the Lord with his people, as appointed, Deuteronomy 11. We must not think to defer covenanting with God till we are settled in the world; nor must any business put us from minding and pursuing the one thing needful. The way to prosper is to begin with God, Matthew 6:33. They built an altar, and offered sacrifice to God, in token of their dedicating themselves to God, as living sacrifices to his honour, in and by a Mediator. By Christ's sacrifice of himself for us, we have peace with God. It is a great mercy to any people to have the law of God in writing, and it is fit that the written law should be in a known tongue, that it may be seen and read of all men.

Joshua 9

Chapter Contents
The kings combine against Israel. (1, 2) The Gibeonites apply for peace. (3-13) They obtain peace, but are soon detected. (14-21) The Gibeonites are to be bondmen. (22-27)
Commentary on Joshua 9:1, 2
Hitherto the Canaanites had defended themselves, but here they consult to attack Israel. Their minds were blinded, and their hearts hardened to their destruction. Though often at enmity with each other, yet they united against Israel. Oh that Israel would learn of Canaanites, to sacrifice private interests to the public welfare, and to lay aside all quarrels among themselves, that they may unite against the enemies of God's kingdom!
Commentary on Joshua 9:3-13
Other people heard these tidings, and were driven thereby to make war upon Israel; but the Gibeonites were led to make peace with them. Thus the discovery of the glory and the grace of God in the gospel, is to some a savour of life unto life, but to others a savour of death unto death, 2 Corinthians 2:16. The same sun softens wax and hardens clay. The falsehood of the Gibeonites cannot be justified. We must not do evil that good may themselves to the God of Israel, we have reason to think Joshua would have been directed by the oracle of God to spare their lives. But

when they had once said, "We are come from a far country," they were led to say it made of skins, and their clothes: one lie brings on another, and that a third, and so on. The way of that sin is especially down-hill. Yet their faith and prudence are to be commended. In submitting to Israel they submitted to the God of Israel, which implied forsaking their idolatries. And how can we do better than cast ourselves upon the mercy of a God of all goodness? The way to avoid judgment is to meet it by repentance. Let us do like these Gibeonites, seek peace with God in the rags of abasement, and godly sorrow; so our sin shall not be our ruin. Let us be servants to Jesus, our blessed Joshua, and we shall live.

Commentary on Joshua 9:14-21

The Israelites, having examined the provisions of the Gibeonites, hastily concluded that they confirmed their account. We make more haste than good speed, when we stay not to take God with us, and do not consult him by the word and prayer. The fraud was soon found out. A lying tongue is but for a moment. Had the oath been in itself unlawful, it would not have been binding; for no obligation can render it our duty to commit a sin. But it was not unlawful to spare the Canaanites who submitted, and left idolatry, desiring only that their lives might be spared. A citizen of Zion swears to his own hurt, and changes not, Psalm 15:4. Joshua and the princes, when they found that they had been deceived, did not apply to Eleazar the high priest to be freed from their engagement, much less did they pretend that no faith is to be kept with those to whom they had sworn. Let this convince us how we ought to keep our promises, and make good our bargains; and what conscience we ought to make of our words.

Commentary on Joshua 9:22-27

The Gibeonites do not justify their lie, but plead that they did it to save their lives. And the fear was not merely of the power of man; one might flee from that to the Divine protection; but of the power of God himself, which they saw engaged against them. Joshua sentences them to perpetual bondage. They must be servants, but any work becomes honourable, when it is done for the house of the Lord, and the offices thereof. Let us, in like manner, submit to our Lord Jesus, saying, We are in thy hand, do unto us as seemeth good and right unto thee, only save our souls; and we shall not repent it. If He appoints us to bear his cross, and serve him, that shall be neither shame nor grief to us, while the meanest office in God's service will entitle us to a dwelling in the house of the Lord all the days of our life. And in coming to the Saviour, we do not proceed upon a peradventure. We are invited to draw nigh, and are assured that him that cometh to Him, he will in nowise cast out. Even those things which sound harsh, and are humbling, and form sharp trials of our sincerity, will prove of real advantage.

Joshua 10

Chapter Contents

Five kings war against Gibeon. (1-6) Joshua succours Gibeon The sun and moon stand still. (7-14) The kings are taken, their armies defeated, and they are put to death. (15-27) Seven other kings defeated and slain. (28-43)

Commentary on Joshua 10:1-6

When sinners leave the service of Satan and the friendship of the world, that they make peace with God and join Israel, they must not marvel if the world hate them, if their former friends become foes. By such methods Satan discourages many who are convinced of their danger, and almost persuaded to be Christians, but fear the cross. These things should quicken us to apply to God for protection, help, and deliverance.

Commentary on Joshua 10:7-14

The meanest and most feeble, who have just begun to trust the Lord, are as much entitled to be protected as those who have long and faithfully been his servants. It is our duty to defend the afflicted, who, like the Gibeonites, are brought into trouble on our account, or for the sake of the gospel. Joshua would not forsake his new vassals. How much less shall our true Joshua fail those who trust in Him! We may be wanting in our trust, but our trust never can want success. Yet God's promises are not to slacken and do away, but to quicken and encourage our endeavours. Notice the great faith of Joshua, and the power of God answering it by the miraculous staying of the sun, that the day of Israel's victories might be made longer. Joshua acted on this occasion by impulse on his mind from the Spirit of God. It was not necessary that Joshua should speak, or the miracle be recorded, according to the modern terms of astronomy. The sun appeared to the Israelites over Gibeon, and the moon over the valley of Ajalon, and there they appeared to be stopped on their course for one whole day. Is any thing too hard for the Lord? forms a sufficient answer to ten thousand difficulties, which objectors have in every age started against the truth of God as revealed in his written word. Proclamation was hereby made to the neighbouring nations, Behold the works of the Lord, and say, What nation is there so great as Israel, who has God so nigh unto them?

Commentary on Joshua 10:15-27

None moved his tongue against any of the children of Israel. This shows their perfect safety. The kings were called to an account, as rebels against the Israel of God. Refuges of lies will but secure for God's judgment. God punished the abominable wickedness of these kings, the measure of whose iniquity was now full. And by this public act of justice, done upon these ringleaders of the Canaanites in sin, he would possess his people with the greater dread and detestation of the sins of the nations that God cast out from before them. Here is a type and figure of Christ's victories over the powers of darkness, and of believers' victories through him. In our spiritual conflicts we must not be satisfied with obtaining some important victory. We must pursue our scattered enemies, searching out the remains of sin as they rise up in our hearts, and thus pursue the conquest. In so doing, the Lord will afford light until the warfare be accomplished.

Commentary on Joshua 10:28-43

Joshua made speed in taking these cities. See what a great deal of work may be done in a little time, if we will be diligent, and improve our opportunities. God here showed his hatred of the idolatries and other abominations of which the Canaanites had been guilty, and shows us how great the provocation was, by the greatness of the destruction brought upon them. Here also was typified the destruction of all the enemies of the Lord Jesus, who, having slighted the riches of his grace, must for ever feel the weight of his wrath. The Lord fought for Israel. They could not have gotten the victory, if God had not undertaken the battle. We conquer when God fights for us; if he be for us, who can be against us?

Joshua 11

Chapter Contents

Divers kings overcome at the waters of Merom. (1-9) Hazor is taken and burned. (10-14) All that country subdued, The Anakims cut off. (15-23)

Commentary on Joshua 11:1-9

The wonders God wrought for the Israelites were to encourage them to act vigorously themselves. Thus the war against Satan's kingdom, carried on by preaching the gospel, was at first forwarded by miracles; but being fully proved to be of God, we are now left to the Divine grace in the usual course, in the use of the sword of the Spirit. God encouraged Joshua. Fresh dangers and difficulties make it necessary to seek fresh supports from the word of God, which we have nigh unto us for use in every time of need. God proportions our trials to our strength, and our strength to our trials. Joshua's obedience in destroying the horses and chariots, shows his self-denial in compliance with God's command. The possession of things on which the carnal heart is prone to depend, is hurtful to the life of faith, and the walk with God; therefore it is better to be without worldly advantages, than to have the soul endangered by them.

Commentary on Joshua 11:10-14

The Canaanites filled up the measure of their iniquity, and were, as a judgment, left to the pride, obstinacy, and enmity of their hearts, and to the power of Satan; all restraints being withdrawn, while the dispensations of Providence tended to drive them to despair. They brought on themselves the vengeance they justly merited, of which the Israelites were to be executioners, by the command the Lord gave to Moses.

Commentary on Joshua 11:15-23

Never let the sons of Anak be a terror to the Israel of God, for their day to fall will come. The land rested from war. It ended not in a peace with the Canaanites, that was forbidden, but in a peace from them. There is a rest, a rest from war, remaining for the people of God, into which they shall enter, when their warfare is accomplished. That which was now done, is compared with what had been said to Moses. God's word and his works, if viewed together, will be found mutually to set each other forth. If we make conscience of our duty, we need not question the performance of the promise. But the believer must never put off his armour, or expect lasting peace, till he closes his eyes in death; nay, as his strength and usefulness increase, he may expect more heavy trials; yet the Lord will not permit any enemies to assault the believer till he has prepared him for the battle. Christ Jesus ever lives to plead for his people, and their faith shall not fail, however Satan may be permitted to assault them. And however tedious, sharp, and difficult the believer's warfare, his patience in tribulation may be encouraged by the joyfulness of hope; for he will, ere long, rest from sin and from sorrow in the Canaan above.

Joshua 12

Chapter Contents

The two kings conquered by Moses. (1-6) The kings whom Joshua smote. (7-24)

Commentary on Joshua 12:1-6

Fresh mercies must not drown the remembrance of former mercies, nor must the glory of the present instruments of good to the church diminish the just honour of those who went before them, since God is the same who wrought by both. Moses gave to one part of Israel a very rich and fruitful country, but it was on the outside of Jordan. Joshua gave to all Israel the holy land, within Jordan. So the law has given to some few of God's spiritual Israel worldly blessings, earnests of good things to come; but our Lord Jesus, the true Joshua, provided for all the children of promise spiritual blessings, and the heavenly Canaan.

Commentary on Joshua 12:7-24

We have here the limits of the country Joshua conquered. A list is given of the kings subdued by Israel: thirty-one in all. This shows how fruitful Canaan then was, in which so many chose to throng together. This was the land God appointed for Israel; yet in our day it is one of the most barren and unprofitable countries in the world. Such is the effect of the curse it lies under, since its possessors rejected Christ and his gospel, as was foretold by Moses, Deuteronomy 29:23. The vengeance of a righteous God, inflicted on all these kings and their subjects, for their wickedness, should make us dread and hate sin. The fruitful land bestowed on his chosen people, should fill our hearts with hope and confidence in his mercy, and with humble gratitude.

Joshua 13

Chapter Contents
Bounds of the land not yet conquered. (1-6) Inheritance of Reuben. (7-33)
Commentary on Joshua 13:1-6
At this chapter begins the account of the dividing of the land of Canaan among the tribes of Israel by lot; a narrative showing the performance of the promise made to the fathers, that this land should be given to the seed of Jacob. We are not to pass over these chapters of hard names as useless. Where God has a mouth to speak, and a hand to write, we should find an ear to hear, and an eye to read; and may God give us a heart to profit! Joshua is supposed to have been about one hundred years old at this time. It is good for those who are old and stricken in years to be put in remembrance of their being so. God considers the frame of his people, and would not have them burdened with work above their strength. And all people, especially old people, should set to do that quickly which must be done before they die, lest death prevent them, Ecclesiastes 9:10. God promise that he would make the Israelites masters of all the countries yet unsubdued, through Joshua was old, and not able to do it; old, and not likely to live to see it done. Whatever becomes of us, and however we may be laid aside as despised, broken vessels, God will do his own work in his own time. We must work out our salvation, then God will work in us, and work with us; we must resist our spiritual enemies, then God will tread them under our feet; we must go forth to our Christian work and warfare, then God will go forth before us.
Commentary on Joshua 13:7-33
The land must be divided among the tribes. It is the will of God that every man should know his own, and not take that which is another's. The world must be governed, not by force, but right. Wherever our habitation is placed, and in whatever honest way our portion is assigned, we should consider them as allotted of God; we should be thankful for, and use them as such, while every prudent method should be used to prevent disputes about property, both at present and in future. Joshua must be herein a type of Christ, who has not only conquered the gates of hell for us, but has opened to us the gates of heaven, and having purchased the eternal

inheritance for all believers, will put them in possession of it. Here is a general description of the country given to the two tribes and a half, by Moses. Israel must know their own, and keep to it; and may not, under pretence of their being God's peculiar people, encroach on their neighbours. Twice in this chapter it is noticed, that to the tribe of Levi Moses gave no inheritance: see Numbers 18:20. Their maintenance must be brought out of all the tribes. The ministers of the Lord should show themselves indifferent about worldly interests, and the people should take care they want nothing suitable. And happy are those who have the Lord God of Israel for their inheritance, though little of this world falls to their lot. His providences will supply their wants, his consolations will support their souls, till they gain heavenly joy and everlasting pleasures.

Joshua 14

Chapter Contents
The nine tribes and a half to have their inheritance. (1-5) Caleb obtains Hebron. (6-15)
Commentary on Joshua 14:1-5
The Israelites must occupy the new conquests. Canaan would have been subdued in vain, if it had not been inhabited. Yet every man might not go and settle where he pleased. God shall choose our inheritance for us. Let us survey our heritage of present mercy, our prospect for the land of promise, eternal in the heavens. Is God any respecter of persons? Is it not better that our place, as to earthly good or sorrow, should be determined by the infinite wisdom of our heavenly Father, than by our own ignorance? Should not those for whom the great mystery of godliness was exhibited, those whose redemption was purchased by Jesus Christ, thankfully refer their earthly concerns to his appointment?
Commentary on Joshua 14:6-15
Caleb's request is, "Give me this mountain," or Hebron, because it was formerly in God's promise to him, and he would let Israel knows how much he valued the promise. Those who live by faith value that which is given by God's promise, far above what is given by his providence only. It was now in the Anakims' possession, and Caleb would let Israel know how little he feared the enemy, and that he would encourage them to push on their conquests. Caleb answered to his name, which signifies "all heart." Hebron was settled on Caleb and his heirs, because he wholly followed the Lord God of Israel. Happy are we if we follow him. Singular piety shall be crowned with singular favour.

Joshua 15

Chapter Contents
The borders of the lot of Judah. (1-12) Caleb's portion, His daughter's blessing. (13-19) The cities of Judah. (20-63)
Commentary on Joshua 15:1-12
Joshua allotted to Judah, Ephraim, and the half of Manasseh, their inheritances before they left Gilgal. Afterwards removing to Shiloh, another survey was made, and the other tribes had their portion assigned. In due time all God's people are settled.
Commentary on Joshua 15:13-19
Achsah obtained some land by Caleb's free grant. He gave her a south land. Land indeed, but a south land, dry and apt to be parched. She obtained more, on her request, and he gave the upper and the nether springs. Those who understand it but of one field, watered both with the rain of heaven, and the springs that issued out of the earth, countenance the allusion commonly made to this, when we pray for spiritual and heavenly blessings which relate to our souls, as blessings of the upper springs, and those which relate to the body and the life that now is, as blessings of the nether springs. All the blessings, both of the upper and the nether springs, belong to the children of God. As related to Christ, they have them freely given of the Father, for the lot of their inheritance.
Commentary on Joshua 15:20-63
Here is a list of the cities of Judah. But we do not here find Bethlehem, afterwards the city of David, and ennobled by the birth of our Lord Jesus in it. That city, which, at the best, was but little among the thousands of Judah, Micah 5:2, except that it was thus honoured, was now so little as not to be accounted one of the cities.

Joshua 16

Chapter Contents
The sons of Joseph.
This and the following chapter should not be separated. They give the lots of Ephraim and Manasseh, the children of Joseph, who, next to Judah, were to have the post of honour, and therefore had the first and best portion in the northern part of Canaan, as Judah in the southern part. God's people now, as of old, suffer his enemies to remain. Blessed Lord, when will all our enemies be subdued? 1 Corinthians 15:26. Do thou drive them all out; thou alone canst do it. These settled boundaries may remind us, that our situation and provision in this life, as well as our future inheritance, are appointed by the only wise and righteous God, and we should be content

with our portion, since he knows what is best for us, and all we have is more than we deserve.

Joshua 17

Chapter Contents

The lot of Manasseh. (1-6) The boundaries of Manasseh, The Canaanites not driven out. (7-13) Joseph desires a larger portion. (14-18)

Commentary on Joshua 17:1-6

Manasseh was but half of the tribe of Joseph, yet it was divided into two parts. The daughters of Zelophehad now reaped the benefit of their pious zeal and prudent forecast. Those who take care in the wilderness of this world, to make sure to themselves a place in the inheritance of the saints in light, will have the comfort of it in the other world; while those who neglect it now, will lose it for ever. Lord, teach us here to believe and obey, and give us an inheritance among thy saints, in glory everlasting.

Commentary on Joshua 17:7-13

There was great communication between Manasseh and Ephraim. Though each tribe had its inheritance, yet they should intermix one with another, to do good offices one to another, as became those, who, though of different tribes, were all one Israel, and were bound to love as brethren. But they suffered the Canaanites to live among them, against the command of God, to serve their own ends.

Commentary on Joshua 17:14-18

Joshua, as a public person, had no more regard to his own tribe than to any other, but would govern without favour or affection; wherein he has left a good example to all in public trusts. Joshua tells them, that what was fallen to their share would be a sufficient lot for them, if they would but work and fight. Men excuse themselves from labour by any pretence; and nothing serves the purpose better than having rich and powerful relations, able to provide for them; and they are apt to desire a partial and unfaithful disposal of what is intrusted to those they think able to give such help. But there is more real kindness in pointing out the advantages within reach, and in encouraging men to make the best of them, than in granting indulgences to sloth and extravagance. True religion gives no countenance to these evils. The rule is, They shall not eat who will not work; and many of our "cannots" are only the language of idleness, which magnifies every difficulty and danger. This is especially the case in our spiritual work and warfare. Without Christ we can do nothing, but we are apt to sit still and attempt nothing. if we belong to Him, he will stir us up to our best endeavours, and to cry to him for help. Then our coast will be enlarged, 1 Chronicles 4:9,10, and complainings silenced, or rather, turned into joyful thanksgivings.

Joshua 18

Chapter Contents
The tabernacle set up at Shiloh. (1) The remainder of the land described and divided. (2-10) The boundaries of Benjamin. (11-28)

Commentary on Joshua 18:1
Shiloh was in the lot of Ephraim, the tribe to which Joshua belonged, and it was proper that the tabernacle should be near the residence of the chief governor. The name of this city is the same as that by which Jacob prophesied of the Messiah, Genesis 49:10. It is supposed by some that the city was thus called, when it was chosen for the resting-place of the ark, which typified our great Peace-maker, and the way by him to a reconciled God.

Commentary on Joshua 18:2-10
After a year or more, Joshua blamed their slackness, and told them how to proceed. God, by his grace, has given us a title to a good land, the heavenly Canaan, but we are slack to take possession of it; we enter not into that rest, as we might by faith, and hope, and holy joy. How long shall it be thus with us? How long shall we thus stand in our own light, and forsake our own mercies for lying vanities? Joshua stirs the Israelites up to take possession of their lots. He is ready to do his part, if they will do theirs.

Commentary on Joshua 18:11-28
The boundaries of each portion were distinctly drawn, and the inheritance of each tribe settled. All contests and selfish claims were prevented by the wise appointment of God, who allotted the hill and the valley, the corn and pasture, the brooks and rivers, the towns and cities. Is the lot of any servant of Christ cast in affliction and sorrow? It is the Lord; let him do what seemeth him good. Are we in prosperity and peace? It is from above. Be humbled when you compare the gift with your own unworthiness. Forget not Him that gave the good, and always be ready to resign it at his command.

Joshua 19

Chapter Contents
The lot of Simeon. (1-9) The lot of Zebulun. (10-16) The lot of Issachar, Asher, Naphtali, and Dan. (17-51)

Commentary on Joshua 19:1-9
The men of Judah did not oppose taking away the cities within their border, when convinced that they had more than was right. If a true believer has obtained an unintended and improper advantage in any thing, he will give it

up without murmuring. Love seeketh not her own, and doth not behave unseemly; it will induce those in whom it richly dwells, to part with their own to supply what is lacking to their brethren.

Commentary on Joshua 19:10-16

In the division to each tribe of Israel, the prophetic blessings of Jacob were fulfilled. They chose for themselves, or it was divided to them by lot, in the manner and places that he foresaw. So sure a rule to go by is the word of prophecy: we see by it what to believe, and it proves beyond all dispute the things that are of God.

Commentary on Joshua 19:17-51

Joshua waited till all the tribes were settled, before he asked any provision for himself. He was content to be unfixed, till he saw them all placed, and herein is an example to all in public places, to prefer the common welfare before private advantage. Those who labour most to do good to others, seek an inheritance in the Canaan above: but it will be soon enough to enter thereon, when they have done all the service to their brethren of which they are capable. Nor can any thing more effectually assure them of their title to it, than endeavouring to bring others to desire, to seek, and to obtain it. Our Lord Jesus came and dwelt on earth, not in pomp but poverty, providing rest for man, yet himself not having where to lay his head; for Christ pleased not himself. Nor would he enter upon his inheritance, till by his obedience to death he secured the eternal inheritance for all his people; nor will he account his own glory completed, till every ransomed sinner is put in possession of his heavenly rest.

Joshua 20

Chapter Contents

The law concerning the cities of refuge. (1-6) The cities appointed as refuges. (7-9)

Commentary on Joshua 20:1-6

When the Israelites were settled in their promised inheritance, they were reminded to set apart the cities of refuge, whose use and typical meaning have been explained, Numbers 35. God's spiritual Israel have, and shall have in Christ and heaven, not only rest to repose in, but refuge to secure themselves in. These cities were designed to typify the relief which the gospel provides for penitent sinners, and their protection from the curse of the law and the wrath of God, in our Lord Jesus, to whom believers flee for refuge, Hebrews 6:18.

Commentary on Joshua 20:7-9

These cities, as those also on the other side Jordan, stood so that a man might in half a day reach one of them from any part of the country. God is ever a Refuge at hand. They were all Levites' cities. It was kindness to the poor fugitive, that when he might not go up to the house of the Lord, yet he had the servants of God with him, to instruct him, and pray for him, and to help to make up the want of public ordinances. Some observe a significance in the names of these cities with application to Christ our Refuge. Kedesh signifies holy, and our Refuge is the holy Jesus. Shechem, a shoulder, and the government is upon his shoulder. Hebron, fellowship, and believers are called into the fellowship of Christ Jesus our Lord. Bezer, a fortification, for he is a strong hold to all those that trust in him. Ramoth, high or exalted, for Him hath God exalted with his own right hand. Golan, joy or exultation, for in Him all the saints are justified, and shall glory.

Joshua 21

Chapter Contents

Cities for the Levites. (1-8) The cities allotted to the Levites. (9-42) God gave the land and rest to the Israelites, according to his promise. (43-45)

Commentary on Joshua 21:1-8

The Levites waited till the other tribes were provided for, before they preferred their claim to Joshua. They build their claim upon a very good foundation; not their own merits or services, but the Divine precept. The maintenance of ministers is not a thing left merely to the will of the people, that they may let them starve if they please; they which preach the gospel should live by the gospel, and should live comfortably.

Commentary on Joshua 21:9-42

By mixing the Levites with the other tribes, they were made to see that the eyes of all Israel were upon them, and therefore it was their concern to walk so that their ministry might not be blamed. Every tribe had its share of Levites' cities. Thus did God graciously provide for keeping up religion among them, and that they might have the word in all parts of the land. Yet, blessed be God, we have the gospel more diffused amongst us.

Commentary on Joshua 21:43-45

God promised to give to the seed of Abraham the land of Canaan for a possession, and now they possessed it, and dwelt therein. And the promise of the heavenly Canaan is as sure to all God's spiritual Israel; for it is the promise of Him that cannot lie. There stood not a man before them. The after-prevalence of the Canaanites was the effect of Israel's slothfulness, and the punishment of their sinful inclination to the idolatries and abominations of the heathen whom they harboured and indulged. There failed not aught of any good thing, which the Lord had spoken to the house of Israel. In due season all his promises will be accomplished; then will his people acknowledge that the Lord has exceeded their largest expectations, the Lord shall inherit the kingdom he prepared for them from the foundation of the world. They will say in admiration of the grace of Jesus, Unto him that loved us, and washed us from our sins in his own blood, and hath made us kings and priests unto God and his Father, to him be glory and dominion for ever and ever. Amen.

Made in the USA
San Bernardino, CA
29 October 2015